The Glovesmen of Goodison

A History of Everton's Goalkeepers

Paul Owens

Foreword by Alan Kelly

pitch

First published by Pitch Publishing, 2025

1

pitch

Pitch Publishing
9 Donnington Park,
85 Birdham Road,
Chichester, West Sussex,
PO20 7AJ
www.pitchpublishing.co.uk
info@pitchpublishing.co.uk

A CIP catalogue record is available for this book
from the British Library.

ISBN 978 1 83680 164 1

Typesetting and origination by Pitch Publishing

MIX
Paper | Supporting
responsible forestry
FSC
www.fsc.org   FSC™ C016779

Printed and bound on FSC® certified paper in line with
our continuing commitment to ethical business practices,
sustainability and the environment.

Printed and bound in India by Replika Press Pvt. Ltd.

Contents

This book is dedicated to my mum and dad, for all their love and encouragement. And for spending hundreds of pounds on the latest Neville Southall-endorsed goalkeeper gloves throughout the 1980s and 1990s.

To Jenny, Lucy and Katie – by far the greatest team the world has ever seen.

To all my Everton friends with whom I spent some very special times at Goodison Park.

To all the budding Neville Southalls, Jordan Pickfords, Rachel Brown-Finnises and Courtney Brosnans I have had the pleasure to coach. Keep getting behind that ball!

Acknowledgements

There are many people I need to thank for their help with this book.

It goes without saying but I am indebted to all the goalkeepers, their coaches and their team-mates who agreed to be interviewed and were so generous with their time and the sharing of their memories. I hope that they are all satisfied with the outcome. With regard to this group of sportsmen and sportswomen, I would especially like to thank Alan Kelly, who kindly agreed to write the book's foreword. The comforting warmth that comes through in his writing on those opening pages is, in many ways, a paper version of the kindness and passion for the project he conveyed during our online meetings last year.

Many of the interviews with ex-players were arranged with the help of the Everton FC Heritage Society, whose members have shown great enthusiasm for this publication. A special mention in this regard must go to Everton historians Jamie Yates and Rob Sawyer, whose support has been unwavering. Furthermore, Rob's detailed articles on several of the goalkeepers mentioned in the early chapters have been invaluable sources of information and, with his permission, leaned on heavily here. A special thank you must go to Dr David France for his encouragement and constructive feedback and also to Brendan Connolly, who has kindly allowed me to use images of some of Everton's early goalkeepers from his personal collection. On the subject of photographs, I would also like to thank Everton Football Club's Darren Griffiths, for allowing me to use some of the club's own images, and the very talented Lewis Guy for giving me permission to use his wonderful image of the giant Jordan Pickford banner on display in the Gwladys Street here.

I am also grateful to several people working for the club and in the wider media for sharing their memories of our goalkeepers.

David Prentice, Alan Myers, Phil McNulty and Brian Viner were all fantastically knowledgeable interviewees. Thank you, Brian, for getting me involved with your article on Jordan Pickford for the *Daily Mail* last year, in which you mentioned and marketed *The Glovesmen of Goodison: A History of Everton's Goalkeepers* despite it not having been written at that point.

Special thanks must also go to the Everton fans and goalkeeping enthusiasts who have contributed to the final chapter of brilliantly written goalkeeping memories from matches played at Goodison Park, and to the friends on social media who helped to confirm essential pieces of information and fill in gaps on the club's goalkeeping timeline, especially concerning the early days of the women's team. Bradley Cates deserves an extra-special mention here.

At Pitch Publishing, I am grateful to Jane Camillin for giving me this opportunity and would like to thank everyone else there who has helped to create this book. I am sure you will all agree with me when I say that Duncan Olner has done a tremendous job with the cover design.

There are many excellent Everton authors out there, whose books have been constant sources of reference. In addition to the aforementioned Rob Sawyer and Dr David France, special mentions must go to Gavin Buckland, Becky Tallentire, James Corbett, Ivan Ponting, Jim Keoghan, Paul McParlan, Lou Reed Foster, Simon Hart and Steve Johnson in this regard. Steve's book *Everton: The Official Complete Record 1878–2016* and website evertonresults.com have been invaluable, and the records and statistics mentioned throughout these pages are mostly from his work.

On a more personal level, I would like to thank my closest friends and family for all their patience and encouragement. I must particularly mention my mum and dad, Tina and Peter Owens, my brother Richard Owens, who provided constructive feedback on early drafts of many of the chapters, my mother-in-law and father in-law Jan and Bill Langhamer, and my two daughters, Lucy and Katie Owens, not only for all their love, support and encouragement, but also for being, at times, much-needed distractions over the last 18 months.

The biggest thank you of all, though, goes to my wife, Jenny, without whom there would be no book. Jen, I am forever grateful for your love, support and patience, and for your normalising of my obsession with everything Everton and goalkeeping related.

Foreword

The goalkeeper. The last line of defence. The most pressurised position on the football pitch. These two phrases highlight the nature and character of the goalkeepers, from all age groups and genders, who have worn the Everton goalkeeper shirt with pride in its long and illustrious history.

You may well know me as Jordan Pickford's former goalkeeping coach, covering over 170 first-team games for Everton during my seven years on Merseyside. During that period, I had the privilege of coaching Everton goalkeepers from the academy to the first team, including several of the club's Women's Super League goalkeepers. Being able to work with Kirstie Levell and observe Ireland's Courtney Brosnan in training and in games was a real privilege. Seeing how hard they worked to hone their skills and strive to be better every day was inspiring.

Goalkeepers have been, and continue to be, central figures in Everton's successes, survivals and everything in between, which have all contributed to an unbroken 71-year run in the top division of English football. Their individuality, brilliance and idiosyncrasies have secured their place in the history of Everton Football Club and in the hearts and minds of the Goodison Park faithful. This leads me perfectly on to the subject of the men's team's former home – the 'Grand Old Lady' – which is steeped in history, unique in the locality of its fans and with as passionate and demanding a crowd as I have ever experienced in world football. Magical!

As an example of what it felt and sounded like when Goodison Park erupted, I can speak from experience, having played there in the Premier League and through standing in the goalmouth, waiting for Jordan Pickford to receive his last six volleys from me, minutes before the start of the match, all in front of the Gwladys

Street. When the siren went off and the *Z-Cars* anthem marked the entrance on to the pitch of the Everton team, the ferocious intensity and wall of sound produced from the whole stadium was truly breathtaking.

In the last few years, the fans, and their unwavering support, have been the team's 12th player on the pitch. To witness first-hand the pre-match bus welcomes, under Frank Lampard in 2022, with the blue flares producing a fog of smoke, the hammering on the bus by the passionate supporters and that wall of sound erupting all around us was utterly amazing. To then top it all off with the experience of that famous pitch invasion, after coming from 2-0 down to beat Crystal Palace to secure our place in the Premier League, still fills me with joy, relief and elation!

We had survived the unthinkable and the Goodison faithful could breathe again, knowing that every fan on that pitch and the thousands outside had played their part in preserving Everton's incredible run of playing in the top tier.

In the mid-1980s, Everton played a small part during the formative years of my eventual 40-year career as a professional goalkeeper and goalkeeping coach at Premier League, English Football League and international levels. After leaving school in 1984, I had been a part-time, non-contract goalkeeper playing for Preston North End's under-18 team on Saturdays and the club's reserve side during the week. I was also working as a full time apprentice at British Leyland Trucks, but, after 15 months of doing both roles, I knew I had to make a decision – either complete my four-year apprenticeship or accept the eight-month professional contract on offer from Preston. I asked my dad for advice and his words are still fresh in my memory, 'No chance. Don't do it, son. Don't give up your trade for a dream that could be over in eight months.'

Dad didn't know during our conversation that I had already signed that contract with Preston on my way home from work that day!

I made my debut in March 1986 and played the last 13 league games of the 1985/86 season, winning the club's young player of the year award. However, the season was a disaster for Preston as we finished 91st out of 92 league clubs and my dad's words of warning from eight months earlier were starting to echo in my head!

But football is unpredictable, and little did I know that two months later I would be making my Everton debut in an international youth tournament, in Italy, against the mighty AC Milan.

So how did I end up playing for Everton? Simple. My dad had been a team-mate of Howard Kendall's at Preston when they reached the 1964 FA Cup Final. Howard had heard Dad had left his manager's job at Preston North End in February 1985 and knew he was the man to keep Neville Southall on top of the world. Dad joined Everton and, in doing so, became one of the world's first full time goalkeeping coaches in professional football.

It was during the 1986/87 pre-season when Dad arrived home from Everton and was sitting at the kitchen table, telling my mum that Ray Minshull, Everton's youth development officer, had asked him if he knew of any young goalkeepers who might like to play for Everton in an international youth tournament in Italy next week. My mum immediately knew it was an opportunity not to be missed for me and she told my dad I was going to Italy – or he could make his own pork chops from that point on! A quick telephone call to Preston to inform them of Everton's request seemed to ignite Preston's interest in a possible transfer fee and the short-term 'work experience loan deal' was agreed. My mum should have been an agent!

My first game was against AC Milan live on TV. We drew 0-0 and I was busy. To be awarded the player of the match award while wearing the famous Everton goalkeeper shirt with NEC blazed across its front was incredible. If Carlsberg did debuts!

To represent Everton Football Club at a time when they were, literally, the best team in English and European football was an amazing experience. I played all three games in Italy, but, in true Toffees style, we were knocked out at the group stage, going down 1-0 to Sampdoria on a cinder-covered pitch. I remember being in the dressing room after that game when Ray Minshull walked in and simply said, 'That's not good enough for Everton. When you wear the Everton shirt, you represent the club, the fans and the spirit of Everton Football Club.' Ray then turned to me and said,

'If we had got through the group stages, you would have been named goalkeeper of the tournament, without a doubt, but that's not going to happen now.'

I loved the experience and saw it as another advancement in my development as a young goalkeeper, even though I had made my league debut for Preston four months earlier. This opportunity took me out of my comfort zone. I had to gel with new players in a very short time. I had to perform in games against top-class opposition and deal with the pressure and expectations of being the last line of defence for a club that was winning the equivalent of Premier League titles, FA Cups and European competitions during that time.

I went back to Preston North End on my return from Italy and trained even harder, determined to take my chance in the first team when the opportunity arose. I ended up playing over 25 games for the Lilywhites as we won promotion, keeping 22 clean sheets as a team in that 1986/87 season. What I didn't know at that time was that my playing and coaching career would go on to cover more than 1,000 first-team and international games over the next 40 years.

As I said earlier, my dad coached Everton's number one goalkeeper, Neville Southall, who was backed up by the impressive Bobby Mimms during that period. Neville was the best goalkeeper in the world at that time and I would sometimes travel in with Dad to Everton's old training ground, Bellefield. It was during those trips that I got to observe Neville and the team in training.

Watching Neville was my 'lightbulb moment'. I was literally in the presence of greatness, standing just four yards away from the action. Graeme Sharp, Adrian 'Inchy' Heath and Kevin Sheedy, all lethal finishers in their own right, were left with their heads in their hands as Neville somehow saved the impossible. Truly amazing goalkeeping!

I couldn't have imagined that seven years later I would be playing against Neville in the Premier League at Goodison Park or that I would make my debut for the Republic of Ireland national team in February 1993 against Wales at Tolka Park in Dublin with Neville in goal for Wales.

Dad only stayed at Everton for 18 months. His time was wedged between the two title-winning teams of 1985 and 1987, and the losing FA Cup team of 1986. Timing really is everything in football!

When I fast-forward to 2017, I bet Dad was looking down and saying, 'Jesus, Alan Junior, you've followed in my footsteps playing for Preston North End; you did the same playing for the Republic of Ireland national team; you then followed my coaching path at both Preston and Ireland – and now you're following in my footsteps at Everton as a goalkeeping coach!' Unbelievable really, especially as I was starting a seven-year stint coaching another world-class Everton goalkeeper – the outstanding Jordan Pickford.

I first worked with Jordan at Preston as he worked his way up the league ladder in 2015 through a series of loan moves, but his stint on loan at Deepdale from Sunderland is still remembered by the Preston faithful for the sheer quality of his performances. He was consistently brilliant, breaking a club-record clean sheet stat and showcasing his amazing distribution talent to all. It was no surprise that he went back to Sunderland and went straight into the Premier League. He really was that good. Little did I know that our paths would cross again and lead to us working together for over 170 first-team games for Everton, where he won the player of the year award on three occasions and established himself as England's first-choice goalkeeper.

Jordan deserves all the success in the world because he gives everything to the game and everything to Everton Football Club. He is adored by the fans, who value his brilliance, his hard work and his loyalty – three qualities I observed watching Neville Southall back in the 1980s.

Paul Owens is a self-confessed Everton goalkeeping fanatic. He lives and breathes all things goalkeeping. His passion, knowledge and joy when talking about the goalkeepers of Everton is amazing. All those qualities are exemplified in the research, detail and love that have produced this unbelievable tribute to all of the Toffees' number ones – from the household names to Preston's former teenage apprentice engineer, whose dad once happened to coach the best goalkeeper in the world.

Alan Kelly
May 2025

Introduction

Since childhood, I have been obsessed with three things: Everton, goalkeepers and Everton goalkeepers.

The multicoloured kits, the goalkeeper gloves (very much the goalkeeper gloves!) and the desire of the very different characters that the position attracts to be part of a team yet simultaneously stand alone fascinated me right from the start of my football journey.

Throughout my school years, I would waste my time trying to imitate my idol, the inimitable Neville Southall, and often take to the field with my socks rolled down around my ankles, in the hope of playing like the then world's greatest goalkeeper. My love for the Welshman grew even more when I started taking the position more seriously and began writing to him for goalkeeping tips and training drills – receiving handwritten replies to my letters every single time. I wanted to be a goalkeeper. I wanted to play for Everton. I wanted to be Neville Southall. Seeing the work that he does today and his constant backing of the underdog in society, I am very proud to call him my hero.

When I wasn't playing football, I was watching videos of Everton's great teams from the past or had my head in books about the club's history. Although stories about the legendary Dixie Dean and the Holy Trinity midfield of Howard Kendall, Alan Ball and Colin Harvey fascinated me, they didn't fascinate me the way the much shorter paragraphs on the likes of goalkeepers Ted Sagar, Gordon West and Neville Southall did. I wanted to find out more about these men and the challenges that they faced during their careers.

It may sound odd but *The Glovesmen of Goodison: A History of Everton's Goalkeepers* is a book I knew I wanted to write long before I *actually* knew I wanted to write it. In my late teens, my grandma used to bring a copy of the *Weekly News* to my house every Saturday and I would spend hours cutting out articles about the club's goalkeepers of that time from the newspaper before adding them to a file I had produced containing football cards of English and Scottish Football League goalkeepers I had collected as a younger child. At the time, I didn't know why I did any of this – after all, the goalkeepers in those articles were not my idols (Southall was out of the team by then), my own dreams of turning professional were no longer alive and I am sure many of my friends would have viewed it as sad behaviour had they known about it – but looking back now it feels as though a lot of what I did back then was the groundwork for this publication.

It is a book that tells the history of Everton through the highs and lows of its goalkeepers and one that I hope does justice to every keeper who has stood between the sticks for this wonderful football club. Of course, there are chapters on two-time title-winners Southall, West and Sagar and a lengthy section on the effervescent Jordan Pickford, but it also shines a light on some lesser-known individuals, who have all played some part in the club's rich history – the likes of David Jardine, Tommy Fern and Arthur Davies, and Billy Coggins, Jim Arnold and Albert Dunlop.

Furthermore, I am very proud to have produced a chapter detailing the careers of the goalkeepers who have played for Everton Women (previously Everton Ladies) since its inception in 1995. The stories of the challenges that many of these women have had to overcome to be taken seriously in a male-dominated environment and, in many cases, to balance playing football with other commitments are truly inspiring.

I am also extremely proud of the book's final chapter, which consists of fans' memories of standout saves and goalkeeping performances at Goodison Park, the club's iconic home for 133 years. Although we are all looking forward to our future at the magnificent new stadium at Bramley-Moore Dock (and delighted that Everton Women are moving into Goodison Park), nobody does nostalgia quite like Evertonians and the collection of goalkeeping memories at the back of this book is truly brilliant.

It takes a very special character to be a goalkeeper – the willingness to put your body on the line and take responsibility for your actions while standing just metres from thousands of barracking supporters should never be undervalued by fans, teammates or those working in the media.

I hope you enjoy reading about these exceptionally brave individuals as much as I enjoyed researching them.

Up the Toffees!

Up the Goalkeepers' Union!

Paul Owens
May 2025

1

Jordan Pickford –
England's Number One

Bold. Brash. Brave. Bonkers. Brilliant. Manic. Magnificent.
Malevolent. Terrific. Terrible. T-rex arms. It is difficult to think
of a goalkeeper in the history of British football performing at the
top of his game who has spawned a greater lexicon of antonyms
or been as heavily criticised by the national media as Everton and
England's mercurial stopper **Jordan Pickford**.

Consistently brilliant for club and country for well over half a
decade, Pickford appeared in two World Cups and two European
Championship finals before turning 31 years old – the age, in
many experts' eyes, when goalkeepers begin to reach the peak of
their powers. In all four of those competitions, the ex-Sunderland
man's performances were of the very highest standard, and in
three of them, including in the Euro 2020 Final against Italy
at Wembley, he made stupendous saves from the penalty spot
as Gareth Southgate's team came tantalisingly close to winning
the country's first piece of senior silverware in the men's game
since 1966.

However, despite Pickford's heroics, ahead of the 2024 Euros
in Germany, the narrative somehow still prevailed that he was the
weakest link in the England team, that his perceived arrogance and
tendency to get emotionally involved with the crowd would be the
difference between winning and losing matches at the business end
of a major tournament – that there were better options out there
available to Southgate, including goalkeepers who were not playing
first-team football for their club sides. All of it was nonsense.

In an attempt to prove that the Everton man was a loose
cannon incapable of handling the pressure, his critics – many

of whom were ex-Liverpool players working for various newspapers and the major TV outlets – would choose to ignore the world-class saves he made week in, week out for his club and the ridiculously brilliant performances he put in to preserve Everton's top-flight status almost single-handedly for three seasons in a row between 2022 and 2024. Instead, they preferred to constantly point to a freak goal he conceded in the dying moments of a Merseyside derby in 2018 and a reckless yet unintended collision with Liverpool skipper Virgil van Dijk at Goodison Park two years later. At times, the stinging abuse coming Pickford's way, especially after the incident with Van Dijk, would become not only extremely personal but unacceptably toxic, and it is testament to his incredible strength of character and mental toughness that he has managed not to let it affect his performances or halt his progress in becoming the finest British keeper of his generation.

Pickford ended the 2024 European Championship finals with the second-highest save percentage of any goalkeeper to have played in a Euros finals tournament and made several excellent reflex saves in the final against Spain before being beaten by Mikel Oyarzabal's close-range strike with only minutes remaining. Of course, there were still those in the media who found the time to criticise him, firstly for celebrating a save late on in the last-16 tie against Slovakia that prevented the game from going to penalties and then for sliding on his knees after Ollie Watkins's last-minute winner against the Netherlands in the semi-final.

In 1996, the great Neville Southall gave an interview to *Goal* magazine, in which the Welshman addressed both the issue of him being dubbed eccentric by the press and his perceived frostiness to many of those working in the media. Southall stated, 'If you want to do something different from how they think things should be done, then you're eccentric, aren't you? If you go along with everyone else, you become a robot. You can't win so you may as well do what you want to do. I'm my own man. If you don't like it, then too bad. It's the only way you can live your life. I just do what I want and if they don't like it, tough.' Almost 30 years later, the same lines may just as well have been uttered by arguably Everton's second-greatest goalkeeper of the postwar era.

One man who has had Pickford's back covered throughout his career to date is goalkeeping coach and mentor Alan Kelly, who knew his protégé was destined for great things after seeing him play as a raw 20-year-old on loan at Carlisle United from Sunderland in 2014, in a game which saw Pickford concede six goals against Kelly's Preston North End. When I spoke to Kelly, he explained what he saw in the young goalkeeper that day, 'After the game, I walked over to my manager Simon Grayson and said, "That's the one for me. That's who we need going forward." Simon looked at me as though I was daft as Jordan had just let six in but I told him, "That's definitely the one we want."

'After a year on loan at Bradford City, Jordan came to us on loan about a week before the start of the 2015/16 season. Straight away, he was fantastic. You talk to any Preston North End fan from that era and they will tell you that they would struggle to think of a better goalkeeper. At one point he kept seven clean sheets on the bounce. We went to Burnley, who were flying at the time, and won 2-0 and he made two outstanding saves in that game. He was an unbelievable shot stopper; he was coming for crosses, he was totally dominating his area and his distribution was at a level that nobody had ever seen before. Karl Robinson, who was managing MK Dons, couldn't believe it when Jordan kept coming for crosses against his team. Their plan had been to isolate our young keeper and put him under pressure, but Jordan caught 12 and punched three of the total crosses in that game and I remember Karl turning round and saying to me, "Who gave me that dud information about your keeper?!"

'Jordan also made his England under-21s debut that season against the USA at Deepdale. Undoubtedly, he saw his time at Preston as his audition for the Premier League and not long after returning to Sunderland forced his way into the first team. He hasn't looked back since. I knew even back then that he would end up playing for England.

'He has always had a real mental toughness about him and never been afraid to put himself out in front of new team-mates and new supporters. He has always backed himself. That was evident in all the loan moves he undertook as a teenager and in his early 20s – Darlington, Alfreton Town, Burton Albion, Carlisle,

Bradford City and Preston. To walk into a dressing room full of people you don't know shows that you have to have a belief in your talent, a resilience in your character and an ability to show your new team-mates that these new surroundings will hold no barrier to your performances. People look at the goalkeeper and think you are alone but Jordan prides himself on being a team player, which was evident when Frank Lampard gave him the captain's armband at Everton. That was a statement of what Jordan is like behind the scenes – a great lad, a good team-mate and a leader. And that is the behind-the-scenes person that people don't always see.

'For me, that person hasn't changed. From being at Preston in 2015 to seeing him at Everton in 2024, he has remained grounded because that is his character. Yes, people see the frustration at times but that is only because he wants better. Surely that is something that you want from all your players on the pitch – you want them to strive to be better, to improve performances and to climb the league ladder. The day you don't want to do that for yourself and the team is the day that your standards will start to slip and the time to pack it all in.'

Having been shortlisted for the PFA Young Player of the Year award in 2017 (at the time of writing, a trophy that no goalkeeper has ever won) after his maiden campaign as a Premier League goalkeeper, Pickford, voted England under-21s' player of the year after some outstanding performances in the UEFA European Under-21 Championship finals that summer, moved to Goodison Park in June 2017 for an initial payment of £25m (plus an extra £5m in add-ons), which made him the third most expensive goalkeeper in world football at the time, after Gianluigi Buffon and Ederson. On signing for the club, Pickford told the BBC Sport website, 'Last season was my first in the Premier League so to get this opportunity with Everton now, to be able to go forward with my career and show everyone what I can do, is unbelievable. This is an exciting time for the club and for me, too, with the ambition being shown. I just want to be the best I can be to help.'

Over the last near-decade, he has done far more than merely help out. In a troubled and turbulent period in Everton's history, which saw Pickford play under eight different 'permanent' managers (and two caretaker bosses) in his first eight years on

Merseyside, the club docked ten points for breaching financial fair play rules and the team embroiled in relegation battle after relegation battle, he has done more than anyone to keep Everton in the top flight of English football. Pulling off big saves at big moments in big games would become the norm for the Washington-born stopper.

According to Kelly, reunited with Pickford just five months into his Everton career, following the sacking of Ronald Koeman and his backroom staff after an awful start to the 2017/18 campaign, 'I have never seen a goalkeeper receive as much stick as Jordan has over the years. Because of his character – and the fact that he likes to interact with the fans as his way of "staying in the game and focused" when dealing with pressurised situations – and because he has performed at such a consistently high level for such a long time, he has often got it in the neck for his actions on the pitch, not only when things have gone wrong and he has conceded goals, but also for celebrating saves, which is absolutely bonkers. His Premier League save of the season against Chelsea at Goodison in 2022 is a prime example: he makes a miraculous save, celebrates with the Everton fans and then quickly refocuses to make another brilliant point-blank save from the resulting corner from Antonio Rüdiger.

'I think when you break down what many of those who have criticised him have had to say, then it is pretty obvious that they haven't really seen him play. He has been brilliant for a long, long time now and it has been the greatest of privileges for me to work with him – both at Preston when he was just 21 years old and then at Everton between 2017 and 2024 after David Unsworth brought me to the club. The negative noise surrounding Jordan has been ridiculous because, in my opinion, he is a modern-day Everton legend.'

It is an opinion shared by many Evertonians, including the media trio David Prentice, Alan Myers and Phil McNulty. According to Prentice, a lifelong Evertonian, the former sports editor at the *Liverpool Echo* and the Toffees' communications manager since 2022, 'We would have gone down at least twice in recent seasons without him. His performance against Chelsea towards the end of the 2021/22 campaign was one of the great

Everton goalkeeping performances and it really frustrates me when I hear people who obviously never watch Everton play say, "He is OK for England but not for his club." He has been so good and so consistent for so long, and is very much a modern goalkeeper in terms of how good he is with his feet to spark attacks. I absolutely love the guy and think we are very lucky to have him.'

Sky Sports News' Alan Myers, Everton's head of media between 1996 and 2001, believes that there are similarities to be made between Pickford and Neville Southall, 'People may shudder a little at the comparison but over the years both Neville and Jordan have made big saves that have won us games. That's what makes them great. Along with Nigel Martyn, Jordan is the closest we have seen at Everton to Neville in terms of consistency but away from the club he doesn't get anywhere near the credit that he deserves.'

Phil McNulty, BBC Sport's chief football writer, is another who believes that Pickford deserves to be talked about in the same breath as Southall, 'All Everton fans will know how good he is and the debt that the club owes to him for keeping them in the Premier League. He is a model professional who consistently makes match-winning and match-saving stops. He is still out there, still wired, but not to the extent that he was and, anyway, wouldn't it be dull if everyone was the same? In my opinion, only Neville Southall sits above him in the Goodison Park goalkeeping pecking order. He makes a compelling case to sit alongside Gordon West, who won two titles and an FA Cup in his Everton career. Jordan Pickford may not have the medals to show for his efforts but his honours list is keeping Everton in the Premier League on at least two occasions with consistently brilliant performances.'

In Chapter 13, Jordan Pickford's excellent Everton career and brilliant performances at club and international level are chronicled and analysed in great detail. However, before we get there, let's go back to the very start, to a time before Goodison Park even existed, and commence a journey that pays tribute to every player to have stood between the posts for the club, starting with banker George Bargery, who first lined up in the Everton goal almost 150 years ago.

To aid with the navigation, the name of every 'regular' goalkeeper who made at least one appearance for Everton has been emboldened here, whereas the names of utility players who played the odd game in goal, outfielders who acted as emergency keepers (after an in-game injury or a sending-off) and goalkeepers who failed to make a first-team appearance have not.

2

The Early Men

The pre-Football League years (1878–1888)

During the Victorian period, Everton Football Club and the role
of the goalkeeper looked very different from those recognised
by football fans today. In 1878, St Domingo's Football Club was
formed when Reverend Ben Swift Chambers decided to give the
cricket-playing boys of the Methodist chapel on Breckfield Road
in Everton something to occupy their time during the winter
months. Having attracted interest from players and followers from
outside the chapel community, the club decided to change its
name to Everton Football Club in November 1879.

Ahead of joining the Football League in 1888, Everton
competed only in local cup competitions and played friendlies
against sides mainly from the Lancashire region. During that
period, goalkeepers usually wore the same colours as their team-
mates and were prohibited from carrying the ball. The use of
hands was strictly limited to protecting the goal and there was
nothing in the laws of the game to stop keepers from being
unfairly charged or obstructed by their opponents.

In their first game, Everton defeated local church side St
Peter's 6-0 on Stanley Park. In the first four years, the team had
no real regular goalkeeper, though **George Bargery** made more
appearances between the posts during that period than anybody
else. Although it is unknown whether he played in the game
against St Peter's, London-born but Kirkdale-raised Bargery
was definitely in goal for the club's first competitive match – a
Lancashire Senior Cup tie against Great Lever in 1880. Having
lost 2-0, Everton protested that the referee had not been impartial,
which led to the game being replayed. Unfortunately for Everton

and Bargery, he was beaten seven times in the replay – which was lost 7-1.

The following season, the goalkeeper and his defensive line fared far better. According to club records, Bargery kept six clean sheets in the nine games he played in during 1881/82 – keeping shutouts against Northwich Victoria, Middleton, Halliwell Jubilee, Liverpool Association, Over Wanderers and St Peter's. In his final appearance that campaign, he was beaten four times, but Everton still came out on top, defeating a Bootle XI 7-4 in their penultimate home game of the season.

Bargery, who spent the final 30 years of his life on the Isle of Man, was the great-grandfather of Tory MP Nadine Dorries, who served as secretary of state for digital, culture, media and sport from 2021 to 2022. In a 2008 news article about Dorries in the *Liverpool Daily Post*, it is claimed that Bargery, a bank clerk by profession, was given a choice – his job, or the 'rough and tumble' of football in 1882. Having a family to feed, he retired from the game and went on to manage his own branch. According to club records, his final appearance for Everton came in a 2-2 draw with Crewe Alexandra in October 1882. Earlier that year, he became the first Everton player to be credited with scoring an own goal after unfortunately netting for the opposition in a 4-1 victory over Bootle.

Other players known to have lined up in goal for Everton during those first four years are Charlie Hiles, John McGregor, William John Clarke, Henry Williams, Frank Brettell, Harry Richards, Tom Marriott, Sidney Chalk, Tom Williams, Harry Glover and John Williams, all of whom also played as outfielders. Furthermore, the following men are credited with making between one and three appearances in goal for Everton during those formative years: **Walter Jones**, **Ed Richards**, **Jack Richardson**, **Jim Houlgrave**, **Jimmy Brownlie**, **John Sharpe**, **John Wilkinson**, **George Jackson** and **Jack Flood**. However, as several team line-ups are missing or incomplete for matches played during that period, some of those keepers may well have played more games in goal for the club. With first names missing from certain early records, it is quite possible that a few of them also made appearances as outfielders. On a similar note, it is unclear whether Edwards, the goalkeeper who lined up against the Birkenhead Association in the second game of the 1879/80 campaign, was **George Edwards**, who played in goal against Birkenhead almost five years later. Another goalkeeper whose first name is missing from the early records is **Ashley**, who, in the opening game of the 1881/82 campaign, kept a clean sheet against Chester Rovers in the one appearance he is known to have made for the club.

The goalkeeping landscape looked very different in those early years. It was not until 1882 that crossbars were introduced or until the following year that goalkeepers were permitted to carry the ball in their hands – though even then they were restricted to moving just two steps with the ball before having to release it. At the time that those rules came into the game, Everton's goal was guarded mainly by **Charlie Lindsay**, who, after making his debut in an 8-2 loss to a far more experienced Bolton Wanderers side in March 1883, became the first Everton goalkeeper to win silverware, 12 months later, when he kept a clean sheet in the 1-0 victory over Earlestown in the Liverpool Senior Cup Final.

During that victorious season, outfielders Robert Morris, John Sinnott and leading scorer Jack McGill, who scored 19 goals in 17 appearances that term, also made appearances in goal, as did **Charles Twemlow** and **Jock Munroe**. Nonetheless, Lindsay led the way with 13 appearances in goal. He was again the main custodian during the 1884/85 campaign, Everton's first at their new Anfield home, when he played in more than two thirds of the club's known 37 fixtures. Unfortunately, in the final of the Liverpool Senior Cup there was heartbreak for Lindsay and his team-mates when, having cleanly taken a high centre, he was swept over the line by a pack of onrushing Earlestown forwards for the only goal of the game.

In the 1884/85 season, appearances between the posts were made by George Edwards, outfielder Joe Pickering, **George Chambers**, and **Charles Jolliffe**. Jolliffe became the regular goalkeeper the following campaign and held that position for the next two years, winning two Liverpool Senior Cups in that time, before making way for **Robert Smalley** in the autumn of

1887. Between 1885 and 1888, on the few occasions that Jolliffe or Smalley were not available or selected, goalkeeping duties were handed back to Lindsay, Pickering and Chambers. **Wally Mee**, **Tom Taylor**, **James Tynsley** and outfielders William Parry and Will George also made appearances in goal during that time. Conversely, on Christmas Day 1888, Jolliffe played the second half of the game against Ulster outfield and scored the final goal in a 3-0 victory in front of 8,000 spectators. According to the *Belfast Evening Telegraph*, 'much merriment was caused by the appearance of Jolliffe among the forwards', though, bizarrely, no reference was made to the makeshift forward grabbing the third goal in its match report. Thankfully for the Liverpudlian, his excellent performances between the Everton posts did result in him gaining some much-deserved recognition from the eloquent football wordsmiths of that period. In the *Liverpool Daily Post*, Jolliffe was described as 'a demon' after a fine early showing for the club, in which he had displayed 'goalkeeping wonderful in the extreme'. Moreover, the *Cricket and Football Field* labelled him a 'clever custodian' and described him as being 'as agile as a pantomime sprite'. Notwithstanding their clear artistry with the pen, many of the late-19th-century reporters struggled with the spelling of his surname, with many referring to him as 'Joliffe' in their prose. There was also some confusion surrounding the correct spelling of the diminutive form of his first name – with both 'Charlie' and 'Charley' often appearing in the sports pages of various publications.

Interestingly, in 1886, Everton entered the FA Cup for the first time and drew Rangers, as Scottish clubs were allowed to enter the competition at that time. However, after realising that they were about to field a team containing ineligible players, Everton forfeited the tie, withdrew from the competition and played the game as a friendly. Jolliffe was selected that day, as he was when Everton entered the FA Cup again the following year – playing in the 2-2 draw with Bolton Wanderers after the game had been replayed due to Bolton fielding an ineligible player in the first tie, which Everton had lost 1-0. However, by the time of the second and third replays, Smalley had been installed as the club's first-choice goalkeeper.

At Preston North End in the next round, the team was hammered 6-0, though that game was struck from the records and Everton were suspended from playing any football for a month after Bolton claimed that their opponents had 'persuaded players to join them by financial inducement' ahead of the previous round's ties. As a consequence, the Liverpool Senior Cup trophy that Jolliffe and his team-mates had won in both of the previous two years was taken back by the Liverpool and District FA, who also disqualified Everton from that season's competition.

Other than those made in the 1887/88 FA Cup ties against Bolton Wanderers, none of the appearances made by Everton players prior to the birth of the Football League in 1888 are counted in the club's official records. However, I believe it is extremely important to make reference to the original goalkeepers here – almost 40 men mentioned above who were brave enough to put their bodies on the line in the club's opening decade of matches. With line-ups missing for many games played during that period, there may have been more. Smalley and Jolliffe both stayed at the club for the next couple of years and made further appearances as Everton entered the brave new world of national football league competition.

* * *

The early years of the Football League – and a title win at Anfield

In the inaugural Football League campaign, 1888/89, Robert 'Bob' Smalley played in 18 of the club's 22 fixtures. Having started in the reserves at Preston North End, where his brother Walter also played, Smalley joined Everton from amateur side Lostock Hall in 1887 and made his debut in the 1-1 draw with Notts County that year, a friendly which had been arranged to coincide with the town's annual Goose Fair – a real high in Nottingham's calendar during that period. In 1890, the goalkeeper, renowned for both 'repelling and fisting out hot shots', was part of the Everton team that destroyed another East Midlands side, Derby County, 11-2, in the first round of the FA Cup, which, at the time of writing, is still Everton's record victory in a competitive match. In the 1889/90 season, he was a near-ever-present before losing his place to Scotsman **Walter Cox** for the final four matches of that campaign.

Charles Jolliffe, who had deputised on four occasions for Smalley in the 1888/89 season, played only one more game for the club, a 4-3 victory over Bolton Wanderers in September 1889, and retired at the end of Everton's second season in the Football League. Sadly, the likeable custodian, affectionately known as the 'smiling goalie', fell on hard times both financially and physically after leaving the game and in 1924 was unable to carry out his work as a decorator – his profession at that time. Mr M. Cowden wrote to the *Liverpool Echo* asking for Everton and its supporters to help their ex-goalkeeper, 'The old-time football enthusiast has had many a bright hour through Charlie's football at Everton and I want to help on his cause in the following manner. First, perhaps Everton could take concern in the affair. Then the 144th Scouts, with whom he was assistant officer, are arranging their side of the "benefit" and these scouts have a capable concert party who would like to give a show anytime anywhere.'

Pleasingly, it would appear that the former stopper got his life back on track with the help of his old club as in 1933 the *Liverpool Echo* stated that Jolliffe was 'still hale and hearty, and is engaged at Goodison during the season on matchdays'. Two years later, at the age of 73, Jolliffe was interviewed by reporter Ernest 'Bee' Edwards of the same newspaper, who described him as being 'straight as a poplar tree, nearly as tall and almost as sprightly as many a man half his years'. In that interview, Jolliffe detailed some of the odd experiences he encountered during his time between the uprights, 'I remember one match when the goalmouth was so under water that I stood on a wooden plank placed on a couple of bricks.' He then went on to explain how he had once been pinned down in a goalmouth scramble by seven or eight opposing players, one of whom had stood on his neck, leaving stud marks that were visible, according to Jolliffe, for some six months afterwards.

Jolliffe described those days as the greatest of his life and stated that he 'wouldn't be without them for a pension'. In the same article, reporter Edwards described the role of the goalkeeper during Jolliffe's time as 'being anything but a bobby's job – no goal nets, no penalty areas, no neutral linesmen; in fact, very nearly "no nothing". Goals were allowed that shot way over the bar or shot wide of the upright. Those were the days when the goal-judges would have been the right people in the right place.'

Walter Cox was signed on a short-term contract by club secretary Richard Molyneux at the goalkeeper's home in Leith after he fell out of favour at Burnley. After coming in to replace Smalley, Cox played in the last four games of the 1889/90 campaign as Everton finished just two points behind champions Preston North End. Although Cox was allowed to leave Merseyside that summer – he moved on to non-league Nottingham Forest before heading back to Scotland to play firstly for Leith Athletic and then Hearts, with whom he won the Scottish FA Cup in 1895 – Robert Smalley found himself usurped by another two Scots: **John 'Jack' Angus**, who started 11 of the club's first 12 matches of 1890/91, Everton's first title-winning campaign, and **David Jardine**, signed from local rivals Bootle that autumn, after a dip in form by his compatriot, who, along with his Everton team-mates, had started the season fantastically well.

Everton began the campaign with five straight victories, winning those games by an aggregate score of 23-2, before picking up a point in a 2-2 draw with Aston Villa at Villa Park in October, a match in which Angus, who had been signed from Football Alliance side Sunderland Albion six months earlier, received praised from the *Liverpool Mercury* reporter for the way he had to 'fist out rather cleverly a beautiful shot from the left'. However, after the team suffered a bad run of results and the young keeper kept just one clean sheet in four matches – ironically, against Sunderland, his old club's city rivals – Angus was replaced in the team by new signing Jardine for the home game against Blackburn Rovers in late November.

On the transfer of Jardine, the *Edinburgh Evening News* reported, 'The glories of Everton goalkeepers are usually transient. Bob Smalley did not like the advent of Cox, and the erstwhile Burnley man grew unhappy before he was long with Everton. Lots of people shook their heads at the engagement of Angus, but he has proved himself good enough, and now he has to go. The transfer of Jardine from Bootle to Everton is a solution to this problem of goalkeeping infallibility. The Lockerbie man has given displays here worthy of a Trainer [a probable reference to Preston North End's goalkeeper and former Everton second-team custodian James Trainer, regarded as the best goalkeeper in the league at that time], not once nor twice.'

Winning seven of the first eight league games in which Jardine kept goal, Everton returned to the top of the league in some style and took the title from Preston North End, after finishing two points ahead of the Lilywhites in a closely fought contest, despite losing 1-0 to them in the penultimate game of the season. After both sides lost their final matches, Everton were crowned league champions and became the first club in the country to be awarded silverware for finishing the season at the top of the Football League. Previous champions Preston had been awarded flags – known as 'standards' – for both of their previous title successes. Along with his team-mates, Jardine was presented with a winners' medal for his efforts that campaign. The silver and blue medals came from the club itself, not the league, and their design included a liver bird, the mythical creature these days synonymous with Everton's city rivals. David Jardine had made an excellent start to his Everton career and would start the next two seasons as the club's first-choice goalkeeper.

In the 1890/91 title-winning season, Robert Smalley made just one appearance, and was at fault for the winning goal in Everton's 2-1 defeat to Blackburn Rovers. The report in the *Liverpool Courier* stated, 'Smalley let a ridiculous soft shot from Southworth roll past him and into the goal.' It was a disappointing way for the popular Smalley's career in competitive football to end. Nonetheless, in April 1892, to acknowledge his six years of sterling service, the club granted him a benefit match, in which he kept a clean sheet and 'fisted out' several second-half efforts in a 2-0 victory over Blackburn Rovers. Ahead of the game, the *Liverpool Mercury* reported that Smalley had 'done a full share in the years preceding to bring Everton up to the high status which it enjoys, and for the many clever exploits achieved in goal by Smalley the followers of the club will be eager to acknowledge in the most practical manner this evening'.

After leaving Everton, Smalley returned to the Preston area, where he worked as a chartered accountant and got involved with many of the city's sports clubs. Following his death in 1947, his obituary in the *Lancashire Evening Post* made reference to his varied sporting career, 'Mr Smalley was a keen active sportsman in his youth and maintained an interest in cycling, football, cricket and bowling through-out his life. A former director and keen supporter of the North End club, he once kept goal for Everton and had the rare distinction of playing for and against the Old Invincibles. He was president of the Preston & District Cricket League and a member of the Fulwood Bowling Club. He was president of the Preston Rotary Club, president of the Preston Reform Club and president of the Preston & District Chartered Accountants' Society.'

John Angus made only one more appearance for the club after Jardine's arrival – in the 1-0 FA Cup loss to Sunderland in January 1891. Tragically, he died during the close season after contracting typhoid fever while back in Scotland. On 10 August 1891, the *Liverpool Mercury* published the following short paragraph, 'John Angus, the Everton Football Club custodian, died at his father's residence, Denny Loanhead, Denny, Scotland, on Saturday. Angus, who was spending the close season at home, was struck by typhoid fever, and gradually growing worse, expired at ten o'clock on Saturday night. The deceased began his career in King's Park FC, but his great fame [came when] reaching England; he was engaged by Sunderland Albion, with whom he remained for three seasons, when he signed for Everton, in whose team he was last year. He was 24 years of age, unmarried, and was a plumber by trade.'

On the same day, the *Sunderland Echo* paid their own tribute to the late stopper, 'Although only 24 years of age, Angus was a player of ripe experience, and as a goalkeeper he had few superiors. He rarely allowed high shots to pass him; if he had a weakness, it was for low shots, which sometimes puzzled him. Tall and strong, Angus was in appearance a model goalkeeper, and his genial disposition won for him lots of friends in Sunderland, among whom there have been many expressions of regret at his demise.'

* * *

Moving to Goodison Park

In the winter after Everton's title victory, a huge split at committee level resulted in Everton leaving their Anfield home. Club president and Anfield landlord John Houlding, who had already increased the annual rent of the ground from £100 to £240 at the onset of league football in 1888, wanted to increase it further – to £370 – following Everton's title success. Such plans, mixed with political and religious differences, spurred George Mahon – the organist from St Domingo's and both a successful politician and highly skilled accountant on Merseyside – into leading the rebellion against Houlding. This culminated in the abandonment of Anfield for a new home at Mere Green Field on the other side of Stanley Park. Within six months, the new stadium was constructed, the land on which it stood was bought within three years and all the monies borrowed paid back within a decade. Named Goodison Park, it would become Everton's home for the next 133 years.

The new ground was officially opened to the public on 1 September 1892, when Everton defeated Bolton Wanderers 4-2 in a friendly ahead of the 1892/93 campaign. Less than 48 hours later, the stadium hosted its first league fixture, which Everton drew 2-2 with Nottingham Forest in front of 14,000 spectators. In goal for both those matches was David Jardine. Jardine had been selected over understudy **Richard 'Dick' Williams** – who had joined the club on professional forms in September 1891 after the tragic passing of John Angus. Although Jardine holds the title of being the first person to keep goal for Everton at Goodison Park, his time at the club was coming to an end. Over the next 18 months, the Scot would make only eight more appearances before leaving the club at the end of the 1893/94 campaign. After initially signing for non-league side Nelson, Jardine moved on to Wrexham, where he won the 1897 Welsh FA Cup. His new team would then finish as runners-up in the competition in both of the following two seasons.

Everton's first season at Goodison Park was an odd one in terms of the goalkeeping position. Eight keepers were used across the 30 matches that term – a club record, at the time of writing, since the inception of the Football League. In addition to Jardine and Williams, who played in eight and 11 league games respectively, **Archibald Pinnell**, **William Thomas**, **Murray** (first name unknown) and **Alex Rennie** all made appearances between the sticks that campaign, as did outfielders Bob Kelso and Hope Robertson. In just the second game of the season, Jardine came off hurt in the 4-1 loss at Aston Villa, resulting in half-back Kelso playing the rest of the game in goal. A month later – with Jardine having broken down again in the return fixture against Aston Villa, and Everton suffering a goalkeeper crisis – Robertson played the full match in goal against Newton Heath (soon to be renamed Manchester United), a feisty encounter which Everton won 4-3. Incidentally, 12 months earlier, he had also taken over from the injured Jardine midway through the first half at Bolton.

It would appear that Robertson was quite a character. In Rob Sawyer's biography of the player, one of the chapters is titled 'The Case of the Missing Crossbar'. After a 4-1 defeat at Bolton, the first-team squad was instructed to attend a meeting called by the club's directors. As Robertson had not played in the game at Pike's Lane, he took umbrage at being summoned to a dressing-down and chose not to attend the meeting. Having received a letter from the secretary demanding an explanation, Robertson 'liberated' a crossbar from the stadium by way of protest and told the club, 'If the directors want it back, they must send a man to remove it.'

During that autumn and winter, Pinnell, Thomas, Murray and Rennie all made their only appearances for Everton. First up was Archibald Pinnell, who came in for the 2-2 draw with Blackburn Rovers, seven days after the defeat at Villa Park. Having performed competently, Pinnell, described as 'a very lengthy chap' by *The Clarion*, retained his place for Everton's next game and kept a clean sheet in the 6-0 demolition of Newton Heath at Goodison Park. Just three days later, the clubs met again but, with the teams locked at 1-1, the game was abandoned by the referee after 75 minutes as it had become too dark for him to distinguish aspects of play.

Sadly for Pinnell, his next game would prove to be his last for the club. After a 4-1 defeat to Sunderland, when, according to reports in both the *Shields Daily News* and the *Athletic News,* the goalkeeper endured a nightmare performance, Pinnell returned to the reserves before leaving for Preston. The *Athletic News* went in particularly strongly on the rookie, who had originally been signed by Everton as a centre-forward, 'Where the real difference in the two teams lay was in the goalkeeping. Pinnell is said to have done well against [Blackburn] Rovers, but I saw nothing in this match to justifying him in claiming ability as a goalkeeper. He never shaped anything like one, and adopted the dangerous experiment of kicking at balls when he could have used his hands, and in other instances he was very undecided what to do. I don't know whether Murray is eligible or not but he gave me the impression that he does know something about keeping goal.'

After joining the Scots Guards and surviving the First World War, Pinnell saw out his working life as a coal miner back in Blantyre, the Scottish town in which he had first come to the attention of Everton's scouts.

Unfortunately for Murray, he endured a similar afternoon to Pinnell's Sunderland experience in just his second outing for the club away at Bolton. In the *Football News*, it was reported that the Everton supporters 'were disgusted with the display of Murray in goal' in a 4-1 loss at Pike's Lane. Although he is credited as playing well in the 6-1 victory over Derby the following week by the *Aberdeen Press and Journal*, he played no more games for the club.

As William Thomas's sole appearance for the club, a 3-0 defeat to West Bromwich Albion, had also failed to convince the team selectors that he was the right man for the job, the club then turned their attention to Alex Rennie, paying Scottish side Halliwell £30 for his signature. Despite him being beaten five times on his debut, a 5-3 defeat to Sheffield Wednesday, initial signs were extremely promising. Rennie kept a clean sheet in the 6-0 victory over Notts County and then again versus West Bromwich Albion just seven days later, when he was in superb form and instrumental in Everton gaining a 1-0 victory at Goodison Park. The *Glasgow Herald* described him as being in 'capital form' that day. However, his outstanding performance against the Throstles turned out to be his last in an Everton shirt as Richard 'Dick' Williams re-emerged from the shadows and played all but one of the remaining 16 games that season. In

July 1893 Rennie signed for Liverpool – a new club that had been established at Anfield the previous year following Everton's departure from their former home. He then went on to play for the Liverpool Police football team.

Everton finished the 1892/93 season in third position – just a point adrift of rivals Preston, but a massive 12 points behind Sunderland. They also reached their first FA Cup Final that campaign and Williams was an ever-present in goal during that cup run. Having defeated West Bromwich Albion 4-1 the week after Rennie's heroics against the same side in the league fixture (Rennie was ineligible for the cup games having signed too late in the season), Everton then beat Nottingham Forest and Sheffield Wednesday in the following rounds, before meeting Preston in the semi-final. After two draws at Bramall Lane, cup ties in which Williams performed extremely well – frequently cutting out attacks by intelligently dashing from his line despite taking an early knock to the thigh in the first game of the semi-final trilogy – Everton overcame the Lilywhites 2-1 in the second replay, staged at Ewood Park.

In the final, Everton were defeated 1-0 by Wolverhampton Wanderers in front of a massive crowd at Fallowfield, Manchester. In some quarters, Williams was blamed for the goal, though many fans believed that he had been distracted by the close proximity of the supporters to him in a stadium ill-equipped to accommodate a reputed crowd of 45,000. In the *Liverpool Echo*, the following excerpt from a letter was printed, which highlighted the less than sporting actions of the opposing supporters behind Williams's goal in the second half, 'The poles which at first supported the net attached to the posts at the Whitworth-Lane end were in the second half loosened and the netting cut by some uncouth ruffian, and when Williams was defending that goal in the second half he was subjected to some very uncomplimentary remarks. One gentleman had so carried out his design that those so disposed could by walking on the netting touch Williams. He very properly took no notice of their "gas" but when the shot was sent in which decided the match these "sportsmen" I should think completely bewildered Williams with their hints and crushing.'

Despite the disappointment, Williams ended the season strongly, keeping three clean sheets in the four games played after the cup final. During the 1893/94 campaign, he played in all but four of Everton's 31 matches, before moving on to Luton Town in 1895. In his final appearance for Everton, away at Sheffield United, he was badly injured after just 25 minutes and had to be replaced in goal by outfielders Bob Kelso and Alf Milward, who shared his duties that day. From Luton, Williams joined Glossop North End and was part of the small Derbyshire club's promotion to the top flight, playing against Everton twice in 1899/1900. However, following Glossop's inevitable relegation from the First Division at the end of that campaign, Williams retired and settled in Leigh, on the outskirts of Manchester, where he found employment as a labourer and also with Leigh Cricket Club.

Richard 'Dick' Williams holds the distinction of being the first Everton goalkeeper to save a penalty, having kept out Hughie Wilson's strike in the Christmas Day fixture against Sunderland at Anfield in 1891. Two years later, in the 8-1 thrashing of Darwen, he became the first keeper to save a penalty at Goodison Park. He is the only custodian in the club's history to save penalties at both stadia. Before the introduction of the penalty spot in 1902, the penalty kick could be taken from any point along a line 12 yards from goal, and goalkeepers could charge up to six yards out of their goal (it was not until 1905 that keepers were required to remain on their line for penalties). Williams also played in the club's first intra-squad friendly to be held at Goodison Park. In August 1894, he lined up for the Blues against the Whites, who had Wearsider Tom Cain in goal, with Cain's side coming out on top 4-2 in front of thousands of supporters. Over the next 75 years, the intra-squad practice matches would regularly take place at the stadium in the summer months. The teams would consist of first-team players, reserves and trialists.

Between January 1894 and January 1895, **John Whitehead**, **Tom Cain** and **William Sutton** all made appearances in goal for Everton. Deputising for the unavailable Williams, Whitehead made his debut in the 3-3 draw with Darwen on New Year's Day in 1894, and then kept a clean sheet in the 2-0 victory over

Newton Heath five days later. Having signed for Everton from Bootle in 1892, he would make it a trio of Merseyside clubs he turned out for when he joined Liverpool for an undisclosed fee in March 1894. At the end of the following campaign, he was selected for Liverpool's 'Test Match' against second-tier side Bury (an early form of a play-off between the First Division's bottom team and the Second Division's top team). After losing, Liverpool were relegated to the Second Division and Whitehead played just two more games for them.

Tom Cain, signed from Stoke in April 1894, made 12 appearances in his brief spell with the club. He played in both Merseyside derbies in 1894/95 – the first season in which the two clubs met in league football – keeping a clean sheet in the comprehensive 3-0 victory at Goodison Park on 13 October before being part of the team that earned a 2-2 draw at Anfield five weeks later. However, having initially been unable to dislodge Williams and with the club then signing **William John Hillman** towards the end of the season, Cain decided to move on to Southern League club Southampton St Mary's before returning to the Football League with Second Division outfit Grimsby Town. He then moved back to his native north-east and played for Hebburn Argyle and West Stanley before tragically passing away at the age of just 23, having contracted typhus fever. The signing of Hillman also spelled the end for William Sutton, who, after playing in the high-profile festive period friendlies against Liverpool and Celtic, made his only competitive first-team appearance against Derby in the 2-2 draw in January 1895.

Controversial character Hillman, known as 'Happy Jack' throughout his career, signed from Burnley, and made six appearances in the final few weeks of the 1894/95 season as the club finished in second position on 42 points – five points behind champions Sunderland. Somewhat bizarrely, the goalkeeper's first two appearances for Everton came against his former club, with his new side coming out on top on both occasions (4-2 at Turf Moor and then 3-2 at Goodison Park just five days later). In the second intra-squad friendly, played on 24 August 1895, Hillman was beaten four times as the Blues lost 4-0 to the Whites, who had a J. Cook playing in goal for them.

In the 1895/96 season, the Tavistock-born custodian was an ever-present until the final day, when he lost his place to **Henry Briggs** – a January signing from Darwen for a fee believed to be £50. In the summer of 1896, Hillman was on the move up north to Scotland, where he signed as a goalkeeper for Dundee and a wicketkeeper for Forfarshire CC. His spell with Dundee proved to be an unhappy one, though, as he was suspended by the cash-strapped club for apparently 'not trying' midway through the 1897/98 season. In March 1898, Hillman moved back to Lancashire and began his second spell with Burnley. A year later, he gained his only international cap – playing in England's 13-2 victory over Ireland in Sunderland. More controversy would soon follow, however, and, after allegedly attempting to bribe the Nottingham Forest players on the final day of the 1899/1900 season, when the Clarets failed to fight off relegation, he was banned for the entire following campaign.

In January 1902, Hillman was transferred to Manchester City, where he won the Second Division title in his first full season and then the FA Cup 12 months later. It wasn't long before he found himself in further trouble with the FA, though: in 1906, along with 16 other players, Hillman was banned from playing for the club after an investigation into the paying of player bonuses. He wound his career down at Millwall Athletic before returning to Burnley to work as a trainer. After an extremely colourful career in football, Hillman went on to open a chocolatier's shop, where he would proudly display the football used in Manchester City's 1904 FA Cup Final victory.

Having taken the goalkeeping position from Hillman, Briggs started the first ten games of the 1896/97 season. However, after both picking up a groin injury and being at fault for two of the goals conceded in the 3-2 loss to Bolton Wanderers, when the *Liverpool Mercury* reported that the Everton goalkeeper had been 'apparently unnerved at the very outset, when a goal was scored against him in the first minute', Briggs was replaced in the team by new signing **Bob Menham** – bought out of the Grenadier Guards in April 1896. Sadly for Briggs, he never played another game for the club. Although Blackburn and Woolwich Arsenal both expressed an interest in signing the Nottingham-born custodian, himself a talented wicketkeeper, they were seemingly put off by the £100 asking price, which was double the fee Everton had paid Darwen for him. In the end, Briggs joined Lancashire League side Nelson for an undisclosed fee. He spent several seasons there before his old injury problems resurfaced and he ended up retiring from the game.

North-east-born Bob Menham made his debut in a goalless draw at Anfield in November 1896 and kept his place for the rest of the season – missing just two of 25 games after coming into the team. The *Sporting Life* described Everton's new goalkeeper glowingly, 'He is active and decides what to do quickly, is a good punter, fists out well, and kicks cleanly and surely.' In an up-and-down season, which saw Everton finish in seventh position – at that point, their lowest finish since their first season in the Football League – the highlight was most definitely their FA Cup run, which saw Menham and his team-mates overcome Burton, Bury, Blackburn and Derby before meeting Aston Villa in the final.

Ahead of the game, Menham was described in the *Morning Leader* as Everton's 'weak spot', and there were conflicting reports regarding his performance on that disappointing afternoon, when Everton were defeated 3-2 by the Midlands club. Everton director and first historian Thomas Keates believed that cup silverware had been lost because of Menham's 'feeble goalkeeping' and it was reported in several newspapers that the stopper had been 'deceived by a swerving shot' and 'caught flat-footed' for two of the Villa goals.

Nonetheless, Menham was also said to have made a 'remarkable double save', and in the *London Echo* the following paragraph describing his performance appeared, 'He acquitted himself well; no goalkeeper could have been blamed for allowing the shots that were scored for escaping him. Several times he cleared magnificently, and Menham can look back with feelings of satisfaction upon his display.' Either way, at the end of the season, he was made available for transfer. After a short spell with Wigan County, he moved to Swindon Town, whom he captained and scored a penalty for in a 1900 FA Cup tie against Staple Hill. He settled in the Wiltshire town and became a publican. In a remarkable turn of events, many decades later, his 1897 FA Cup runners-up medal was located in a garden and now takes pride of place in the collection of Brendan Connolly, a member of the Everton FC Heritage Society.

In the 1896/97 season, goalkeepers **John Patrick** and **John Palmer** both made one appearance for Everton. Interestingly, Patrick came in on trial for the 6-0 victory over Burnley in November, which caused great excitement in the *Liverpool Echo*, whose reporter appeared to forget the goalkeeper's nationality, 'For their match tomorrow Everton have arranged a big surprise for their supporters. Patrick, the goalkeeper of Paisley St Mirren, who signed a league form for Everton a couple of seasons ago, has been prevailed upon to visit Liverpool, and will appear between the sticks against Burnley tomorrow. He is in splendid form just now and is looked upon as the only man who can expect with confidence his English cap this season.' Although Patrick only played the one game for the club, returning to St Mirren after the match against Burnley, the Kilsyth-born custodian did go on to receive international honours – playing for Scotland against Ireland and England in 1897.

Unfortunately for young stopper John Palmer, his own career was less successful. After impressing for the reserves, the rookie was handed his only Everton start at Blackburn Rovers, but was at fault for one of the goals in a 4-2 loss, when his goal kick went straight to opponent John Proudfoot, who finished with ease. After leaving the club, Palmer moved to Luton, for whom he also made just the one first-team appearance.

According to Thomas Keates, 'In the season 1896/97 the club had got together an array of talented players for every position except in goal, and the weak link in the side cost the side dearly.' Wholesale changes were made in the goalkeeping department that summer and Scottish international **Robert 'Rab' Macfarlane** started the 1897/98 season as Everton's first-choice custodian having joined the club from Third Lanark. However, after just nine games – and a heavy defeat at home to Sheffield United – he was replaced by another new signing, compatriot **Willie Muir**, who, over the next five years, would become the first Everton goalkeeper to play more than 100 competitive matches for the club. Macfarlane would go on to reach the same milestone himself, back in Scotland with Aberdeen, but not before a nomadic spell either side of the border, which saw him turn out for Bristol St George's, East Stirlingshire, New Brompton, Grimsby Town, Celtic and Middlesbrough within a six-year period.

Muir joined the club for £45 from Kilmarnock and made a strong start to his Goodison Park career. After coming into the side at the start of November, he was an ever-present in the team for the rest of his maiden campaign, saving two penalties early in the new year. He then missed just one game the following season – when Everton matched the previous term's fourth-placed finish. The *Liverpool Mercury* labelled Muir a 'capable custodian' and described him as 'steady, cool and fast' after his performance in the 1898 Christmas Eve 1-0 victory over Burnley, when he 'excelled himself between the uprights, saving his charge from Torran when a score appeared a certainty'.

As Everton entered the 20th century, Muir again kept a clean sheet, in the 1900 New Year's Day home victory over Preston North End, and was on the winning side in both derbies, having played in both defeats to an improving Liverpool side the previous season. An ever-present in 1900/01, the Scot started the 1901/02 campaign still in possession of the first-team goalkeeper spot. However, after a heavy defeat at Nottingham Forest in mid-October, he was replaced by patient understudy George Kitchen, who had signed for the club three years earlier but had been restricted to just three appearances in that time.

After losing his place in the team, Muir returned north of the border in the summer of 1902 and signed for Dundee. Again, he provided sterling service to his employers, making 147 appearances for the Dens Park club – ten more than he made for Everton. His fine form for Dundee resulted in him being selected for the Scottish League XI, for whom he kept a clean sheet in the 0-0 draw with their English counterparts on 2 March 1907, and his country – playing for Scotland in their 3-0 victory over Ireland at Celtic Park just two weeks later. After short spells with Bradford City (where he won a Second Division championship medal), Hearts and Dumbarton, Muir retired at the age of 33. Everton's first centurion stopper had enjoyed an excellent career.

3

20th-Century Boys

As Britain entered the Edwardian period, Everton finished the 1901/02 season as First Division runners-up – just three points behind winners Sunderland. Eight games into that campaign, **George Kitchen** had been installed as the club's first-choice goalkeeper, a position he would hold for the next three years.

Born in Fairfield in 1876, Kitchen became a golf professional at the age of 15. However, just two years later, he joined Buxton as a goalkeeper and spent 18 months in Derbyshire – catching the eye of several top-flight sides, including Everton, after an excellent performance against the Blues' second team. Having declined the opportunity to sign amateur forms with Everton in 1895, Kitchen eventually moved to Goodison Park in 1898, after a brief spell at Stockport County. In total, he played 90 times for Everton, keeping clean sheets in almost a third of those matches. Described by the *Scottish Referee* newspaper as both 'the saviour' and 'the hero of the Everton v Bolton match' – a 1-0 victory played on 21 December 1901 – Kitchen made 47 consecutive appearances between October 1901 and December 1902, before being replaced in the team by **Jack Whitley** for the Christmas Day meeting away at Grimsby Town.

Signed from Aston Villa in 1902, Whitley would make only 14 appearances for Everton before moving on to Stoke. In his two years at the club, possibly his biggest achievement came at the other end of the pitch – as he once scored a hat-trick for the reserves after being employed as an emergency centre-forward following the non-arrival of frontman Charles O'Hagan for the Lancashire Combination fixture against Rossendale. After leaving Stoke, Whitley took in brief spells at Leeds City and Lincoln City before settling at Chelsea in 1907, for whom he made 138 appearances over seven years. He was the first Chelsea goalkeeper to play for more than one season at the club and their first top-flight custodian. Following his retirement in 1914, Whitley became the first-team trainer at Stamford Bridge, a position he held until 1939. According to the Chelsea Supporters' Trust, he was 'a father figure to generations of Stamford Bridge players'.

Although Kitchen played the majority of games in 1903/04 – a campaign in which Everton finished third and conceded, on average, less than a goal a game for the first time since joining the Football League – his Goodison Park career came to a close after a poor display at home to Stoke in early April. The returning Whitley kept three clean sheets and Everton won all three of their remaining games that season, but neither man played for the club again after May 1904. Whitley moved on to Stoke and Kitchen signed for West Ham United, for whom he scored a penalty on his debut against Swindon Town. After seven years with the Hammers, Kitchen moved on to Southampton and then signed for Boscombe FC, later to be known as AFC Bournemouth. During his time on the south coast, he was employed as the resident professional at Queens Park Golf Club.

Everton's next custodian, 22-year-old Irishman **William 'Billy' Scott**, would go on to become a true club great, making almost 300 appearances over an eight-year period, but not before a shoulder injury sustained just 12 games into his Blues career resulted in the club drafting in Welsh international **Leigh Richmond Roose**. At The Wednesday (later to be renamed Sheffield Wednesday) in November 1904, Scott retired hurt midway through the second half and was replaced by outfielder Walter Abbott in an entertaining 5-5 draw. According to the *Liverpool Echo* correspondent 'Red Rick', just a couple of months earlier, in a 2-0 victory over Wednesday's city rivals Sheffield United, Scott only just avoided being badly hurt. Displaying 'a sample of his wonderful coolness', the goalkeeper 'had just made a full-length save and on rising to his knees was confronted by three Sheffield forwards; Scott coolly threw the ball over the line for a corner and rolled into the net to avoid the ugly clash. They were hard on goalies in those days.'

The son of a Presbyterian minister, a school friend of the writer H.G. Wells and once voted London's second most eligible bachelor, 'Dick' Roose was one of the game's first great goalkeeping extroverts. After leaving his North Wales home to study medicine, the Holt-born stopper joined Aberystwyth Town in 1895 and would go on to change the goalkeeping landscape during his colourful career. In addition to frequently leaving his goal and acting as an auxiliary defender, or 'sweeper keeper' to use the common parlance, Roose often bounced the ball all the way to the halfway line before sending it forward towards the opponents' goal – an extremely clever way of getting round the rule stating that goalkeepers could handle the ball anywhere in their own half of the pitch but not carry it for more than two steps. In 1912, a new rule was introduced which stated that goalkeepers could handle the ball only in their goal areas – markings which had been added to the pitch in 1902.

On his buccaneering style and surges upfield, Roose later said, 'A goalkeeper should take in the position [of the opposing players] at once and, if deemed necessary, come out of his goal immediately. He must be regardless of personal consequences and, if necessary, go head-first into a pack into which many men would hesitate to insert a foot, and take the consequent gruelling like a Spartan.'

After winning the treble with Aberystwyth Town and gaining his first Wales cap against Ireland in 1900, when he kept a clean sheet and also knocked opponent Harry O'Reilly unconscious after bundling him into touch, Roose moved to London, combining playing for London Welsh with working as an assistant at King's College Hospital. Despite James Catton of the *Athletic News* describing him as the 'Prince of Goalkeepers', Roose refused to go professional as doing so would have resulted in him having to give up his medical career. Furthermore, after a three-year spell with Stoke, where Roose had signed amateur forms but been given money to pay for first-class travel to matches from his London home, stays in luxury hotels, and also to help fund his lavish lifestyle, the eccentric custodian decided to quit league football and begin the next part of his medical studies. However, he was soon coaxed back. With Scott sidelined through injury and Kitchen out with flu, Everton turned to Roose in November 1904.

After showing signs of rustiness and fumbling a cross that gifted Sunderland a late winner on his debut, Roose spent 15 minutes before kick-off the following week apologising to the Everton fans for his error. He endeared himself further to the Goodison Park faithful that day by keeping a clean sheet in a 0-0 draw with Derby County and by, somewhat bizarrely, sitting on top of the crossbar during a stoppage in play. The shot-stopping showman, described by writer 'Red Rick' as a regular 'dancing doll' in his 1937 article 'The Star Goalkeepers', saved a penalty in his next match, at old club Stoke, and stayed in the side for all but four of the remaining games that campaign – which saw Everton finish as league runners-up and reach the semi-finals of the FA Cup.

Throughout his short time at Goodison, Roose performed extremely well. However, after a fall-out with club secretary Will Cuff about the playing of several important matches over a short period of time (Everton lost two games in two days in the final week of the season, which ultimately cost them the league title), he was dropped for the final game of the season away at Nottingham Forest and refused to travel with the team. With that, his Everton career came to an end. He returned to Stoke for the start of the new season and later played for Sunderland, Celtic, Port Vale, Huddersfield Town, Aston Villa and Woolwich Arsenal. In total, he made 24 appearances for Wales, often wearing his old Aberystwyth Town top, which had remained unwashed since the Welsh Cup Final win over Druids in 1900. According to 'Red Rick', Roose also refused to change his 'knickers' (playing shorts) while Everton remained in the 1905 FA Cup – changing them only after the semi-final defeat to eventual winners Aston Villa.

Off the pitch, Roose continued to make headlines too. He had a relationship with music hall star Marie Lloyd and, following retirement, became a popular after-dinner speaker. In 1914, he signed up to fight in the First World War and was awarded the Military Cross two years later for his brave actions in a battle at Agny, where he suffered damaged lungs after a flame-thrower attack. As his body was never found in battle, mystery surrounds the war hero's final days. His remarkable life story is told in *Lost in France*, by Spencer Vignes.

Returning to the topic of goalkeeping, it feels appropriate to end Leigh Richmond Roose's profile with his thoughts on life between the sticks, 'There is a proverb which says, "Before you go to war, say a prayer; before going to sea, say two prayers; before marrying, say three prayers." One might add, "Before deciding to become a goalkeeper, say four prayers." He's the Aunt Sally.' He concluded the same article on goalkeeping, which appeared in the 1906 publication *Association Football and the Men who Made it*, by stating the following, 'To a goalkeeper alone is the true delight of goalkeeping known. He must be an instinctive lover of the game; otherwise, goalkeeping will take it out of a man if he is not devoted to it.'

With Roose having departed and with his own injury concerns behind him, Billy Scott's Everton career began in earnest at the start of the 1905/06 season – a campaign which saw the Blues crowned FA Cup winners for the first time and Scott keep clean sheets in the semi-final victory over Liverpool at Villa Park and the defeat of Newcastle United in the final held at the Crystal Palace, London, three weeks later. Having barely touched the ball in Everton's dominant display in the final, Scott was happy to be far busier just 48 hours later, away in the league at The Wednesday, where, in addition to pulling off a series of brave diving saves, he kept out a penalty from Harry Wilson – just as he had done at Goodison Park six weeks earlier in Everton's 4-3 quarter-final win over the South Yorkshire outfit.

The Belfast-born stopper signed for the club in 1904 from Linfield, where his sound performances had already gained him international honours. However, just a year into his Everton career, Scott's place in the Ireland goal was thrown into question after a story appeared in the press claiming that he had thrown a punch at a committee member of the Irish FA after a game against Scotland. The *Liverpool Echo* reported, 'It seems the Irish goalkeeper on one occasion while discussing with Mr Foy, the chairman of the Irish Association, certain financial matters struck the latter official a heavy blow in the face with his clenched fist. The Irish Association, having privately discussed the affair, have officially reported the entire facts to the committee of the

Everton Football Club, to which the player belongs. It is almost certain the same individual will never again be chosen for the Irish international team.' As it turned out, Scott continued to represent his country with distinction for a further eight years, gaining 25 caps in the process and lining up in goal for Ireland when they defeated England for the first time in their history at Windsor Park in 1913.

At club level, he impressed throughout his time at Everton, with the *Liverpool Mercury* reporting that on his debut, against Notts County in 1904, Scott 'showed that he is a custodian of real ability'. A near-ever-present in every campaign between 1905/06 and 1911/12, the Irishman continued to receive the plaudits from the pressmen throughout his time on Merseyside. Away at Newcastle in September 1906, he was the team's top performer, with the *Liverpool Evening Express* stating, 'Scott showed a resourcefulness in goal which imparted just that requisite degree of confidence to his colleagues. Appreciating that the goalkeeper was safe as a rock, the visiting attack gave of their best.' It was a similar story the following campaign against lower-league opposition Oldham Athletic in a tricky away tie in the second round of the FA Cup. Scott's courageous performance that day earned his side a replay, which they won 6-1 back at Goodison Park, and himself the man of the match award in the *Liverpool Echo*.

In 1910, even though he was still very much the Blues' first-choice goalkeeper, Scott, along with team-mate Jack Sharp – the illustrious Everton winger and an England international in both football and cricket – was afforded the proceeds of the league encounter at Goodison Park against Chelsea. According to the *Liverpool Daily Post*, it was a 'fitting occasion for local enthusiasts to show their admiration of the Irish goalkeeper and their high opinion of Sharp' in the outfielder's final season of league football. For a further two seasons, Scott continued to be the club's reliable last line of defence and in 1912 narrowly missed out on a championship medal when Everton finished just three points behind Blackburn Rovers at the top of the Football League.

Despite his consistently brilliant performances and the 1906 FA Cup victory, Billy Scott is regarded as one of Everton's great 'nearly men' – one of the unluckiest players to be associated with the club. In his eight-year spell at Goodison Park, he finished as a league runner-up on three occasions: in 1904/05, 1908/09 and 1911/12. He was also an FA Cup Final loser in 1907 and a defeated semi-finalist in the same competition on two occasions, including in 1910, when he suffered a serious hand injury after conceding the first goal in the catastrophic 3-0 defeat to Barnsley at Old Trafford. With blood gushing from two of his fingers, Scott had to leave the pitch to have his hand bound up – his place in goal taken by left-back John 'Jock' Maconnachie, who, according to the *Birmingham Mail*, pulled off a great save to deny forward George Lillycrop. Bizarrely, Scott then returned to the field before having to come off again minutes from the end of the game, as the wounds had reopened.

At the time of writing, Billy Scott's 251 league outings for the club is bettered by only Neville Southall, Ted Sagar, Gordon West, Tim Howard and Jordan Pickford. In total, he made 289 appearances before signing for Leeds City for £400 in July 1912. According to the Leeds United fan website Mighty Leeds, as part of the deal, City manager Herbert Chapman agreed to pay Scott a full year's salary of £208 for ten months' work, meaning that he received more than the maximum wage. As a result, and much to his annoyance, he had to pay back some of his salary – the 'bonus' payment had been a major factor in him signing for the club in the first place.

After two years in West Yorkshire, Scott returned to Merseyside and signed for Liverpool. Although he failed to make a league appearance for the Anfield club, he did play in several wartime fixtures for the Reds (the Football League was replaced with regional leagues between 1915 and 1919 and there was no FA Cup between 1915 and 1920). Furthermore, he was Liverpool's goalkeeper in the Lancashire Cup Final victory over Everton on New Year's Day in 1919. His younger brother, Elisha, would go on to take his place in the Ireland national team and become one of Liverpool's greatest custodians, but only after Everton had reportedly decided against signing him in 1910 on the grounds of the then-17-year-old being too young to take a chance on. Elisha Scott would go on to make over 400 appearances for Liverpool in a career on Merseyside that lasted over two decades.

In later years, comparisons were inevitably made between the two goalkeepers. In 1936, following Billy Scott's death from pneumonia, reporter Ernest 'Bee' Edwards stated in the *Liverpool Echo*, 'I don't suppose there were two such contrasting characters as William and Elisha, but in spite of that they were parallel cases when they took the sport and kept goal. In fact, one would call William Scott the stolid goalkeeper; and in dealing with the best shot of old times, namely the ball that rose a little, William Scott was unequalled in his ability, using a knuckle to knock down a shot from a Hampton, a Shepherd or any other driving force.' A year later, 'Red Rick' also paid tribute to him in the same newspaper, 'William Scott, the nonchalant Irishman, seemed to be always chewing, had wonderful anticipation, rarely left his goal, and did everything in a quiet, cool manner that evoked admiration.' In 2017, the Everton FC Heritage Society, working in partnership with Linfield FC, had Scott's grave in Anfield Cemetery restored with a new headstone. Family members joined representatives of his clubs to mark the rededication.

Between August 1904 and May 1912, good friends Leigh Richmond Roose and Billy Scott started all bar 32 of Everton's 344 matches. When Roose failed to arrive in Liverpool for the 1904 Christmas Eve encounter with Manchester City, full-back Jack Crelley started in goal, before Scott was tracked down and entered the field eight minutes into the game. The following autumn, the outfielder had another run-out in goal – taking over from the injured Scott at half-time in the 3-2 loss to Sheffield United. According to the *Athletic News*, Crelley had little to do after the break 'but twice he saved his citadel very cleverly'. The following week, Irishman **Harry Collins**, a £75 signing from Burnley the previous month, came into the side to make the first of only three appearances for the club – he made his debut in the 6-2 victory over Notts County and then played in two April defeats ahead of the 1906 FA Cup Final before being released at the end of the season.

After Collins's exit that summer, former Wallasey amateur **Robert Depledge** and ex-Belfast Distillery stopper **Donald Sloan** joined the squad as cover for Scott. With Scott away on international duty, Depledge made his only competitive first-team appearance, in a 3-0 victory over Stoke just a week before the Blues' semi-final showdown in March 1907. Despite keeping a clean sheet, he was released at the end of his contract that May and later had brief spells at Linfield and Wrexham. Over a two-year period, Sloan managed just six appearances in the Everton first team. Having been unable to dislodge Scott from the starting XI, the Ayrshire-born young stopper moved across Stanley Park to join Liverpool in May 1908 for £300, resulting in Everton making a £50 profit on him. After just a handful of appearances for the Anfield club, he returned to Distillery as player-trainer and won the Irish Cup with them in 1909/10. Two years later, he was on the move again, this time heading back to Scotland, where he played for Bathgate and East Stirlingshire.

Tragically, Sloan and three of his brothers were all killed during the Great War. He lost his life when a heavy German mortar hit the dugout he was in near St Laurent-Blagny, Arras, on New Year's Day in 1917.

At the start of the 1908/09 season, following a successful trial towards the end of the previous campaign, rugby league player **Clarence Berry** decided to switch codes and join Everton. In his four seasons with the club, the former Warrington RLFC man made just three appearances in goal – though never finished on the losing side. After making his debut in a 2-2 draw at Bury in February 1909, when Billy Scott was away on international duty, Berry then made his Goodison bow a month later, when a Bert Freeman hat-trick helped Everton get the better of Chelsea for the first time in their history. The 3-2 victory scoreline was repeated in Berry's final game for the club, almost three years later in February 1912, when Sheffield United were vanquished at Goodison Park.

Throughout his time at Everton, Berry received numerous plaudits for his performances in the reserve team. In 1911, the *Liverpool Echo* wrote the following about Everton's stand-in keeper, 'The club is indeed fortunate that it can replace a great goalkeeper like William Scott by Berry, than whom there is not a better goalkeeper in the Lancashire Combination.' Following the expiry of his contract, Berry continued his goalkeeping career at St Helens Town before switching back to rugby league and returning to Warrington.

Having gained a reputation as a penalty-saving expert at Grimsby Town, where he saved 14 of the 17 spot kicks he faced in the 1908/09 season and became the first goalkeeper to save three penalties in one game, **Walter Scott** made the switch to Goodison Park in January 1910 for a fee of £750. During his 18-month stay at Everton, the Worksop-born keeper made 18 appearances – and played in the final eight games of his first season with the club, following namesake Billy Scott's hand injury in the FA Cup semi-final against Barnsley. Indeed, in just his third game, Walter repeated his penalty-saving heroics of the previous term when keeping out Henry Low's spot kick in a 1-0 victory over Sunderland at Roker Park.

In his second season at Goodison Park, Walter kept four clean sheets in seven games, which yielded two wins and five draws. That summer, the *Sheffield Star Green 'Un* claimed that the goalkeeper, who was enjoying a game of cricket back in Worksop with his hometown club's second string, 'made a catch which out-rivalled anything ever seen in that neighbourhood. He sprang four or five yards, took the ball with one hand outstretched and held on while turning a complete somersault.' A month later, the agile custodian moved to Sunderland for the same £750 fee that Everton had paid Grimsby for his services.

Sadly, he endured a miserable spell in the north-east and had his contract terminated by the Sunderland directors for 'palpable inefficiency' four weeks into the 1912/13 season. Following his exit, Scott spent time in Ireland with Shelbourne, and represented the Irish Football League on five occasions. He wound down his career back near his birthplace – signing for Worksop Town, Gainsborough Trinity and Grimsby. During the First World War, he also guested for Millwall Athletic and Brentford.

Ahead of the 1912/13 campaign, more changes were made in the goalkeeping ranks, with Scottish duo **James Caldwell** and **William Hodge** joining, and Billy Scott and Clarence Berry departing. Caldwell, a £500 signing from Reading, started the season as first choice, but lost his place in the March after an awful performance against Oldham Athletic in the FA Cup, a game in which his erratic kicking and handling error in the lead-up to the visitors' winning goal drew strong criticism from supporters and newspaper reporters alike. At the end of the season, having played just three more first-team games, Caldwell left for a reduced transfer fee of £200. After short spells with Woolwich Arsenal and at former club Reading, the goalkeeper served as a private in the Black Watch during the Great War. He then returned to Scotland, where he won the Second Division title with Alloa Athletic before finishing his career at East Stirlingshire.

After Everton's FA Cup exit to Oldham, William Hodge was handed his chance at home to Sheffield United and received huge praise for his debut display – with the *Liverpool Echo* describing him as being 'safe, acute and swift in clearance', and reporting that he received great applause from the Goodison crowd. A week later he dislocated a finger in a 3-1 win at Chelsea. Although the Scot returned for the last four matches of the season – after missing the same number of games over a busy Easter period, during which local stopper **William Bromilow** made his one appearance in the Football League for the club – Hodge played only four more times for Everton's first team and was released at the end of his contract in May 1914. Incidentally, Bromilow, the elder brother of the future Liverpool and England left-half Tom Bromilow, would go on to make six further Everton appearances during the First World War football period (1915/16 to 1918/19). He was released in May 1920 and subsequently joined Oldham Athletic – the club against whom he had made his solitary competitive appearance for Everton over seven years earlier.

Ahead of the first 14 seasons of the 20th century, Everton played a total of 21 intra-squad friendlies. In addition to many of the goalkeepers mentioned so far in this chapter, Frank Joyce, W. Kelly and Gilbert Turner lined up between the posts in those fixtures. None of the three played a competitive game for the club.

Everton's next custodian, Elgin-born **Frank Mitchell**, made 24 competitive first-team appearances during his war-interrupted spell at Goodison. After starting the first nine games of the 1913/14 campaign, Mitchell lost his place in the team following an error-strewn display against Manchester City, when, according to the *Daily Citizen*, his poor handling and indecision 'made his colleagues tremble'. From that point on, the former Motherwell man was mainly employed as the Blues' understudy goalkeeper – winning the Central League with the reserves in his first season on Merseyside. After William Hodge returned to the Everton starting XI for a short spell that autumn, Tommy Fern was signed from Lincoln City in the December. The new arrival would instantly make the first-team spot his own.

Although Mitchell held the first-team position for only a short period, it must be noted that he did play three games in the victorious 1914/15 campaign, when the club won the league title for only the second time in their history, and that he made an impressive 99 appearances for Everton during the wartime football period – a total bettered by only five Everton players during that time. Mitchell also played in all eight of the intra-squad friendlies during that period – with Fern lining up in the opposing goal for the first five and Johnny Best, Pritchard and Lawson making appearances in the final three. Having started the first campaign after the Great War between the posts at Goodison Park, Mitchell moved on to Liverpool in 1920 and later joined Tranmere Rovers, meaning he shares the distinction of turning out for all three Merseyside clubs with 1950s legendary forward Dave Hickson.

After making his debut in the 1-1 draw with The Wednesday in December 1913, courageous keeper **Tommy Fern** would go on to play for more than a decade in goal for the club – making 231 competitive appearances (as well as 40 more during the wartime period). According to historian Rob Sawyer's article on the goalkeeper for the Everton FC Heritage Society's website, Fern's transfer to Goodison Park came about quite by chance. Having been sent to West Yorkshire to run the rule over Lincoln City forward David MacFarlane in a game against Leeds City at Elland Road, one of Everton's directors returned to Merseyside strongly recommending that the club signed the Lincoln goalkeeper instead. Soon after Fern's arrival, the *Liverpool Courier* reported, 'Everton's angling at Lincoln has resulted in a big catch. Though he has figured for such a long time in Second Division football, Fern is reckoned a keeper of the highest class, and certainly he has performed wonderful work for Lincoln City during the four and a half seasons he has been with them. On his only appearance in the city – against Everton Reserves in a Central League game – Fern, in addition to making several grand clearances, had the distinction of stopping a couple of penalty kicks.'

The *Athletic News* were just as generous with their praise for Everton's new goalkeeper, 'The ease with which he can grasp a ball under the bar shows his reach, but he is equally at home with low shots. Putting all his weight into a blow, he can fist a ball nearly to the halfway line. With agility and anticipation, he fields beautifully, and is probably the best keeper Everton have had since William Scott was at his zenith.'

In his first full season at Goodison Park, Fern was a crucial figure and near-ever-present as Everton pipped Oldham to the league title by one point. Indeed, the Blues may have gone on to achieve a historic double had he not missed the FA Cup semi-final clash against Chelsea at Villa Park with a finger injury. The unfortunate Frank Mitchell was widely blamed for both goals in the 2-0 loss that day – having had a clearance charged down for the first goal and then being slow to react to a long-range effort for the second. Because of his courageous style, injuries were a common theme throughout Fern's time at the club. On five different occasions, he had to leave the pitch and be replaced by outfielders Jock Maconnachie (who had deputised for Billy Scott in 1910), Harry Makepeace, Jack Page and Tom Fleetwood.

At the end of the 1914/15 campaign, the Football League was suspended for four years – and Fern was stationed at a support and supply depot in Catterick, Yorkshire, where he would remain with the Royal Garrison Artillery until 1919. During the wartime period, he had the misfortune of being kicked by a horse not long after being hospitalised for eight weeks with persistent leg trouble.

Although Fern remained Everton's first-choice goalkeeper for four and a half seasons after the hostilities ended, the team had very much lost its way. Over the festive period in the difficult 1921/22 campaign, Fern experienced the highs and lows that a career as a goalkeeper inevitably brings. On Boxing Day, away at Sunderland, he brilliantly saved two penalties in a 2-1 victory before being beaten six times in the FA Cup defeat to Crystal

Palace early in the new year – a fixture he should not really have played in as he was wearing a splint on his wrist after sustaining an injury against Bolton Wanderers on New Year's Eve. Two years later, the burly Fern lost his place after a poor display in a 3-0 loss at Sunderland on New Year's Day – which turned out to be his final appearance for the club. Later that year, Fern, by then in his late 30s, moved on to Port Vale, for whom he made 90 appearances. He ended his career in Wales with Colwyn Bay United. In total, he kept an impressive 67 clean sheets in 231 competitive matches for Everton.

Two goalkeepers who deputised for Fern in postwar matches were **Ernie Salt** and **Benjamin Howard Baker** (Howard was Baker's middle name but it was later adopted as part of a double-barrelled surname by his sons). Walsall-born Salt played in a handful of matches either side of the heavy FA Cup defeat to Crystal Palace in January 1922. Having kept a debut clean sheet in a 3-0 win over Sunderland, the former Talbot Stead stopper then played in the loss to Bolton Wanderers and victory over Aston Villa, the latter a game in which he recovered extremely well after gifting the opposition a goal following a sloppy handling error. His last Everton appearance came in the 3-1 loss at Middlesbrough in February 1922 – a fixture Fern missed because of the death of his father. Having recovered from a broken collarbone, sustained in a reserve-team fixture at Anfield, Salt moved to Accrington Stanley in search of more game time in July 1923 and later signed for Wigan Borough.

The story of Baker's sporting career is a truly remarkable one and worthy of far more than the three paragraphs afforded here. The holder of the British high jump record on three separate occasions, Baker represented Great Britain in jump events at the 1912 and 1920 Summer Olympic Games. In November 1920, he signed for Everton from Liverpool after impressing in a reserve-team derby fixture. Although he played just twice for his new club during the 1920/21 campaign, the Anfield-born custodian became Everton's first England international goalkeeper in May 1921 – keeping a clean sheet in a 2-0 victory over Belgium. In all truthfulness, Baker's international recognition had mainly come about because of his fine form for the famous London-based amateur side Corinthian, for whom he had a parallel amateur career throughout his time as a professional player.

In October 1921, Baker left Goodison Park when work (and perhaps the promise of the bright lights) took him to London. He duly signed for Chelsea. However, he returned to Merseyside ahead of the 1926/27 campaign – with Everton bereft of fit goalkeepers. After an extremely tough start to the new season, which saw the team lose its first five matches, Baker became the first goalkeeper to captain the club in a competitive fixture – a 0-0 draw at home to West Bromwich Albion – and was instrumental in the 1-0 derby victory over Liverpool in late September. However, after a poor display the following month, he was dropped from the starting XI, and subsequently signed for Oldham. After making just the one competitive appearance for the Boundary Park club, this great Corinthian retired from professional football and turned his attention to tennis – a sport in which he won the Lancashire Doubles Championship Welsh Indoor Open in 1932. He would later hold a position on the management committee of the Wimbledon Lawn Tennis Championships.

In 1962, Basil Easterbrook of the *Lancashire Evening Telegraph* wrote the following about Benjamin Howard Baker's remarkable sporting life, 'Howard Baker loved football, but very properly he only sought it as a balance from his other life as a manufacturing chemist. Baker played for fun outside of the shadow of the pay envelope.'

Between Baker's two spells at the club, **Alfie Harland, Jack Kendall**, **Robert 'Bob' Jones** and **Charles 'George' Menham** all made appearances between the posts for Everton. In addition, McIlroy, Gough and Stephenson (first names unknown) lined up in goal for the intra-squad friendly fixtures during that period.

Having impressed Everton director Andrew Coffey with his tremendous performance for the Irish League against their English League counterparts, Linfield's Irish international Alfie Harland signed in October 1922 and vied with Fern for first-team duties for 18 months before seeing off the elder custodian. Following his debut against Arsenal a month after his arrival, the *Evening Express* reported, 'That Harland is a clever keeper was demonstrated by the manner in which he saved the few shots which came his way. He had very little to do, but when he is more fully tested, I expect him to prove exceptionally skilful.'

The brave Harland's four years at Goodison Park were blighted by injuries and illness. In his debut season, on Valentine's Day 1923, he was knocked unconscious after taking a blow to the head when making a courageous diving save at Chelsea. Full-back Richard 'Dickie' Downs took over in goal that day. Towards the end of the following season, he was again knocked out in a defeat at St James' Park, where, according to the *Newcastle Daily Journal and North Star*, Harland had put in an 'outstanding' display. Although he had to be taken from the field following the clash, with full-back David Raitt taking over in goal, Harland returned for the second half – an incident which highlights how different the sport was back then. In 2016, the FA and Premier League set out clear 'return to play' guidelines for players who are suspected to have suffered concussion – with no player being allowed to return for a competitive game for at least six days, let alone re-enter the pitch on the same day. On a more positive note, on the two Saturdays either side of Christmas Day 1924, Harland saved penalties against Sheffield United and Birmingham City, helping Everton to claim three points from a possible four after two extremely tight encounters.

In the early months of the 1925/26 season, Harland, renowned for wearing an oversized cap, made just four appearances for the club. Having come off with a leg injury in the 1-1 draw with West Bromwich Albion in September, when left-back John O'Donnell took over in goal, he returned to the pitch that day in the outside-left position. After missing the next six games, including the defeat at Birmingham City, when O'Donnell again took over in goal – replacing Jack Kendall after just 15 minutes – Harland was back in goal for the 5-1 hammering at Anfield later that month. His next game, a 3-2 defeat at home to Huddersfield Town seven days later, turned out to be his final appearance in an Everton shirt. Having been hospitalised with appendicitis, the luckless goalkeeper spent the rest of the 1925/26 season recovering. He was released at the end of his contract in the close season and subsequently joined Cheshire County League outfit Runcorn

AFC, where he was made captain. Following his retirement, he served on Runcorn's board for almost 30 years.

During Harland's various spells out of the Everton side through injury, Jack Kendall made 23 appearances in his three seasons with the club. Signed from Lincoln City in April 1924, Kendall made his debut in the 4-2 victory over Tottenham Hotspur in Everton's penultimate game of the 1923/24 season and started 11 of Everton's first 13 matches the following campaign. However, after losing his place, firstly to local youngster Robert 'Bob' Jones – the great Dixie Dean's closest friend, according to the *Lancashire Telegraph* – and then the returning Harland, Kendall made just 11 more appearances for Everton over the next two seasons and signed for Preston North End in 1927. Later in his career, after a short stint back at Lincoln and a four-year spell with Sheffield United, Kendall became Peterborough United's first full time professional and made over a century of appearances for the London Road club.

Although Jones made only three appearances for Everton, he did go on to have a successful career at Cardiff City and Bolton Wanderers, sandwiched between two spells with Southport, where he later became the first-team trainer. His son, Robert Jones Junior, was also a professional goalkeeper – for Blackburn Rovers, with whom he enjoyed an eight-year spell after signing in 1958.

Like Jones Senior, Charles Menham, an amateur stopper with Northern Nomads and the nephew of Bob Menham – Everton's goalkeeper in the disappointing 1897 FA Cup Final loss to Aston Villa – played only three times for the club. All three of his appearances came in October 1925 and on his debut he shipped seven goals as the Blues went down 7-3 at Sunderland. Nonetheless, he emerged from the game with great credit – the *Daily Courier* reported that he was blameless for any of the goals on a trying afternoon at Roker Park and that his 'fine clearances' were 'deservedly cheered' by the travelling support. After his second game, a 3-1 victory over Burnley courtesy of a Dixie Dean hat-trick at Turf Moor, Ernest 'Bee' Edwards wrote in the *Liverpool Echo*, 'Menham was the guardian of the goal, and after his baptism of seven goals one wondered how the old Wallaseyan would shape. I liked his run-out; I liked his general style of punching away and his pick-up; twice the wet ball might have eluded him, but he had it "clutched" to his body. His save from Roberts was really a bonny one. All this served to stem Burnley's confidence, and after a gruelling first half Everton fought back uphill against the rival side.'

A week later, Menham made his Goodison bow in another Everton win, a 4-2 victory over Leeds United, thanks largely again to a Dean hat-trick. Although the club's directors tried to persuade him to extend his stay and join full time, Menham declined – seemingly reluctant to forsake his other commitments, which included turning out for amateur side Northern Nomads. Interestingly, Menham often wore spectacles while warming up for matches but, prudently, removed them prior to kick-off. Furthermore, he was one of the first keepers to be spotted sporting a visor when defending his goal while facing the sun. After leaving Everton, he continued to play amateur football for Northern Nomads, for whom he played in the 1926 FA Amateur Cup Final win over Stockton.

After hitting the net an impressive 53 times in the league in his first two seasons at the club and recovering from a horrific motorbike accident, the irrepressible Dixie Dean would go on to score an incredible 60 league goals in 1927/28, a campaign which saw Everton return to the top of the Football League. At the other end of the pitch, the club employed three goalkeepers during that campaign – two of whom had already gained full international honours with England.

Having signed from Huddersfield Town in February 1927, veteran **Ted Taylor** started the 1927/28 season as the Blues' first-choice goalkeeper and played in all bar two of Everton's first 30 matches. Already a three-time title winner with his previous club, and the recipient of eight England caps during his time in West Yorkshire, the 40-year-old Liverpool-born custodian was regarded as one of the best goalkeepers of the 1920s, and, in Everton's battle for survival, the previous season had brought some much-needed experience to a backline that had conceded over 70 goals in the 32 games played prior to him coming into the team. Notwithstanding a couple of heavy defeats away at Newcastle and Bolton, Taylor managed to stem the tide somewhat – putting in some big performances, most notably at Highbury in a 2-1 win and at his former employers in a 0-0 draw. In total, he kept five clean sheets in the 14 games he played in 1926/27 (the Blues had kept just three clean sheets all season before his arrival) – and Everton managed to get themselves above the relegation zone.

After such a poor campaign, it is fair to say that nobody saw the blistering start Everton made to 1927/28 coming. On New Year's Day, they sat top of the table, having lost just four of the 23 games they played before the turn of the year, and Taylor, despite his ageing years, showed no real signs of slowing down. However, after he sustained a nasty finger injury in a 2-2 draw away at Birmingham in January (a game which saw outfielder O'Donnell complete his hat-trick of appearances as an emergency stopper for Everton when taking over in goal for a few minutes midway through the first half) and then back-to-back heavy defeats in early February, Taylor was replaced in the team by one-time England international **Harry Hardy** for the derby at Anfield on 25 February 1928. Hardy had made his Everton debut almost two and a half years previously, after signing from Stockport County, where he went an impressive 755 minutes without conceding a goal in 1921. Being the only County player to have received an England cap, he is widely regarded as the Hatters' greatest-ever goalkeeper.

Everton's poor form continued throughout February and March, failing to register a victory in the six games Hardy played in that season (they drew four and lost two during that spell). Although he kept two clean sheets and conceded more than one goal in a game only once during that run of matches (in the 3-3 draw with Liverpool, when Dixie Dean netted another hat-trick), he was dropped after a defeat at Leicester City, where he seemed to be deceived by a wind-assisted long-range effort for the game's only goal. That gave local custodian **Arthur Davies** a second sustained run in the first team – the former New Brighton keeper having played in ten games the previous season after replacing Benjamin Howard Baker in the starting XI before losing his place to Hardy and then Taylor.

This time, things went much better for Davies – with Everton getting back to winning ways to clinch the league title by two points from Huddersfield Town, and the returning goalkeeper playing his part in six victories and two draws in the final six weeks of the season. Davies was in goal on the final day when Dean's hat-trick against Arsenal meant that the forward had beaten George Camsell's record of 59 league goals in a single campaign by one. As Dean's final goal came with only eight minutes of the season remaining, it looked for large periods as though opposing goalkeeper Bill Paterson's fine display was going to prevent the prolific scorer from achieving the 60-goal record. However, in a true act of sportsmanship, the Scottish stopper was the first to shake hands with Dean and congratulate him on his incredible achievement after the Everton man beat him for a third time with a powerful header into the net.

Neither Taylor nor Hardy played another game for Everton after the victorious 1927/28 campaign ended. In total, Taylor played 42 games for the club before moving to Cheshire League outfit Ashton National in September 1928 and then to Wrexham two months later. Hardy made 45 Everton appearances before joining Bury. Although Arthur Davies would remain at Goodison Park for a further two years, and chalk up almost 100 appearances, his time at the club came crashing to an end after a disastrous display at Arsenal in February 1930. Reporter Thomas Moult of the *Sunday Dispatch* highlighted the lack of communication clearly evident between the goalkeeper and his defenders that day, 'Everton were incredibly poor. Williams and O'Donnell defended without understanding either of each other or of Davies in the goal behind them. When the Arsenal opened the scoring in the eighth minute, Williams and Davies were left staring at each other in bewilderment.' That summer, Davies, who had played a massive part in the 1928 Charity Shield victory over Blackburn Rovers – saving England international Arthur Rigby's spot kick in the 2-1 victory at Old Trafford – left for Exeter City, where he enjoyed five excellent seasons. He later signed for Southport and Plymouth Argyle. Sadly, at just 35 years old, Davies died from peritonitis and a perforated duodenal ulcer. He is widely considered to be one of the finest goalkeepers in Exeter's history.

In this chapter, 23 goalkeepers (and several outfield players standing in) have been profiled, which, on average, works out as almost one goalkeeper for every year of the three decades covered. Less than a month before Arthur Davies's Highbury horror show in 1930, a teenage goalkeeper from the other side of the Pennines made the first of almost 500 competitive appearances for Everton. Although the young man in question would not become a first-team regular for a further 18 months, short-term fixes, indecision regarding goalkeeper selection and brief careers between the posts at Goodison Park were soon to become a thing of the past.

4

The Boss – Ted Sagar

In Grand National week 1929, following a successful trial against Stockport County at Goodison Park, Everton signed a young player from South Yorkshire who would stay at the club for almost a quarter of a century and go on to become a true Everton great. Having played 497 games in goal for the Blues and with two league titles and an FA Cup to his name, **Ted Sagar**, affectionately known as 'The Boss', is one of the most decorated and renowned goalkeepers in the club's history.

Sagar was born in the village of Brodsworth, near Doncaster, in 1910 and began his working life as a miner in the South Yorkshire coal pits. He became the family breadwinner when his father died at the age of 32 in the Battle of the Somme, and worked permanent night shifts so that the family home would not be taken away from his mother and his four siblings. After impressing Hull City scouts while playing for Thorne Colliery in the Doncaster Senior League, Sagar went on trial with the Boothferry Park club and was set to sign for the Tigers until they mislaid his contact details, leaving Everton, who he had always supported from afar, with the opportunity to claim his signature.

Having moved into digs above the corner shop at 33 Goodison Road, with fellow new signings Johnny Wilkinson, Tommy Robson and room-mate Ted Common, Sagar quickly settled into life on Merseyside. In his first game after signing professional forms, he saved a penalty for the reserves in a draw with Aston Villa in the Central League, and continued to impress throughout the rest of the spring, with the *Liverpool Daily Post* stating that he had made 'a number of fine saves' in the second-team's victory over Blackpool and that he had 'effected some brilliant saves' in their narrow loss to Wolverhampton Wanderers.

It was a similar story at the start of the ill-fated 1929/30 campaign. After again impressing in 'the stiffs', particularly against Sheffield Wednesday in the 4-3 victory over the festive period, when the *Liverpool Daily Post* reported that 'Sagar was brilliant, saving shots from all angles', he was given his first-team debut early in the new year. With Everton languishing just one place above the bottom of the table, Sagar came in for the out-of-form Arthur Davies at Derby County and kept a clean sheet in the team's first league victory for over a month. Following such a composed debut, in which Sagar 'showed pluck when he fell at Bedford's feet', it was no surprise to see him keep his place the following week – in a disastrous 4-1 loss to Blackburn Rovers in the FA Cup fourth round. Wing wizard Jimmy Stein and Sagar, injured early on after being clattered into by the Rovers frontline despite the ball apparently being nowhere near him, were the only two Everton players to come out of the game with any real credit. The *Liverpool Daily Post* reported, 'It would be wasteful of time and energy to go into the state of the Everton market in this game, other than to say that Sagar was brilliant throughout despite his great limp.' An even greater description of his performance was found in the *Athletic News*, which called Sagar 'a giant among defensive dwarfs' for his club that day. His courageous style of goalkeeping, often involving him diving head first at the feet of onrushing forwards, would remain a key feature of Sagar's style throughout his career and result in him becoming an early hero of legendary German goalkeeper Bert Trautmann, who famously broke his neck while keeping goal for Manchester City in the 1956 FA Cup Final.

The thigh injury Sagar sustained against Blackburn kept him out of Everton's next three games, with Davies making appearances against Portsmouth, Manchester City and Arsenal. After coming back into the side following the 4-0 defeat at Highbury, Sagar played in the next seven games, saving a penalty on his return at Middlesbrough. However, in a struggling side, the rookie endured a tough spell of his own, and after a run of five successive defeats, including one at home to West Ham United when Sagar completely misjudged the flight of the ball, and a 5-4 reverse at Leicester City, Everton decided to bring in the more experienced keeper **Billy Coggins** from Bristol City for the final month of the campaign, as they battled against relegation.

Alas, despite being victorious in four of their last six games, it was a battle they would not win and Everton, champions of England only two years previously, would start the 1930/31 campaign outside the First Division for the first time in their history.

Coggins began the new season as the first-choice goalkeeper while Sagar, still only 20 years old, continued his development in the reserves. The Bristolian first came to Everton's attention after a fine display for his hometown club against Barnsley in March 1930. However, according to the *Western Daily Press*, ahead of putting pen to paper on a £2,000 move to Goodison Park, the Bristol Babes' regular goalkeeper of the past five years 'had to study how he would be affected by the loss of his newsagent's business' before agreeing to sign professional forms with the Toffees. In the six games he played in the relegation season, Coggins performed extremely well, finishing on the losing team only once. Indeed, after a super showing against Sheffield United in April, the *Liverpool Football Echo* ran with the headline 'Coggins keeps grandly'. Consequently, it was no surprise when he began the new season ahead of Sagar in the first team.

Writing in his weekly column in the *Liverpool Echo* almost 20 years later, Sagar had the following to say about the 1930/31 campaign, which saw Everton crowned Second Division champions and Coggins play in every league and cup fixture for the Blues, 'The team practically chose itself each week and it was hardly surprising that I did not get a chance in the first team that season. Coggins, with his greater experience, was the automatic choice. We were good friends and I was quite happy in the Central League side, for whom I played 42 times. I was still a youngster – not yet 21 – and was still willing to learn.'

Away to Nottingham Forest in October, Coggins was outstanding in a 2-2 draw, which saw Ernest 'Bee' Edwards write, 'Coggins had two shots in two seconds, each from the former Huddersfield man, Dent, who made two stunning shots, and Coggins saved wonderfully each time.' As the goalkeeper continued to gain the plaudits, just before Christmas, artist George Green's caricature drawing of Coggins appeared in the local newspaper, along with the wording 'One of the best – Coggins, the goalkeeper who has played a big part in Everton's success this season. Has been mentioned as England's coming custodian.'

At Port Vale in January, Coggins was involved in a bizarre incident, when 'an intruder' left the stands and stood in the goal with him, leading to the *Liverpool Echo* reporting, 'He [Coggins] was dumbstruck when an enthusiastic young man of good physique joined the Everton "board" and kept goal with Coggins for fully two minutes. Coggins said nothing. The man had his coat off and his hat was thrown into the corner of the net, in approved fashion. They say all good goalkeepers are mad; when this man entered the goal I said, "It's a case of like to like!" Well, Coggins did his part with very fine judgement.'

An almost flawless personal campaign for Coggins was tarnished slightly in March when he was at fault for the only goal in the disappointing all-Second Division FA Cup semi-final loss to West Bromwich Albion. Misjudging the flight of Tommy Glidden's inswinging headed centre, Coggins looked on in disbelief as he saw the ball drop in underneath the angle of bar and post. Despite the cup heartbreak, Coggins, who captained the side and received a warm welcome back at his old club Bristol City in April, could reflect on an excellent season. Indeed, reporter Edwards was gushing with his praise, 'In goal today he is handling positions of rare danger with extreme ability. He has not the average goalkeeper's huge size eights in hands; it is his quick brain that carries him to the spot he divines the shot must come.'

However, just days after the final game of the season, Coggins was operated on for appendicitis and endured a difficult time of convalescence – unable to walk unaided for a long period of that summer and at one point, according to Liverpool full-back James Jackson, fearing for his life. It was a crushing blow for the popular custodian who had played a major part in Everton's return to the First Division. Although he remained on the Blues' books for another four years, Coggins appeared in the first team on only three more occasions – such would be the incredible development of Ted Sagar during that period. In 1935, Coggins signed for Queens Park Rangers before moving back to the West Country and joining Bath City.

With Coggins hospitalised, Everton went into the transfer market in the summer of 1931 and signed Darlington goalkeeper George Henry 'Harry' Holdcroft for a four-figure fee. In the annual intra-club friendly fixture between Blues and Whites ahead of the new campaign, Sagar and Holdcroft lined up at different ends of the pitch, with both receiving vast amounts of praise in the press for their performances in an entertaining 5-5 draw in front of 13,000 spectators. Edwards wrote, 'When you have both goalkeepers praised for skilled work, someone must have been faulted in defence to countenance the glut of goals to either side.' Boxing promoter John Best, a former goalkeeper himself, was in attendance at the game. Afterwards, he told the *Liverpool Echo* that 'Holdcroft's manner of catching and leaping to the crossed centres is excellent' and that 'Sagar is very daring, yet he is inspiring, and his final save when he was seemingly overloaded by Cunliffe was the save of the match'.

Sagar was given the nod to start the 1931/32 season, with goalkeepers now permitted to take up to four steps while carrying the ball. Along with his team-mates, he began the new campaign in fine form. In September, a Dixie Dean hat-trick gave Everton a 3-1 victory in Sagar's first Merseyside derby. At the end of the game, Liverpool's legendary goalkeeper Elisha Scott sought Sagar out and told him that he would be capped by England if he carried on progressing the way that he was. After beating the two Sheffield clubs by an aggregate score of 14-4 over consecutive weekends, the Toffees hit the top of the table in October and stayed there for the rest of the campaign. There was only the occasional blip. Against Leicester City towards the end of November, Everton won 9-2, with one of the opponents' goals going down as an own goal by the unlucky Sagar. He told the *Liverpool Echo*, 'I was experimenting with a new pair of gloves with rubber palms. It was a wet day and one of the first shots I tried to deal with spun out of my rubber-palmed gloves and into the net. I spent the rest of the game, while our forwards were pounding the Leicester goal, tearing the rubber palms off the gloves.' Prior to the Leicester game, Sagar, like all other keepers during that period, had always played either barehanded or in a pair of simple woollen or cotton gardening gloves. The development of high-quality gloves designed specifically for goalkeeping was still decades away.

In total, 84 league goals were scored at home as Everton finished the season two points ahead of challengers Arsenal. In the second league derby of the season, Sagar was instrumental in helping his team to a priceless 2-1 victory, with reporter Joe 'Stork' Wiggall writing in the *Liverpool Echo*, 'The more I see of Sagar, the more I like him. He reminds me of Elisha Scott in the latter's greatest days. He fields the ball in the same way and has the same cat-like agility of the Irishman.' Against Leicester in April, Sagar was in even better form in a victory that went a long way to clinching the title. However, the unassuming goalkeeper was keen to deflect the praise away from himself, 'Some of the newspapers said I won the match, but it was a team victory. Everton's championship belonged to no one player or group of players, but the whole of the playing staff, officials and board.'

At the end of that victorious campaign, Harry Holdcroft, having been unable to dislodge Sagar from the team, left Goodison for Preston North End, without making a first-team appearance for the club (Billy Coggins had deputised for Sagar at home to Sunderland in the only game Sagar missed that year). With the fit-again Coggins also being the preferred choice for the Blues' second team throughout that season, Holdcroft had come in for some rough treatment while playing for the thirds, against local sides who, in his words, 'seemed to think a pro was super-human where feelings were concerned'. In one game, after diving low to his left and turning the ball around the post, he was intentionally kicked in the ribs and feared that he had suffered serious damage to his kidneys. Luckily for him, it turned out to be no more than severe bruising and when the chance to swap Everton's third team for the first team at Preston came about he 'accepted like a shot'. At Deepdale, Holdcroft became a regular, playing over 250 times for the club, and won the FA Cup in 1938. In the same competition two years earlier, he had saved a penalty from Everton's Tommy White as Preston ran out 3-1 winners in a third-round tie at Goodison Park. During his time with the Lilywhites, Holdcroft gained two England caps.

An FA Cup winners' medal and international recognition would also come Sagar's way over the next few seasons. In April 1933, he became Everton's first number one and the first goalkeeper of any club to wear the number one shirt at Wembley, when the Everton players lined up with the numbers 1–11 on their backs while their opponents Manchester City wore the numbers 12–22 on FA Cup Final day. In Becky Tallentire's book *Real Footballers' Wives,* Ted's wife, Dolly Sagar, recalled that special occasion, when goals from Dixie Dean, Jimmy Stein and Jimmy Dunn gave Everton a 3-0 victory over their Lancashire rivals in front of 93,000 supporters, 'Ted made a great save in the first minutes of the game and his confidence rubbed off on the other players. When the team arrived back in Liverpool on the Monday, there were thousands of people waiting at Lime Street station to congratulate them. The team went on a horse-drawn coach from the Town Hall, along Scotland Road, into County Road and all the way to Goodison Park, and there were another 60,000 people inside the ground waiting. I think the players got a £25 bonus for winning the cup, which was an absolute fortune back then.'

More personal accolades followed over the next few seasons. An ever-present throughout the 1932/33 season, Sagar was forced to miss the Merseyside derby in February 1934 after being selected to play for the Football League against their Scottish League contemporaries at Ibrox. In Sagar's place, Billy Coggins kept a clean sheet in his final appearance for the club; incidentally, in his only other outing that season, Coggins had to be replaced by outfielder Warney Cresswell just before half-time, after his leg gave way on him in the 3-2 loss to Sheffield Wednesday. Representing the Football League was a huge honour for Sagar but being selected to play for England for the first time against Northern Ireland in October 1935 was an even prouder moment and he told the *Liverpool Echo*, 'I was gratified that Elisha Scott, who two seasons before had predicted I would be "capped", should be in the opposite goal to see his prediction come true.' Further caps came his way – against Scotland, Austria and Belgium. However, playing during a period that is often described as the 'Golden Age' of British goalkeepers, with the brilliant Harry Hibbs of Birmingham City at the peak of his powers throughout most of the 1930s and then Frank Swift of Manchester City coming to real prominence on the international stage towards the end of the decade, Sagar was up against some stiff competition for an England starting berth. Nonetheless, he was perhaps a little unfortunate not to gain more than the four caps he received.

Towards the end of the 1934/35 season, young keepers **George Bradshaw** and **Frank King** were handed rare starts in Sagar's absence. Bradshaw, an autumn signing from local side New Brighton, played against Aston Villa, Bolton Wanderers and Leeds United in March 1935 as Sagar was nursing a shoulder injury after a heavy coming together in a game at Chelsea. Just ten days after playing the last of those three matches, the 21-year-old rookie was on his way to champions Arsenal after a bizarre bit of business took place just hours before the end of transfer deadline day. In the game between the two clubs at Goodison on 16 March 1935, Arsenal's England international goalkeeper Frank Moss dislocated his shoulder and could not continue. Ironically, he returned to the field as an outfielder that day and scored the opener past Sagar from the outside-left position. Facing a keeper crisis for the next few months and needing to get a deal done that day, the Gunners moved quickly to secure the signing of young Bradshaw for around £2,000, before leaving Merseyside that evening. Sagar told the *Liverpool Echo*, 'I believe my name was mentioned by Arsenal, but Everton would not part and compromised by allowing Bradshaw to sign in one of the slickest deals in football's history.'

Described by Sagar as one of the 'smallest and slimmest goalkeepers in league football', Bradshaw moved on from the Gunners the following year, signing for Doncaster Rovers, where he played for two years, before moving back to the north-west and signing for Bury. Although he later joined Oldham Athletic, he never made a league appearance for the Boundary Park side and retired from football in 1950.

With Bradshaw departed and Sagar still not fully fit, Frank King, the 'brilliant boy goalkeeper', was selected to play in

Everton's final five games of the 1934/35 season. A year earlier, the teenager, signed from Blyth Spartans, had received rave reviews in the *Liverpool Echo*, 'Built for his job, he has a wonderfully clean pick-up and has no trace of nerves; it is very evident that Everton do not intend to lose the service of Frank King. A career that seems well-assured, King has given a very creditable performance in several reserve-team Central League games.' However, although a further nine appearances were made over the next two seasons (King deputised for Sagar six times in 1935/36 and then on three occasions in 1936/37), Sagar's dominance resulted in the Alnwick-born stopper seeking first-team football elsewhere and in 1937 he signed for Derby County for £200.

On the final day of the 1937/38 season, King lined up opposite Sagar and was in splendid form against his old employers in a 1-1 draw. Only six months later, though, the goalkeeper left the professional game. In his final season at Goodison Park, King had become disillusioned with life as a professional footballer and lost a lot of his early confidence after, in his words, the home crowd had 'barracked me so much that I got the idea they were comparing me to Sagar – very much to my disadvantage'.

Sadly for King, his move to Derby failed to restore his passion for professional football and at just 21 years of age he decided on a career change. He joined the Southport police force, before transferring to the fire service during the Second World War.

Throughout the wartime period, King remained a known presence on Merseyside, lining up for Southport and Tranmere Rovers against Everton and participating in sporting events such as the 'Battle of the Roses' football match between the Yorkshire and Lancashire fire services in February 1944 and the National Fire Service (E Division) sporting fun day held in Crosby in July of the same year, when he won both the firemen's 100 yard sprint and the long jump competition. After injury cut short his playing career, King became a referee in the Lancashire Football League and then returned to the professional game as the assistant trainer at Leicester City and later Luton Town. On the opening day of the 1959/60 season, he was harshly booked at Goodison Park for entering the field without the referee's permission to sponge several of the injured Luton players.

In the six seasons directly following Everton's 1932 title triumph, the team's form had been extremely disappointing. After finishing 11th, 14th and eighth in 1932/33, 1933/34 and 1934/35 respectively, the Blues ended the next three campaigns only a few points above the relegation zone. Incidentally, midway through the last of those seasons, at home to Leicester on the day after Boxing Day in 1937, Sagar ended up playing as a left-winger after dislocating his shoulder in a collision with Joe Mercer and handing over goalkeeping duties to outfielder Robert 'Bunny' Bell early on in the game. Having returned from the local hospital 15 minutes into the second half, Sagar, still wearing his black goalkeeper shorts and therefore dressed differently from the rest of the team, entered the field smoking a cigarette. He almost scored when his shot hit the side netting after the Leicester keeper had saved magnificently from Douglas Trentham. Sagar recalled, 'Sandy McLaren, the Leicester goalkeeper, said to me, "If you had scored, I would have reported you to the Goalkeepers' Union!" I believe I acquitted myself quite well.' Two years earlier, Sagar had temporarily passed goalkeeping duties on to another outfielder – outside-right Albert Geldard – after coming off injured in the Boxing Day victory over Sheffield Wednesday midway through the 1935/36 campaign. Sagar had also missed the intra-squad friendly on 17 August 1935, with King and teenager Fred White, later of Sheffield United, playing in the 3-3 draw between the Blues and the Whites.

In 1938, for the first time in 14 years, the club entered a new season without the presence of Dixie Dean, who, after scoring 349 goals in 399 games for the Blues, moved on to Notts County. In his weekly column in the *Liverpool Echo*, Sagar wrote glowingly about Everton's greatest-ever centre-forward, 'As readers of this series will know, Billy Dean has always been my football idol. I don't think anybody before or since could turn a ball on a curl like William Ralph Dean.' Nonetheless, his replacement, 18-year-old Tommy Lawton, had scored 28 goals during the previous campaign, and with cultured centre-half Thomas George 'T.G.' Jones having come of age in the second half of that season, Everton lined up against Blackpool on the opening day of the 1938/39 season with cautious optimism.

In the first six games, all resulting in Everton wins, Lawton bagged eight goals, while, at the other end, Sagar, ably assisted by Jones in front of him, conceded just three goals. According to Dolly Sagar, Welshman T.G. Jones was her husband's favourite team-mate, 'They had an understanding between each other and they worked really well together. The pair of them used to talk for hours before the match about players who they thought could give them problems – and they continued their natter off the park.'

In a truly outstanding season, the team occupied one of the top two positions throughout, and after defeating Liverpool 3-0 at Anfield in early February, thanks to another brace from Lawton and a goal from Stan Bentham, Everton went top of the league and stayed there for the rest of the campaign. Just as he had been in the 1931/32 title-winning season, Sagar was once again instrumental, leading the *Liverpool Echo*'s columnist Louis T. Kelly to describe him as 'the father of First Division goalkeepers' and state that the evergreen stopper was good for another ten years. In close games, he often came up with hugely important saves, such as the one in the 'fortunate' 1-0 win away at Portsmouth three days before the derby, a save described as 'superlative' by reporter Wiggall in the *Liverpool Echo*.

On 22 February 1939, Sagar missed his only game of the season – a 7-0 drubbing at the hands of title rivals Wolverhampton Wanderers. In goal that day was the unlucky **Harry Morton**, who had been acquired from Aston Villa two years previously. Having been a near-ever-present for over half a decade at Villa Park, Morton, who had saved penalties from Dixie Dean, Jimmy Stein and Tommy Johnson in games against Everton during his time at the Midlands club, saw his Aston Villa career come to an abrupt end in February 1937 after he was cautioned for drunken behaviour following an incident involving fellow inebriated team-mate George Cummings, who had lost control of his car and collided with a pedestrian. In his first two seasons at Everton, Morton, who had been signed for £1,100 soon after the drink-driving incident involving Cummings, was handed several starts as Sagar struggled with cartilage injuries during that period. The Chadderton-born keeper had acquitted himself very well. In Ernest 'Bee' Edwards's column in March

1937, after an excellent display by the goalkeeper against West Bromwich Albion, the journalist wrote, 'Morton kept goal remarkably well. He has a flourishing style not to be confused with theatricalism. Sound work is allied to secure pick-up or punch away.'

Later that year, Morton, a former soldier, fireman and rugby league full-back, was handed the Everton captaincy for their annual game against the British Army – which was played at Aldershot, where Morton had once been stationed. His superb performances for the reserves were a key factor in Everton winning the Central League for only the second time in their history in 1937/38.

Sadly, the heavy defeat to Wolves in the club's title-winning season turned out to be Harry Morton's final game in an Everton shirt as he was transferred to Burnley three months later. At Turf Moor, with no Sagar in front of him, regular first-team opportunities appeared to be heading his way. However, Morton's league career was brought to an end following the outbreak of the Second World War and a significant knee injury sustained in a wartime East Lancashire derby against Blackburn Rovers. He ended his playing career at Ashton United.

The Football League was abandoned after just three games of the 1939/40 campaign following Germany's invasion of Poland. Over the next seven years, Everton competed in regional football leagues, firstly the Western Division and then the Northern Division (or North Division, as it was called in 1945/46), and the Football League War Cup, which replaced the FA Cup between 1940 and 1945. Although wartime appearances are not counted in any official records, it is important to make reference to the goalkeepers who played during that period – especially as Everton had to make do without Sagar for over 200 of the 275 games played between September 1939 and May 1946. Incidentally, in one of his final appearances before heading off to war, Sagar missed a penalty – against Tranmere – something he had once described as being 'a crime'. With his team 9-0 up, he was given the chance to score from the spot, only to strike the ball at the opposing keeper Hassall and then have to scamper back to avoid conceding a goal himself.

In 1940, Sagar joined the Royal Corps of Signals, and after training as a driver mechanic and guesting for Barnsley, he was stationed in County Armagh, Northern Ireland. During his time there, he played for Portadown and Glentoran, which led to him being selected for the Northern Ireland Football League XI. On Sagar's Portadown debut, the *Derry Journal* reported, 'Sagar, the Everton and England international goalkeeper, made his bow to Irish football fans for Portadown. He had a real baptism of fire. Kelly, Kelso and McLaughlin gave him exacting tests. After stopping a typical Kelly drive, which he fielded well, the Englishman was seen to collapse on the goal line. After attention, he was able to carry on. A great keeper, he made goalkeeping look simple.' Sagar then went on to be stationed out in Syria and spent time in India, where he played with and against several Football League greats, including Middlesbrough's Wilf Mannion, who went on to score 11 goals for England in 26 postwar internationals, including one against Chile in the 1950 World Cup. From India, Sagar moved on to Italy and was part of the first Sicily and Anzio landings. Sagar recalled, 'For days, we were constantly subjected to heavy shelling but even then with tin hats as part of our football equipment, we managed to get several matches in on the beaches.'

In Sagar's absence, Everton employed numerous men between the sticks, including outfielders George Jackson, Harry Jones and Gordon Watson. **Percy Lovett**, a teenage member of the Blues' Central League title-winning side in 1938, played 18 times between 1940 and 1942, and Crystal Palace's **Edgar Williams** guested on one occasion – in a 4-1 loss to Wrexham towards the end of the 1942/43 campaign. **Wilf Birkett** also played 11 games during that season. The Haydock-born goalkeeper went on to enjoy a lengthy career with Southport while Lovett moved on to Wrexham before finishing his career at Hereford United.

Everton's main goalkeeper during the wartime years, though, was **George Burnett**, who made 181 appearances over that period, after seeing off the challenge of Lovett in the battle of the highly rated young keepers. Burnett's debut came in a 3-2 defeat to Chester in November 1939. According to Bob 'Ranger' Prole, writing for the *Liverpool Echo*, 'For Everton, Burnett, their young goalkeeper, did outstanding work, his saves from Sanders and

Horsman being the highlights of his game.' Interestingly, in 1943, Burnett was fined £20 on three summonses of being absent from work and one of persistent lateness. Although the Liverpool-born custodian, a brass finisher by trade, pleaded not guilty to being absent through playing football, his case highlights the dilemma that footballers desperate to continue playing faced during that period. Incidentally, that same year, Burnett also guested for Wrexham against the Blues in the aforementioned 4-1 defeat to the Welsh club in April 1943, having travelled to the game with the Everton team. Just 15 minutes before kick-off, Wrexham found themselves without a goalkeeper so in stepped Burnett, who went on to deny his usual team-mates on numerous occasions in the second half. Towards the end of the wartime period, the ever-present from 1943 onwards was again in magnificent form, against Grimsby Town, in a 2-1 victory just three days before Christmas in 1945, which saw Everton go top of the league. When peace was restored and First Division football returned, the Everton selectors had a huge decision to make regarding their first-choice goalkeeper: would it be best to go with the in-form Burnett or the returning twice-title-winner Sagar?

At the start of the new campaign, Burnett was given the nod and kept his place for the first 12 games. However, after a 3-3 draw at home to Grimsby, Sagar was recalled. Speaking of his return, Sagar told the *Liverpool Echo*, 'Although judged by army football standards, I was still playing well enough to hold my place, I felt I had gone back a mile after my long lay-off and that my First Division career was finished. My reflexes were dulled and I really believed that the last chapter had been written to the story of "Ted Sagar – Footballer". But here and now let me express my thanks to Mr Theo Kelly, whose cordial greeting made me feel immediately at home and more important made me feel that I was "wanted". It was something I will never forget. Burnett was playing well and I was not optimistic about getting my place back in the first team however hard I tried to recover my prewar form. I felt that a run in the reserves might help me to get the "feel" of the ball, and I felt that there was a chance it might come back to me.' After returning to the team in November, Sagar missed only one game that season and then went on to play in every league and cup game the following campaign. According to the *Liverpool Echo* reporter Prole, it was not a surprise move to recall the experienced custodian, 'The inclusion of Sagar is not altogether unexpected. Burnett, usually so reliable, has been off-form recently, and the coolness and experience of Sagar will steady the rearguard.'

In a 2-2 draw with Manchester United, in only his second game back, Sagar was in top form and made a save from Jack Rowley late in the first half that was, according to the *Liverpool Echo*, of 'international class'. After the break, Sagar went on to make one of his trademark 'daring' saves, when he dived bravely at the feet of Johnny Morris to stop a certain goal. Dolly Sagar recalled, 'When the war was over, everything went back to normal again and the boys [Ted and Dolly's sons] wanted to go to matches, so we would all go to Goodison Park to watch him play. They were big Evertonians and we'd look forward to the game on a Saturday. We saw some great matches but, whenever the ball was near the net, I was really anxious. Sometimes it was strange to watch him play; it was like he was another person when he was on the pitch. When I was pregnant with Margaret [their daughter], I asked the doctor if it was wise for me to go to the games, but he said it was OK as long as I sat near him. Not many women went to the match in those days.'

Although the returning Sagar looked to have recaptured his prewar form, the much-changed Everton team certainly had not, with the loss of key players ultimately proving to be costly. After a falling-out with secretary-manager Theo Kelly over which position to play, Joe Mercer joined Arsenal for £9,000; Tommy Lawton, who was having marital problems, also headed to the capital and signed for Chelsea; and the 'Prince of Centre-Halves', AS Roma transfer target T.G. Jones, spent time in the reserves after falling out with new manager Cliff Britton before eventually returning to Wales in 1950. Two 18th-placed finishes preceded the inevitable, and in 1951 Everton dropped out of the top flight for only the second time in their history. According to Charles Mills Senior, a match-going Evertonian of that time, who served as a navigator in RAF bomber crews, 'From being at the heights [prior to the outbreak of war], we plunged to the depths [of the Second Division].'

In the intra-squad friendlies played in the years directly after the war, Sagar lined up against George Burnett, youngster Jimmy Jones and amateur Keith Mitton, who was signed after impressing for the Central League team in a fixture against Derby County towards the end of the 1948/49 campaign. Mitton would later play for Preston North End.

In his final season in the First Division, Sagar received standing ovations at many away grounds. In the *Liverpool Echo*, Prole wrote the following about the goalkeeper's reception at Villa Park just before Christmas in 1950, 'It was indeed impressive to hear the tremendous ovation accorded Ted Sagar by the Villa supporters as he took his place between the sticks prior to the start of the game and again after the interval, when he went to the far end of the ground. It was just another tribute on a visiting ground to a great sportsman. There may have been better keepers than Ted, though I doubt it, but he must be one of the greatest of club men.

'I hope that when the time comes for him to hang up his boots for keeps, the people of Merseyside to whom he has given such great pleasure and enjoyment for the past 21 years in the colours of his one and only club during that period will give him a send-off which he will remember for the rest of his days.'

Just four weeks from the end of his final season as a First Division goalkeeper, Sagar saved a penalty in the 1-1 draw with Wolves at Goodison Park, which maintained his fine record of saving a spot kick in each of the five top-flight campaigns he played in after the Second World War.

On Saturday, 9 May 1953, Goodison Park bid farewell to the 43-year-old, who had signed for the club over 24 years earlier. At the end of the Liverpool Senior Cup Final victory over Tranmere, opposing captains Peter Farrell and Tom Bell carried Sagar off on their shoulders, to rapturous applause from all sides of the ground. It was fitting that in his final appearance for the Blues he should add another medal to his impressive collection and pull off a save from Davies that the *Liverpool Echo* described as 'immaculate' and as 'good as any save he made in his palmy days'.

Following his retirement from the professional game and a brief spell on the ground staff at Goodison Park, Sagar went into the pub business and became the landlord of several public houses on Merseyside. According to Dolly, 'He'd catch beer glasses and say that the first lad who could get one past him would get a pint. They never got one past him because he had those great big hands.' Sagar also became a regular columnist in the *Liverpool Echo*, often commenting on the custodians who followed him. After his sad passing in 1986, his ashes were buried at the Gwladys Street End of Goodison Park, because, according to Dolly, 'that was where he made the best saves'. In his 1937 article 'Star Goalkeepers', correspondent 'Red Rick' described the Yorkshireman as the most 'daring goalkeeper' to have played for the club, before going on to state, 'He should be locked up for stealing – look at the times without number he has snatched the ball from bobbing heads in the goalmouth!'

It feels fitting to end this chapter with the following extract from goalkeeping aficionado Bob Wilson's portrait of Sagar from his book *You've Got to be Crazy*, 'So what sort of goalkeeper was Ted Sagar? One word sums him up – commanding. Such was the domination of his area that his team-mates nicknamed him "The Boss". The courage that saw the lithe goalkeeper plunge in amongst flying feet carried over to that other sort of courage required by keepers to leave their charge and take a high cross. That was the most eye-catching aspect of Sagar's keeping, but his agility and anticipation were equally brilliant. One of Ted's colleagues in the prewar Everton league and cup-winning sides was quoted as saying, "You never had to worry about Ted; you didn't have to look round half the time either. You just knew that he wouldn't make a mistake." It's easy to understand why Ted Sagar established himself so quickly as a first-team fixture and a favourite.'

It is also easy to understand why those who followed him found it difficult to do so. Although Jimmy O'Neill, Harry Leyland, Bert Harris and Albert Dunlop all enjoyed some fine moments in the Everton goal during the 1950s, it would take Everton a whole decade to find a successor truly worthy of following the great man. Indeed, the final name mentioned in this paragraph would turn out to be a hugely controversial character in the club's history.

The 1950s would prove to be an interesting decade.

5

Postwar Blues

In August 1949, frustrated by the lack of first-team opportunities at Goodison Park, regular wartime goalkeeper George Burnett dropped out of professional football and signed for non-league South Liverpool, only to re-sign for Everton just 24 hours later after an ankle injury to Ted Sagar on the opening day of the 1949/50 campaign resulted in a keeper crisis at the club and gave the experienced ex-Bootle Juniors man a three-match run in the side. Sandwiched between two shaky displays against Newcastle United was a fine performance and a clean sheet in the goalless Goodison derby. In the *Liverpool Echo*, Bob 'Ranger' Prole wrote, 'Strangely enough, despite Everton's second-half territorial superiority, Burnett had rather more work to do than Sidlow. And right well he did it. While he is in this form, Everton need have no anxiety about the last line of defence during Sagar's absence.'

In December 1949, following a loss of form by the ageing Sagar, Burnett was again recalled to the starting XI. From that point on, he stayed in the team until the final game of the season, when Sagar, who had turned 40 a couple of months earlier, returned to captain the side in the 3-1 victory over Manchester City. In doing so, the veteran set a new Football League record for appearances, surpassing old friend and rival Elisha Scott's previous record of 429 league games. Nonetheless, his time at Goodison was clearly coming towards the end.

In Everton's disastrous 1950/51 relegation season, three goalkeepers made first-team appearances. Having recovered from a pre-season cartilage operation, Burnett started the campaign in goal for the Blues. However, after pulling a thigh muscle in the opening-day victory over Huddersfield Town, he was replaced, firstly by young Irish prospect **Jimmy O'Neill** and then Sagar. After a woeful run of results in March and April, Everton went into the final game of the season, against fellow strugglers Sheffield Wednesday, needing to match Chelsea's result to avoid dropping into the second tier. Burnett, who despite being transfer-listed earlier that season, had returned for six games during the autumn when Sagar and O'Neill were both sidelined through injury, was recalled for the showdown with the Owls after Sagar pulled a thigh muscle in the lead-up to the game. On a truly calamitous final day, Burnett conceded six and Everton were relegated on goal average, along with their South Yorkshire opponents, with Chelsea gaining the point they needed for safety. The Hillsborough horror show turned out to be Burnett's final game in an Everton shirt. After failing to secure a first-team spot at the start of the new campaign, he was offloaded to Third Division Oldham Athletic for £2,000.

Although Sagar started the first ten games of 1951/52, Everton were now looking to the future, and goalkeeping duties for the remaining 34 games that campaign were shared between 20-year-old Jimmy O'Neill and 21-year-old **Harry Leyland**.

O'Neill, the son of the famous golfer Moses O'Neill, joined the club as a 17-year-old for £100 from Irish outfit Bulfin United after impressing in several trial games towards the end of the 1948/49 campaign. The youngster was recommended to Everton by Shelbourne FC committee member Michael Douglas, who, more than 20 years earlier, had been involved in the IRA's bombing of the King William of Orange statue in College Green, Dublin. In January 1949, Douglas wrote to Everton manager Cliff Britton, inviting him to have a look at the willowy teenager, 'I recommend to you a boy who is playing goalkeeper for a schoolboys' team, and he is certainly playing great. I know of two League of Ireland clubs who are interested in him, but he is not inclined to sign for either of them. He has informed me that if he got the chance then he would like a trip across [to England].'

In his first couple of seasons at Goodison Park, O'Neill vied with Burnett and fellow newcomer Keith Mitton for the role of Sagar's understudy. Reflecting on the start of his Everton career, O'Neill told the *Liverpool Echo* in 1996, 'In all honesty, Ted didn't help me out too much. The job was his and he wasn't going to show me how to take it over. His strengths were his keenness and dedication. If you are dedicated and work hard, you will get to the top. That is what I tried to do.'

In a friendly against Notts County in February 1951, O'Neill drew praise from reporter Joe 'Stork' Wiggall, who stated, 'The young Irishman is getting better and better. He was as confident as Sagar when the County were slashing in all manner of shots at him – good shots too – but he dealt with them in masterly style.' After a ten-game run in Everton's relegation season, O'Neill was afforded more opportunities the following year. In his first appearance of the 1951/52 season, at home to Sheffield United in early December, he made a splendid diving save in the first half that proved crucial in earning Everton a 1-0 victory. In the same month, against Sheffield Wednesday, O'Neill again performed admirably despite being on the wrong end of a 4-0 defeat. In the *Liverpool Echo*, reporter 'Contact' described an acrobatic save that would soon become O'Neill's trademark style, 'Wednesday were playing confidently and O'Neill had to bring off a magnificent one-handed save from Davies, getting the ball around the post when it seemed certain to cross the line.'

Benefitting from a sustained run in the side, O'Neill grew in confidence and in the close season made his international debut against Spain. Despite conceding six goals that day, two before he had even touched the ball, O'Neill, horribly exposed and let down by those in front of him, was deemed blameless and kept his place for the next international.

Back on Merseyside, the Irishman was an almost ever-present in the disappointing 1952/53 campaign, which saw Everton finish 16th in the second tier – at the time of writing, their lowest final position in the Football League. O'Neill, still only 21 at the start of that season, continued to gain the plaudits for his gymnastic style throughout that campaign and missed only one full game (in November 1952, Ted Sagar made his final league appearance against Plymouth Argyle when O'Neill was away on international duty) before a horrific showing in the FA Cup semi-final defeat to Bolton Wanderers in March 1953. Taking to the field without his lucky mascot – a silver cardboard horseshoe with a cat attached to it, made by his niece – O'Neill looked nervy throughout and was widely blamed for two of the goals he conceded in the 4-3 loss. Incidentally, earlier in the competition, at home to Nottingham Forest in the fourth round, O'Neill had been replaced in goal by half-back Cyril Lello for two minutes while the goalkeeper received treatment for cramp.

On the opening day of the new season, O'Neill endured another torrid time. Against Nottingham Forest, he let a simple header slip through his hands with ten minutes remaining to gift the hosts a point in a 3-3 draw. Nonetheless, he would soon bounce back. After a spell out of the side, O'Neill reclaimed the number one position in the autumn and featured in every game from that point onwards as Everton gained promotion back to the First Division. Against Brentford, in the February, he was in phenomenal form, with Prole writing in the *Liverpool Echo*, 'We have had cause many times this season to reflect on the frequency with which opposing goalkeepers have come to Goodison and played a "blinder". Yesterday the boot was on the other leg. O'Neill has never produced a better display in his life than this and may go a long time before he gives another so crammed with brilliance.'

During O'Neill's early season spell on the sidelines, local lad Harry Leyland had come into the side, and his run of 12 consecutive appearances at the start of the campaign was the longest stretch he put together in his Everton career. Leyland signed for the club as an amateur in 1947 and made his debut four years later, in September 1951, at Leicester City in a 2-1 win. Ahead of that game, Wiggall wrote, 'When I saw him [Leyland] in the public practice game at Goodison Park, he was the hero of the match, and I said then that he was ready for top-class football. He is the type who takes complete control round about the penalty area and has the build suitable to a goalkeeper.'

In his early appearances, young Leyland played exceptionally well. On his debut, he pulled off a leaping save from Arthur Rowley's header to earn the Blues the win at Filbert Street, and then a week later prevented a rugby-score defeat to Blackburn Rovers, producing a series of fine saves which Wiggall described as both 'miraculous' and 'spanking'. However, he also made a handful of errors in his maiden first-team campaign, including one at home to Bury in November, when he let a tame effort slip through his hands in a 2-2 draw. In the *Liverpool Echo*, Wiggall wrote, 'He [Leyland] knew he had erred for he dropped down on his knees in despair. He must have been the unhappiest young man in the ground, but I noticed he received a pat on the back from captain Farrell, as he went down to the depths.'

After that dreadful mistake, Leyland found himself in and out of the first team, sharing duties with O'Neill for the next two months. However, after a shocking performance in the 3-1 home FA Cup third-round defeat to Leyton Orient, when Leyland was blamed for all three goals, he found himself playing second fiddle to the Irishman for the next two years, making just six appearances in 1952/53 and then 14 in total in 1953/54. In both of those campaigns he failed to fully convince the Goodison faithful that he was worthy of the number one spot.

In the *Liverpool Echo*, at the end of the 1953/54 campaign, the following line appeared about the goalkeeping position at Everton, 'Goodison goalkeepers must always be on top form; otherwise, their rival is likely to replace them. Leyland lost his place to O'Neill after the home defeat to Leicester and could not regain it, but the burly Liverpool boy is a capable reserve.' Away from the first-team spotlight, Leyland was a key member of the Central League title-winning squad in 1954.

On the final day of the promotion season, Everton, needing a 6-0 victory to secure the Second Division title, played Oldham Athletic, who lined up with George Burnett between their sticks. By half-time the Blues found themselves 4-0 up, with the ex-Goodison man at fault for two of the goals. Although Everton failed to add to their tally after the break and Burnett made a string of fine saves from Dave Hickson, in James Corbett's *The Everton Encyclopedia*, it is stated that 'for years dark rumours that he [Burnett] had been too generous to his former team-mates followed him'. A year later, Burnett signed for Ellesmere Port. Although he is mostly remembered for his less-than-convincing final-day appearances for and against Everton, his commitment to the club and willingness to step in for Ted Sagar, especially during the wartime period, should not go unnoticed. His run of over 130 consecutive appearances is extremely impressive, especially when one considers how much troop movements and guest appearances by players from other clubs affected team line-ups during that period. Incidentally, Burnett was also a member of the Everton baseball team that played matches at Goodison Park and Bellefield during the 1940s, when the sport became hugely popular on Merseyside.

Back in the top division, Jimmy O'Neill continued to be the preferred first-team choice, playing every game bar one, a 5-0 loss away at Portsmouth, when he was away on international duty. Early in the season, he made his 100th Football League appearance for the Blues at home to Leicester. In the week after that game, in celebration of him reaching the milestone, the local newspaper ran a piece on the Eire international, 'Lithe, agile and with a wonderful sense of anticipation, O'Neill is one of the finest custodians in the country today. His catching of high balls is one of his many strong points.' For a few weeks that season, he penned his own column in the *Liverpool Echo*, in which he gave hopeful young goalkeepers handy hints to help improve their game. On the art of saving penalties, O'Neill wrote, 'If you are better diving to your right than your left, then leave a little more space to cover on that side, or vice-versa,' before going on to provide sound advice regarding taking high balls from corners, narrowing the angle and getting your body behind the ball for waist-high shots. Just days after this sage advice was printed, he saved a penalty away at Manchester City, keeping out Fionan 'Paddy' Fagan's centrally struck spot kick with ease. Towards the end of an excellent maiden top-flight campaign, the Dubliner was again outstanding in an exciting 2-2 draw at Sheffield Wednesday, making a string of fine saves – the pick of the bunch, according to Bob 'Ranger' Prole, being an acrobatic tip over the bar of Albert Quixall's powerful strike.

With O'Neill playing so well and first-team chances therefore at a premium, Harry Leyland left the club at the end of the 1955/56 season, having played just five times that campaign. On Everton's decision to let their reserve keeper go, Prole wrote in the *Liverpool Echo*, 'I confess to a feeling of disappointment at the decision to part with Harry Leyland, who though not always without fault – and which goalkeeper is? – has never lacked courage and determination, and with greater and more extended opportunities might have eventually made the first-team place his own.'

After initially agreeing to sign for Ron Saunders's Tonbridge Wells in the summer of 1956, Leyland quickly moved to Johnny Carey's Blackburn Rovers before the start of the new campaign. Within two seasons, he helped the Lancashire outfit gain promotion to the First Division and in 1960 played in the FA Cup Final defeat to Wolverhampton Wanderers, having been tremendous in Rovers' semi-final victory over Sheffield Wednesday. The following year, Leyland returned to Merseyside and signed for Tranmere Rovers, making 180 appearances between 1961 and 1967, before having a season in charge of Cheshire League outfit Wigan Athletic, where he was employed as player-manager.

Following his death in 2006, Leyland, despite having never played a game of rugby union in his life, had a 400-seater stand named after him at New Brighton Rugby Union Football Club, as a tribute to his hard work and devotion at the head of the community-focused club in his later years. According to a 2021 article in the *Rugby Paper*, shortly after their 1994/95 Premier League title triumph, Blackburn chairman Jack Walker invited some of the club's more distinguished past players back to Ewood Park as guests of honour at a top-flight match. However, the devoted Leyland politely declined the offer as it clashed with a match his New Brighton rugby union team had that day and he 'didn't want to let the lads down'.

Towards the end of the 1955/56 season, **Bert Harris** was given a five-match spell in the team after O'Neill had gifted Sheffield United a couple of goals in the embarrassing Good Friday 4-1 home loss to the Blades. The *Liverpool Echo* described it as O'Neill's 'worst-ever performance' for the club and stated that he was very lucky to get away without conceding more goals after uncharacteristically going into challenges timidly instead of diving bravely on the ball. Maghull-born Harris, who had played at Old Trafford in a friendly shortly after joining Everton in early 1955 and starred for the reserves in several Central League outings, came into the side away at Aston Villa. In a 2-0 defeat, the 23-year-old part-timer performed competently, with the

Liverpool Echo reporting that he had given a 'promising display in goal' and 'had come through the ordeal of making his debut remarkably well'.

After keeping his place the following week – in a 1-1 draw away at Sheffield United – Harris then made his Goodison bow and 'kept goal coolly and confidently' in a 2-1 victory. Unfortunately, the following week, at Chelsea, he, along with the rest of the Everton team, endured a miserable afternoon. The rookie conceded six goals, with the *Liverpool Echo* claiming that a more experienced goalkeeper might have saved at least three of them. Nonetheless, his season and Everton career finished on a real high with a strong performance and a clean sheet in the 1-0 final-day victory over Blackpool at Goodison Park. Unable to force his way past O'Neill in the first team, and with **Albert Dunlop** beginning to make a name for himself in the reserves, Harris left for Tranmere in 1957 and then moved on to Southport in 1960. He later managed Kirkby Town.

In a 2024 conversation with Everton fan Ian Maher, 93-year-old Harris fondly recalled his time at the club, 'Everything at Everton was geared for the first team. I remember when I was told I was going to make my debut that all of a sudden my boots got cleaned! I can recall the greenness of the pitch and how the noise swirled around the stadium. It might start in one corner and would travel around the Gwladys Street End, the Bullens, the Park End and back down Goodison Road. I was good friends with Jimmy O'Neill, who, in my opinion, was a much better goalkeeper than I was!'

Just 13 games into the 1956/57 season, though, after his own poor showing against Chelsea, O'Neill lost his first-team place to the promising Dunlop and never really gained it back, despite staying at the club for a further four years. On numerous occasions during that period he almost left Goodison Park. Indeed, just days after the Chelsea horror show, he came close to signing for Charlton Athletic, in a swap deal involving inside-forward Jimmy Gauld, who was later imprisoned and kicked out of professional football for his leading role in the 1964 football betting scandal which also cost Everton wing-half Tony Kay his career. However, having failed to agree terms with the London outfit, O'Neill travelled back to Merseyside and, the following month, submitted a formal transfer request.

Sheffield Wednesday showed some interest in taking the goalkeeper to Hillsborough that autumn, but no deal could be agreed with any potential suitor until Stoke City manager Tony Waddington signed O'Neill for £5,000 in July 1960. Alongside Dennis Viollet, surprisingly discarded by Manchester United, and the veteran Stanley Matthews, the experienced custodian helped the Potters gain promotion to the First Division in 1963, before winding down his career at Darlington and subsquently Port Vale, by then managed by his former team-mate Matthews. Following a short spell back in Ireland with Cork Celtic, O'Neill, who made 213 appearances for Everton and gained 17 caps for his country, retired from the game in 1968 and returned to Merseyside, where he raised his family and ran a small taxi firm. His place in the Eire international team was taken by Alan Kelly Senior, who would later have huge goalkeeping links with Everton.

In retirement, O'Neill was often interviewed by local journalists, and in 1997 had the following to say about the different challenges goalkeepers at that time faced compared with the problems he faced when playing, 'Players are under so much pressure these days. Some of the criticism they come in for today I find hard to understand. All goalkeepers go through spells where they are not at their best. There isn't a goalkeeper playing that hasn't made a mistake. But it is how you react to those mistakes that determines how good you become. I think a goalkeeper's job is easier now than in my day because they have all the time on the ball and half the time we were dodging opposing forwards, but I still wouldn't like to be playing.'

After the goalkeeper's death in 2007, *The Independent's* football historian Ivan Ponting described O'Neill as 'the sort of goalkeeper that football fans love to watch. Whether plunging acrobatically to repel shots on his line or springing skywards to pluck crosses from the heads of rampaging centre-forwards, the slim almost willowy Republic of Ireland international was a natural crowd-pleaser.' O'Neill kept goal in all nine of Everton's intra-squad friendly fixtures played during the 1950s. After facing Burnett, Sagar, Leyland, Harris and youngster Bryan Caldwell in matches in the early part of the decade, the Irishman was twice replaced by substitute Graham Griffiths, in 1957 and 1959, in games which saw Albert Dunlop line up in the opposing goal. Dunlop's first taste of Goodison action had come in a junior practice match in August 1953, when he and Caldwell shared goalkeeping duties for the Blues in a 2-0 defeat to the Whites, who had Peter Fairclough in goal that day.

Albert Dunlop's performance against Manchester United in October 1956 must be in contention for the title of the greatest first-team debut by an Everton goalkeeper. Having joined the club from school, the stocky youngster signed professional terms in 1955 and performed superbly well in the reserve and junior teams. His Central League performance against Liverpool was described in the *Liverpool Echo* as 'one of the finest displays of goalkeeping ever seen at Anfield'. However, his performance at Old Trafford, in front of 43,677 fans, was even more impressive and went a long way to helping Everton become the first team to beat Matt Busby's side on their home soil for 18 months. In the 5-2 victory, Dunlop made an outstanding double-handed save from Tommy Taylor before cleanly collecting a high ball under pressure from three opposing forwards and then going on to deny Bobby Charlton almost certain goals on at least two occasions. In the *Liverpool Echo*, captain Peter Farrell paid tribute to the performance of the young custodian, 'I don't think I can let the occasion pass without my own personal tribute to the display of Albert Dunlop, and I know the rest of the side who all played such a valiant part in the win will not mind if I single out Albert for special mention. He certainly showed his skill as a goalkeeper and inspired the rest of the defence to greater efforts by his safe handling and uncanny anticipation.'

The plaudits continued to come his way over the next few months. In addition to receiving column inches for his terrific one-handed save against Newcastle United and his bravery in the draw with Portsmouth, Dunlop received more praise from Farrell for his quick thinking in launching an attack that led to a goal in the 4-0 win over Arsenal, 'The goalkeeper is not only in the side to prevent goals but also to use the ball like the other ten players constructively when possible. I was facing my own goal about eight yards out and nodded the ball back to Dunlop, who in turn threw it to Eglington, from whom the ball travelled to Kirby and Gauld and finally to Fielding, who crashed it into the back of the Arsenal net for the Blues' fourth goal. I mention that incident to prove how a constructive back pass can be the means of leading to a goal.'

Over the next 17 months, Dunlop, wearing a more lightweight jersey than the heavy-duty turtle-neck jumpers worn by the majority of his predecessors over the previous 50 years, was an ever-present and continued to perform solidly, notwithstanding one nightmare performance at Stamford Bridge, when, according to reporter Prole, he 'made more errors in this game than in all others I have seen him play'. His awful day in the capital was compounded when he was credited with an own goal after misjudging the flight of a corner, which hit his legs before crossing the goal line. Nonetheless, his consistently high level of performances had certain reporters suggesting he was close to international recognition. Consequently, it was a great surprise to many when he was dropped after a 65-match run in the side for the game at Burnley in March 1958. The *Liverpool Echo* noted, 'The omission of Dunlop is likely to meet with a very mixed reception, for in the vast majority of games this season he has played extremely well, and in some cases so brilliantly that he alone has staved off defeat.' After a four-game spell out of the side, Dunlop returned for six matches in place of Jimmy O'Neill before again making way for the Irishman for the final two games of 1957/58. Earlier that season, Dunlop had become the first Everton goalkeeper to play under the floodlights at Goodison Park, having been selected to line up between the posts for the autumn friendly with Liverpool. He kept a clean sheet in a game Everton won 2-0.

During the close season he switched sports and put his throwing and catching skills to good use playing for Liverpool Cricket Club. An accomplished bowler, he also captained an Everton team that took on Bootle Cricket Club at their own game in a light-hearted fixture staged over two nights in July 1958. Just over 12 months earlier, Dunlop had played both sports on the same day – having played in Everton's home draw with Manchester City, he pulled on his cricket whites, only to be dismissed for a duck in Liverpool Cricket Club's contest with the Lancashire Club and Ground side at Aigburth in April 1957.

After starting the first two games of the 1958/59 season, Dunlop again found himself replaced by O'Neill, after a poor display at home to Preston North End in a 4-1 defeat. After nine games out, he returned to the starting XI when the Irishman aggravated a knee injury, initially sustained on international duty, in Everton's 7-4 friendly victory over the touring South Africa amateur team that October. On his return, Dunlop suffered the ignominy of shipping double figures at White Hart Lane in a 10-4 loss – at the time of writing, the only game in which Everton have conceded double digits in a game of competitive football. In all truthfulness, Dunlop was offered very little protection by those in front of him in a dismal defensive display; likewise, O'Neill had been hugely let down by his backline against Arsenal in a 6-1 loss five weeks earlier – incidentally, Ivan Ponting described O'Neill's performance at Goodison that day as one of the Irishman's finest displays in goal for the Blues.

A fortnight after the hammering at Tottenham, a change in management was deemed necessary and former Manchester United defender Johnny Carey, who had twice guested for Everton during the wartime period, took over at Goodison Park. During his 30 months in charge, Carey was extremely keen on Dunlop, selecting him for all but five of the 122 matches the team played under his stewardship. However, in December 1958, it was an opposing manager, Wolves' Stan Cullis, who paid tribute to Dunlop in the local press. Following an excellent display in a 1-0 away defeat, Cullis told the *Liverpool Echo*, 'This man always does well against us – he seems to reserve his best work for Molineux. I remember his display last season; he was terrific.'

Journalist Michael Charters went even further with his praise, stating that Dunlop had 'never given a greater performance in his life' and that 'his positional play was perfect, his anticipation uncanny and his handling of the ball as sure as the most professional juggler'. The following week, the football special edition of the *Liverpool Echo* used five action images of Dunlop on its front cover, accompanied by the headline 'Wolves faced a Dunlop in the plural', to emphasise how brilliant he had been in that game.

Sadly, for everyone concerned with the club, the love Dunlop received from Carey, opposing managers like Stan Cullis and the local media was not forthcoming from many of his team-mates, who were less than enamoured with their controversial custodian. According to Ponting, the goalkeeper earned himself the nickname 'The Bandit' because of his small-time wheeler-dealing on Merseyside and involvement in the licensed club trade. By many of his colleagues, though, he was viewed far more sinisterly. In particular, legendary centre-forward Alex Young heavily criticised Dunlop, who, after falling out of favour at Goodison Park and signing for Wrexham in 1963, would go on to make some extremely strong allegations against his former team-mates – accusing them of taking performance-enhancing drugs during their victorious 1962/63 title-winning season. Interestingly, and perhaps somewhat tellingly, that campaign was the first in half a decade in which Dunlop had not been Everton's first-choice goalkeeper, following the signing of Gordon West from Blackpool by new manager Harry Catterick, a far stricter disciplinarian than Carey, towards the end of the previous campaign.

In his autobiography, the graceful Young, affectionately known as the 'Golden Vision' – a nickname which contrasts strikingly with Dunlop's more minacious moniker – is quoted as saying, 'Albert had few friends at the club and was known as something of a menacing character. He had always been a troublemaker and, like most of my team-mates, I thought of him as someone to be avoided.' The Scottish forward then went on to state that Dunlop had 'sworn to get even' with the club following his sale to Wrexham. Young claimed that Dunlop's actions of going to *The People* in September 1964 with tales of the pushing of the 'purple hearts' drug Drinamyl by Everton's coaching staff on their players for performance-enhancing purposes were those of 'a troubled soul who had been discarded by his employer'.

In the same tabloid article, Dunlop, who also claimed that opposing players had been bribed and told to take it easy against Everton towards the end of the 1962/63 campaign, alleged the following, 'Drug-taking had previously been virtually unknown in the club. But once it had started we could have as many tablets as we liked. On matchdays they were handed out to most of the players as a matter of course. Soon some of the players could not do without the drugs. It became a sort of ritual for them to be handed out on Saturdays and other matchdays by our head trainer, Tommy Eggleston. During training we could have the tablets on request from Eggleston or from our other trainer, Gordon Watson.'

Young refuted such claims and went as far as to say that it was only Dunlop himself who had become an addict, and that 'the only substance that [team-mate] Alex Parker and I ever resorted to before a match was a wee dram of whisky from an old bottle of Bell's kept in the dressing room'. The article in *The People* supports this view of Dunlop and claims that his addiction to the drugs left him weakened and confused, ultimately costing him his Everton career, 'His play deteriorated. In the end, Dunlop was playing so badly that in March 1962 he lost his first-team place to a new youngster, Gordon West. In despair, he took more and more drugs, drank more and more in Liverpool's clubs and dives and spent more and more money he could ill afford. In a fit of depression, Dunlop tried to end his life with an overdose of sleeping tablets. He was unconscious for two days. But doctors managed to pull him through.'

The tale of Albert Dunlop's final couple of years as an Everton player is an exceptionally sorry one, though it is worth noting that he did save a penalty on his return to the team for the injured Gordon West against West Ham in April 1962 and then played the final four games of the championship-winning season 12 months later.

Dunlop's lack of respect for his former employers and team-mates incensed several people associated with the club, none more so than Tony Kay, Everton's outstanding wing-half during the 1962/63 title-winning campaign. Via the Everton fan website Toffeeweb in 2015, Kay responded to the reprinting of Dunlop's allegations in the *Liverpool Echo* that year, 'On behalf of my team-mates, the league champions of 1962/63, by far the greatest team in the land at that time, I'm writing this riposte because there are only a few of us left and they're not local so are unable to defend themselves. I was part of that incredible team and there wasn't a man more proud than me when we did our lap of honour at Goodison Park having stuffed Fulham 4-1 in the last game of the season. I even smoked a celebratory cigar, such was the level of my jubilation. I have no idea where it came from; I can only imagine a fan handed it to me and I never did get a chance to thank him for it. To put this ludicrous story into perspective, the accusation that we were all drug-addled cheats was made by our then goalkeeper, Albert Dunlop, who was rapidly in decline and nearing the end of his very average professional career.

'At that time, Dunlop was dating a nurse so may have had some second-hand knowledge about drugs. He was an unpopular person who never socialised with any of his team-mates and had his own problems. To give you a measure of the man, he was the only person my lovely, kind, gentle, gifted, much-loved and sorely missed team-mate, Gordon West, ever openly disliked. I never heard Gordon say a bad word about anybody, from any walk of life, professionally or socially, but in his words, Albert Dunlop was "a nasty piece of work, a bully and a thug". He made Westy's introduction to Everton from Blackpool a torrid time when he was really just a kid, straight out of school. He was embittered, cruel and deeply unpopular. He certainly picked his battles though; he never said a word to me; I imagine that was because my reputation, as a robust player and personality, preceded me.

'Every single man in the championship-winning team of 1962/63 was a truly dedicated, talented professional who worked hard every single day. The matches were just the icing on the cake; behind those fantastic performances were endless hours of hard training: tactics, skipping, sprinting, cross country runs up and down the sand dunes and in the sea at Ainsdale come hell or high water, set pieces, discipline, blood, sweat and tears. We all missed our kids growing up, Christmas, parties, family holidays, births, deaths and marriages, because we were hungry for success, and nothing would stand in our way.

'Harry Catterick was a winner; he carefully built his teams on a sturdy foundation of talent, youth, belief and dedication. Nobody was allowed to slack and our coach, Tommy Eggleston, worked us until we were spent. The 90 minutes on a Saturday afternoon was a welcome relief from the hard graft we'd put in prior to that. Everybody respected Catterick and, to be honest, we were all a bit scared of him. Backed by the might of Sir John Moores' personal fortune, he orchestrated the birth of the Mersey Millionaires; he commanded respect and got it.

'The only whisper of any kind of tablet I ever heard mentioned was the availability of a sleeping pill the night before an away game when we were staying in a hotel and a glucose pill in the dressing room before kick-off if the player asked for one. I've never taken an illegal drug in my life, and I can't imagine any of my team-mates doing it either. It certainly didn't happen in front of me, and I never heard a whisper of it during my short yet glorious time at Everton Football Club. I find it deeply offensive to my colleagues that these accusations have been raked up again when they're not here to defend themselves.

'As an aside, the story referred to in the article was published in the *Sunday People* and penned by another man I dislike intensely, one Mike Gabbert. He is the one who was to become my nemesis by ending my glorious football career and, for all intents and purposes, my life. He exposed a betting syndicate myself and my then team-mates, Peter Swan and David Layne, at Sheffield Wednesday had inadvertently become a part of by placing a single bet against our own team a couple of years earlier ... but that's another story. Following my global life ban for the next 40 years, I continued to play for any football team who'd have me, usually for charity. From time to time, I came up against a team in which Dunlop was the opposing goalkeeper. He always came over to me to shake my hand. I always refused.'

Albert Dunlop spent two years with Wrexham, making 15 appearances in the lower divisions of the Football League. He then went on to manage Rhyl Town in 1966. Sadly, even after he retired from playing, controversy continued to follow him around and in 1979 he was found guilty of three charges of deception – after stealing £27, obtaining £156.72 board and lodgings, and dishonestly obtaining over £200 by purporting to be a reporter probing corruption in racehorse circles and drugs during a three-week stay in a Southport hotel. In 1987, he was jailed for 15 months after admitting seven further charges of theft and deception. He died from a heart attack in 1990, at the age of just 57.

For all his faults, and despite his Everton career ending so sourly, nobody can deny that Dunlop had many fine moments in his 231 appearances or take from him his impressive debut against Matt Busby's Manchester United at Old Trafford in 1956. Nonetheless, in March 1962, the Goodison Park goalkeeping bar was raised significantly, when a young man named Gordon West penned a deal with the club. Over the next decade, Westy would become a true club great and a much-loved figure among the Everton faithful.

6

Westy – Gordon West

Unconvinced by the long-term goalkeeping options at the club, Harry Catterick made teenager **Gordon West** his first signing as Everton manager when he paid Blackpool £27,500 – a then world-record fee for a goalkeeper – for his services in March 1962. Having previously been linked with Gordon Banks of Leicester City and Burnley's Jim Furnell, who opted to sign for Second Division Liverpool, Catterick turned his attention back to West, an England under-23 international, who had initially caught his eye and made headlines with several stellar top-flight performances in Blackpool's successful battle against the drop towards the end of the 1960/61 campaign.

Writing in the *Liverpool Echo* in April 1961, Blackpool captain Jimmy Armfield was full of praise for his team's young goalkeeper, 'Spare a thought for our goalkeeper Gordon West. He isn't 18 until next month, yet he is playing brilliant games in the tension-filled arenas of relegation dog-eats-dog fights. Young Gordon is a great prospect. He is 6ft 1in and 14 stone but as agile as a cat. I may be biased but Manchester United players were not when we played them twice over Easter. They said young West was the best prospect they had seen for years.' Over the next ten years, Armfield and the Manchester United squad would be proven correct. During his time at Everton, West went on to win an FA Cup, two league titles and three England caps, and firmly establish himself as one of the country's leading goalkeepers.

In an interview with author Steve Zocek for his book *For the Boys in the Royal Blue Jersey*, the South Yorkshire-born custodian admitted to being 'petrified' when he first signed for Everton. Although most players made him feel extremely welcome in his new environment, West admitted that Albert Dunlop had given him a tough time during his first 12 months on Merseyside, 'I'd taken Dunlop's place in goal at Everton and he made life hell for me at the time. He'd hammer the ball at me from only a few yards away, and was horrible to me for about a year, before he left the club. I wanted to tell him to stop but I was only a young kid and I thought it might make him worse.'

Replacing Dunlop in the side straight away, West played in all but one of Everton's remaining 13 games of the 1961/62 campaign. On his debut, he kept a clean sheet in an emphatic 4-0 victory over Wolverhampton Wanderers. Although he had little to do in a dominant Everton display, the new boy received high praise from the *Liverpool Echo* reporter Leslie Edwards for his excellent throws when distributing the ball to his team-mates – a feature of his game that would regularly be on display throughout his career, 'West, left to his own devices, favoured on nearly every occasion the throw to a full-back or half-back. He did it quickly, effectively and almost with the overarm action of a fast bowler. Everton built up from that position. Every ball he sent through was easily acceptable.'

The only game that West missed that spring was the 3-0 victory at home to West Ham, which took place seven days after his outstanding display at Blackburn Rovers, where he dislocated a finger when punching away a Bryan Douglas cross, having already made four terrific saves, including one from Ian Lawther, which, according to the *Liverpool Daily Post* reporter Horace Yates, 'bordered on the miraculous'. Incidentally, while West received treatment at Ewood Park, the versatile Brian Harris had taken over in goal for five minutes in the second half. Notwithstanding a poor showing in a 3-1 defeat at White Hart Lane in his fourth outing, 'Westy' had settled in splendidly at his new club, impressing management, team-mates and supporters alike with his bravery, agility and cat-like reflexes, as well as his tremendous distribution.

Having lost just one of their final 13 games of the previous campaign, Everton carried on where they had left off, starting the 1962/63 season in superb form, with four consecutive victories in 11 days that took them to the top of the league at the end of August. In May, Catterick's expensively assembled side were crowned champions of England for the first time since 1939, conceding just 42 league goals all campaign – a then club record for the fewest number of goals conceded in a league season. In the November, West had put in a brilliant performance at home against his old club, who were trounced 5-0 in a match that was much closer than the scoreline would suggest, with the goalkeeper making two excellent diving saves from former team-mate Dave Durie at important times in the game.

With just over a month of the season remaining, he was in heroic form again on the road at Villa Park, receiving praise from team-mate Alex Young in the forward's column in the *Liverpool Echo* for two exceptional low saves that went a long way to winning the game for the Blues, despite having taken a nasty knock in the first half. Furthermore, at home to Spurs just over a fortnight later, West's clean sheet proved to be vital, as Everton, third in the league at the start of the day, climbed back to the top of the table after a 1-0 victory over their closest rivals for the title.

Having performed so well and been an ever-present all campaign, West's season was cruelly curtailed with just four games remaining as, on the day he was celebrating his 20th birthday, he suffered a serious shoulder injury in the 1-1 draw at home to Arsenal. According to reporter Leslie Edwards, 'But for a courageous performance by their goalkeeper, Gordon West, who played the whole of the second half after having painkilling injections for what is feared to be a serious shoulder injury, Everton might well have surrendered both points to Arsenal at Goodison Park last night. The accident happened after 19 minutes. Eastham's free kick was floating into the goalmouth when Skirton and the goalkeeper collided and West was thrown violently to the ground. The game was stopped for three minutes while he received attention. After such a crunching fall, the miracle was that he was able to continue.'

The injured West was replaced in the side by Dunlop for the final four games. At West Ham, the returning Dunlop was on top form in a crucial 2-1 victory and received high praise from reporter Michael Charters ahead of Everton's final game of their victorious campaign, 'I think words of praise are due to goalkeeper

Albert Dunlop, on the sidelines since the arrival of Gordon West last season. Dunlop has risen to the challenge like the top-flight professional he is. The only goal he has conceded has been an own goal; his confidence and self-assurance have been invaluable. He has more than played his part in the club's triumph.'

In his first full season with the club, West had more than played his part in helping Everton clinch their sixth league title by putting in some impressive performances and his body on the line when doing so. However, although the next campaign would start with more silverware coming the club's way (the Charity Shield, following a 4-0 victory over Manchester United), West found himself dropped from the first team after a poor run of form in the autumn, which culminated in a 4-2 loss at home to Blackburn in early November. With Dunlop having departed for Wrexham, West would vie for the number one spot with local lad **Andy Rankin** – at the time of writing, the last Scouser to play a competitive game in goal for Everton and, in many people's eyes, the greatest backup goalkeeper in England in the 1960s.

Bootle-born Rankin had signed for Everton two years previously after a successful trial, and had impressed Catterick with several terrific displays for Everton's Central League team. Ahead of the 19-year-old's debut away at Nottingham Forest, the manager told the *Liverpool Echo*, 'He is a mild-mannered boy and if he repeats his reserve team form he should do very well.'

According to the *Echo*, the former Liverpool Police cadet enjoyed a 'top-class debut' in a 2-2 draw at the City Ground and then kept clean sheets in his next two games, at home to Stoke City in a 2-0 victory and at Molineux in a goalless draw with Wolves. Sandwiched between those outings, Rankin saved a penalty and was in outstanding form against Rangers in the first leg of the unofficial British Home Championship tie between England and Scotland's title winners, which led to the Ibrox club's chairman John Lawrence describing the stopper and his performance in glowing terms. He told the *Liverpool Echo*, 'If this is Everton's reserve goalkeeper, do us a favour and play your first-team man on Monday. He was out of this world.'

In an early piece on young Rankin – the third member of his family to play for Everton, after grandfather Bruce and cousin

George – the same newspaper wrote, 'Rankin, 19 years of age, is only four months younger than West so no club in the land has better, younger goalkeepers. Rankin, tall and slim, has cat-like reactions, being particularly fast around his goalkeeping area, and with his fine positional play only needing more experience, he could keep West out of the first team for some time.'

Over the next couple of months, his performances continued to be of the same high standard before a shoulder injury sustained in training ahead of the FA Cup tie with Leeds United in January 1964 let West in for a nine-game run in the side. Despite the returning goalkeeper performing very well during that period, conceding just eight goals and being on the losing side only once, West was replaced by Rankin once the latter was fit again, with the Merseysider playing the remaining nine games of the season.

The 1964/65 campaign is an unusual season in Everton's history, in the sense that both goalkeepers made the same number of appearances – 26 – with Rankin being an ever-present until mid-December and West playing every game from that point onwards. In September, Everton went to Anfield and won 4-0. Despite the flattering scoreline, the Blues were indebted to Rankin, who put on the performance of his career in his first taste of a Merseyside derby, thwarting Scottish duo Gordon Wallace and Ian St John on numerous occasions with a string of incredible stops. After the game, Horace Yates of the *Liverpool Echo* wrote the following about Everton's phenomenal young goalkeeper, 'I think I owe an apology to Everton's Andy Rankin. In the last few weeks, I have suggested that he must be a formidable candidate for the next *Young* England team. I should have omitted the word "Young" for if there is a better goalkeeper in England than Rankin on the form he has consistently shown this season, then I have neither seen nor heard of the claimant.'

In November, he deservedly earned an England under-23 cap, playing in a 3-2 victory over Wales at the Racecourse Ground in Wrexham. Unfortunately, he looked far more nervous in an England shirt and was not selected for the next under-23 fixture – missing out to William Glazier, who had taken West's title as the most expensive goalkeeper in world football just a few months earlier, when Coventry City paid Crystal Palace £35,000 for his services. In an eventful week, Rankin was back on club duties just four days later, playing in the infamous 'Battle of Goodison' against Leeds United, when referee Ken Stokes ordered both teams off the pitch in one of the most fractious games in English football's history. Rankin was one of the few players to escape injury that day. However, at home to Stoke just a month later, he broke a bone in his right hand when diving at the feet of Eric Skeels and had to be replaced in goal by full-back 'Sandy' Brown. Although Rankin returned after ten minutes of treatment, playing the rest of the match on the left wing, it would be the last time he would play in that campaign.

Having waited patiently for his chance, West returned to the side the following week – at Tottenham Hotspur. His fine form over the next few months saw him return to the England under-23 set-up and, in the March, he was singled out for special praise by reporter Michael Charters, 'Everton's brilliant defensive work spotlights, I think, the quality of Gordon West, who must have despaired at getting back into the first team. He carried on in the reserves without complaint as Andy Rankin became a permanency in the league side. Then after Rankin had broken a bone in his hand in the Stoke game on December 12, the positions of the two top-class goalkeepers became reversed. West moved up and Rankin waited in the wings for his injury to heal and now fit again is as far away from the first team as West appeared to be earlier in the season. It is a tale as old as football itself but it is particularly good to see the two young men accept misfortune with sportsmanship and in the best spirit.'

With both goalkeepers fully fit, Harry Catterick picked West as his first choice ahead of the start of the 1965/66 campaign. In early September, he was in tremendous form at home to Burnley, making several brave saves to help his side to a 1-0 victory. However, just a month later, he suffered injury heartbreak in the second leg of the Inter-Cities Fairs Cup tie against 1. FC Nürnberg, breaking his right collarbone after falling awkwardly over the German centre-forward Rudolf Bast. The injury would rule him out for over three months.

As a consequence, the door had seemingly re-opened for Andy Rankin to enjoy a sustained run back in the side. However, after several unusually unconvincing displays – in the league, at Fulham, Leicester City and West Ham United, and in the Inter-Cities Fairs Cup tie with Hungarian outfit Újpesti Dózsa – Rankin was taken out of the team. During that period, he had cost his side several goals by being too far off his line and susceptible to the chipped finish. After the Leicester defeat in November, journalist Leslie Edwards wrote, 'Rankin's propensity for leaving his line and thus giving Leicester forwards opportunity to float the ball over his head was only one weakness in an Everton defence which degenerated markedly as the match progressed.'

In for the next nine matches was Northwich-born stopper **Geoff Barnett**, who had won the FA Youth Cup with Everton six months earlier. The academic former England youth international, who was fluent in both French and German, kept a clean sheet on his debut in a 2-0 victory over Sunderland at Goodison Park. However, in each of his next appearances, at Villa Park and Old Trafford, the inexperienced keeper shipped three goals, and though little blame could be apportioned to him in the first of those games, he did experience an unhappy afternoon against Matt Busby's Manchester United side, often displaying indecision when leaving his line. In the 2-0 home victory over Fulham three days later, Barnett looked far more comfortable, showing clean handling in difficult conditions and making a smart full-length save from Scottish forward Graham Leggat.

Sadly for Barnett, in his final game before West's return, he made a calamitous error early in the second half at Blackpool. Horace Yates wrote, 'Barnett, one of the three of the latest colts to be tossed in at the deep end of First Division football, had merely to collect the most innocent of back passes, directed at him from no more than 15 yards by Harvey. Instead of taking the ball that would have been child's play to him 999 times out of 1,000, he looked up at the vital moment and lost sight of the ball, which could only trickle over the line.'

After the defeat, Harry Catterick – who had rested Alex Young and midfielder Jimmy Gabriel – was allegedly assaulted by a crowd of angry Evertonians, which, according to reporter Michael Charters, resulted in the manager receiving a sprained ankle and multiple bruises. Six years later, Catterick told the

Liverpool Post that Barnett had felt guilty about his performance at Bloomfield Road – believing that his error had contributed to the unsavoury events that followed. In his piece in the newspaper, Catterick wrote, 'Barnett was always terribly disturbed about this and his future in football, and I always felt Everton lost a player because of it.'

Although Barnett would play only one more game for the club, he did go on to make almost 50 first-team appearances for Arsenal, having signed for the Gunners after regular goalkeeper Bob Wilson broke his arm early in 1969/70. In his first season there, he saved a penalty in an Inter-Cities Fairs Cup tie against Sporting Lisbon and two years later played in the FA Cup Final defeat to Leeds United. He ended his career in the US with Minnesota Kicks, whom he would later coach for a brief period in the early 1980s. In 2021, Barnett sadly passed away at the age of 74 from complications of Covid-19. In his autobiography, *Behind the Network*, Bob Wilson paid tribute to his one-time Highbury understudy, 'Geoff was hugely likeable and played a starring role against Sporting Lisbon. He was known as Marty because he looked similar to comedian Marty Feldman. He was great company, got on with everyone and proved his ability on many occasions.'

In the early 1960s, having accepted that first-team football at Everton was highly unlikely, a trio of talented teenage keepers departed Merseyside. Like Barnett, Pat Dunne, Willie Mailey and Ken Mulhearn would all go on to have successful careers away from Goodison Park.

West's arrival in 1962 marked the end of 18-year-old Pat Dunne's time at the club. After a two-year spell with Shamrock Rovers, the Dubliner, who was known for having one arm longer than the other, enjoyed a splendid season as Manchester United's first-choice goalkeeper. Alongside fellow Irishmen Shay Brennan, Tony Dunne and captain Noel Cantwell, Dunne played a huge role in helping the Red Devils to the First Division title in 1965, before making way for Alex Stepney. After leaving Old Trafford in 1967, Dunne signed for Plymouth Argyle and then returned to Shamrock Rovers. During his time at Manchester United, he won five international caps.

In March 1963, Scotsman Willie Mailey signed for Crewe Alexandra, for whom he played over 200 games over seven years and kept 17 clean sheets in their 1967/68 Fourth Division promotion campaign. At 5ft 8in, Mailey, an FA Youth Cup runner-up with Everton in 1961, was more than likely considered to be too small for a career at the very top of the game, but his shot-stopping abilities and general awareness made him one of the stronger keepers in the lower divisions during the 1960s.

Ken Mulhearn holds the distinction of being the only player to win the English Fourth Division and First Division titles in consecutive seasons. Having joined Stockport County in August 1964, Mulhearn was part of the Edgeley Park club's title-winning team three years later. His fine form for the Hatters brought him to the attention of Manchester City, for whom he made his debut in the Manchester derby in September 1967. That season, Mulhearn played in the 1-1 draw at Goodison Park and kept a clean sheet in City's 2-0 victory over Everton at Maine Road in April 1968. A month later, he picked up a league winners' medal after Joe Mercer and Malcolm Allison's talented side took the title by two points from their city rivals.

Back to Gordon West. His first game on his return to the starting XI in January 1966 was an FA Cup third-round tie against Sunderland, which Everton won 3-0. Impressively, he would keep clean sheets in the next four rounds of the competition, including in all three games of the mammoth quarter-final clash with Manchester City, and the 1-0 semi-final victory over Manchester United at Bolton's Burnden Park. Playing in 20 of the remaining 22 games of 1965/66, West was on the losing side only once during that spell (incidentally, Everton lost both of the games that he missed somewhat heavily, though many of the team's other stars were also rested for those matches as they took place ahead of the club's FA Cup semi-final and final) and kept eight clean sheets in a row in all competitions – at the time of writing, still an Everton club record. At Highbury, in the March, he pulled off two tremendous saves in a 1-0 victory that resulted in the travelling Evertonians chanting, 'Gordon West is the greatest!' Without doubt, he was about to enter his best spell of form at the club and build a truly special relationship with the supporters.

Ahead of the FA Cup Final, many players received several cards and telegrams from well-wishers. Years later, West told author Steve Zocek, 'I opened mine before the match and there was one from Albert Dunlop. It said, "Dear Gordon, I've finally plucked up the courage to apologise for what I did to you all those years ago and I realise what a great keeper you are now. Please accept my apology." I was made up.' Although the big keeper conceded his first FA Cup goals of the season at Wembley, he and his team-mates enjoyed a triumphant afternoon and returned to Merseyside with the trophy after an incredible comeback from two goals down saw them run out 3-2 winners over Sheffield Wednesday. Following Mike Trebilcock's equaliser that day, supporter Eddie Cavanagh ran on to the pitch in celebration, only to be rugby-tackled by a policeman on the edge of West's goal area. Over 30 years later, in conversation with author Becky Tallentire, for her book *Still Talking Blue*, West recalled the incident vividly, 'I just told the policeman to leave him alone. Eddie was one of us and I didn't want him to get arrested or go to prison or anything like that. He just couldn't stop himself, he started running and nobody could catch him. It was marvellous to witness and I'm so glad it was captured on film.'

The summer of 1966 was a jubilant one for the country's football fans, with England captain Bobby Moore lifting the World Cup at Wembley on 30 July. Goodison Park had been selected as one of the stadia for the tournament and supporters on Merseyside were lucky enough to see the likes of Pelé, Eusébio and the legendary Soviet Union stopper Lev Yashin – still the only goalkeeper to have won the coveted Ballon d'Or trophy – play in the flesh. In his country's semi-final loss to West Germany, Yashin made several fine saves at the Gwladys Street End and received warm applause from supporters inside the ground for his tremendous act of sportsmanship when he ran out of his area to help injured opponent Uwe Seeler while play carried on.

Over the next four seasons, West would miss only nine of Everton's 201 matches and undoubtedly play the most consistent football of his career. He would also firmly establish himself as one of the country's leading goalkeepers. At Wolverhampton Wanderers in the fourth round of the FA Cup, he put on a magnificent display, making a string of outstanding saves to deny, among others, Mick Bailey, Hughie McIlmoyle and Ernie Hunt – with his stop from Hunt's stinging volley late on being described by many fans as the best of his career. In his match report, Michael Charters described West as the 'maestro of Molineux, who touched the peaks of goalkeeping agility and ability' that day. In the same article, Charters added, 'By his sustained excellence this season, capped by his tremendous display on Saturday, West has moved up alongside Leicester's Gordon Banks as the best in the country.' West himself was very pleased with his performance at Molineux, telling Steve Zocek years later that he had bought every newspaper after that game and that he had got a rating of 10/10 in every publication!

In the next round, Everton defeated Liverpool 1-0 at home and looked a good bet for retaining the trophy. However, West suffered a broken bone in his hand at Tottenham Hotspur a fortnight later and was ruled out of the quarter-final with Nottingham Forest. At the City Ground, a rusty-looking Andy Rankin, playing his first competitive game in nearly a year, was at fault for Forest's first goal in the 3-2 defeat, parrying former team-mate Frank Wignall's effort, which was pounced on by Ian Storey-Moore, who bagged a hat-trick that day. Still highly regarded by everyone at the club, to the point that Harry Catterick had turned down numerous offers for his second-choice goalkeeper, Rankin played eight games during West's spell on the sidelines and finished on the losing side on only one other occasion.

Despite beating reigning champions and eventual European Cup winners Manchester United 3-1 on the opening day of the season, a new-look Everton, now containing the much-revered midfield trio of Howard Kendall, Alan Ball and Colin Harvey, started the 1967/68 campaign extremely slowly, losing six of their next dozen league matches. In the last of those defeats, West was sent off at Newcastle for striking Albert Bennett and went on to throw dirt at the home team's dugout. In Dr David France and Becky Tallentire's book, *Gwladys Street's Holy Trinity*, West recounted the incident that saw Sandy Brown end up between the posts for the second time in his Everton career, 'In those days it wasn't uncommon for the nastier forwards to bad-mouth or spit at the keeper. So I learned to retaliate by throwing the ball out with a clenched fist and if they didn't get out of my way then it was their own fault. Well, this day a fella called Burton [sic] happened to get on to the end of my fist and, shortly after he hit the deck, the referee directed me towards the showers. Sandy Brown, who would play anywhere for Everton, pulled on my green shirt and the first time that he touched the ball was to pick it out of the net from the penalty kick. I sulked most of the way home on the coach until Sandy tried to console me by informing me that I'd ruined the game for him. I simply glared at him, "I don't know what you are going on about. It was 0-0 when I came off!" I had expected Bally to have a go at me, not an unsung hero like Alexander Dewar Brown.'

In the new year, Everton's form really improved, winning 12 and drawing two of their 18 league matches from January onwards. West and his team-mates also reached their second FA Cup Final in three seasons but finished as runners-up after West Bromwich Albion forward Jeff Astle's pinpoint strike from the edge of the box proved to be the difference at Wembley. In the same month, having finished runners-up the previous year, Everton's second team lifted the Central League title. In goal, Geoff Barnett was preferred over Andy Rankin for all but three of the reserves' games that season. In fact, it looked as though Rankin's time on Merseyside was up when the *Liverpool Echo* reported that he had signed for Huddersfield Town for £25,000 on transfer deadline day in March 1968. However, four days later, Everton secretary Bill Dickinson told the newspaper, 'The negotiations between the clubs and player were so contracted that he could not sign before the midnight deadline so the transaction was called off and Rankin remains an Everton player.'

Later that year, West won the first of three much-deserved England caps inside seven months, playing in the 1-1 draw with Bulgaria a fortnight before Christmas. The following May, he lined up against Wales in England's 2-1 British Home Championship victory before playing against Mexico on the Three Lions' acclimatisation tour ahead of the 1970 World Cup finals, a tournament for which West was pretty much odds-on to be selected as Gordon Banks's understudy. Although England's top division was home to many excellent English goalkeepers in the late 1960s, the two Gordons were viewed by many as being in a class of their own. Certainly, in Westy's eyes, Banks was the greatest of the lot, 'Gordon Banks was the best and it's as simple as that. I played three games for England and I could have played more. I was sub a few times, but there's no doubt that Banksy was the best.'

Considering West had described receiving his first international cap as 'the proudest moment of my career', it was something of a surprise when he ruled himself out of contention for Sir Alf Ramsey's squad ahead of the 1969/70 campaign. According to Stan Osborne, an Everton apprentice at the time, several theories began to circulate within the club. In his book, *Making the Grade*, Osborne stated that rumours regarding West's own concerns about his weight and nervous disposition began to do the rounds.

Neither rumour held much credence, however. Undoubtedly, the muscular goalkeeper struggled at times to keep the pounds off at different points in his career – he was often found trying to 'sweat down' his weight by wearing extra layers of training kit and admitted to holding on to the side of the table when being weighed every Friday morning. In his own words, 'My problem was simple – if we'd had a good result, I'd put on seven pounds celebrating over the weekend. I was terrified of being overweight and would starve myself on Thursdays in a vain attempt to reach my target weight.' However, he was also widely recognised as being the hardest trainer at the club and had been in the form of his life for the past three seasons.

It is common knowledge that West struggled with nerves throughout his playing career. Before many games, anxiety would take a massive hold of him and turn his face white, though stories of him throwing up before games were heavily exaggerated. In his 1970 autobiography, *The Championship in my Keeping*, West dedicated a whole chapter, titled 'Nervous Torture', to the subject, in which he mentioned how his stomach would often tie up in knots before kick-off and admitted, 'If I let through even one goal, I used to torture myself, whether that goal had been my fault or not. I would go home after a match worrying about the one that had got past me. I found that my sleep was being disturbed, that I was having nightmares about letting goals through.'

In Becky Tallentire's book *Real Footballers' Wives*, Ann West, Gordon's wife during his time at Everton, provided more detail on her ex-husband's nervous disposition, 'Gordon did get very uptight and nervous before a game and I think that's well documented. The players and coaching staff didn't know much about digestion and diets back then, and they used to eat the wrong food – their pre-match meal was steak and toast. He used to get very anxious before a match because he is a nervy kind of bloke – I think it's folklore now about how ill he was – but that's the way it should be. Nerves play a big part when you're a performer and it puts the edge on your game.' It could be argued that it was those nerves that had given him the edge over the other First Division English goalkeepers in the first place and on the brink of selection for the 1970 World Cup. As Osborne stated, 'His nervous temperament was largely contained and overcome as Everton keeper.' Therefore, to suggest it played a part in a league title and FA Cup winner's decision not to represent his country was, frankly, ludicrous.

West aimed to put the record straight in his autobiography, stating that his decision was down to him not wanting to be away from his family for up to ten weeks. Later in life, he claimed that Ann had threatened to divorce him had he gone to Mexico, something she strongly refuted, 'I know I got blamed for him not going and, thinking back, there were times when I asked him not to go on tour. Who would want their husband to go away for a long time? But, to be honest, I'd have been quite pleased for him to go.'

Whatever the actual reason, by deciding early, West was free to concentrate solely on club duties during the victorious 1969/70 campaign – which saw Everton return to the top of English football, and the ever-present goalkeeper concede just 34 league goals in 42 matches. Although most of the campaign was a resounding success, there were a couple of major bumps in the road for the temperamental West, who, according to his close friend and captain Brian Labone, had always taken defeat and criticism badly. In December, the Blues were thrashed 3-0 at home by Liverpool, in a game which saw West beaten by own defender Sandy Brown's header. Then, after a poor performance in a 2-1 defeat at Southampton in January, which saw Everton knocked off the top of the table, it was reported that a traumatised West had left the ground early, telling the waiting press that he would be submitting a transfer request on the following Monday. He never did. It turned out to be Everton's final defeat of the season and over the next few months West played a massive part in bringing the title to Goodison Park. At Stoke City on Easter Monday he was in incredible form – making courageous saves to deny both Terry Conroy and Peter Dobing, as well as forward Jimmy Greenhoff on two other occasions.

Just nine days earlier, at Anfield, West had infuriated the home supporters by celebrating in front of the Kop as Everton ran out 2-0 winners. Throughout his career he enjoyed a love–hate relationship with the Liverpool crowd. Having been shocked by the barrage of abuse that had come his way on his first trip to Anfield in 1963, he decided to get his own back the following campaign, by blowing kisses in their direction and showing them his backside. On many of his subsequent visits to Anfield, West would be greeted by a supporter presenting him with a handbag, often emblazoned with the moniker 'Honey' or 'Mae'. In conversation with Becky Tallentire, West recalled, 'I'd learned that we hated each other and I thought I would shut them up. Gordon, the miner's son and conker champion of Barnsley, was going to shut the Kop up! So I sauntered along, showed them my bum and blew them some kisses. A year later, I got the handbag. It shut me up – it stuck with me for the rest of my life!'

In June 1970, Evertonians and football fans in general were left to wonder what might have been when Gordon Banks contracted Montezuma's revenge and was replaced by Chelsea's Peter Bonetti for England's World Cup quarter-final against West Germany. Unfortunately, Bonetti, an excellent keeper himself, was at fault for at least two of the goals in a 3-2 defeat. West would later go on record as saying, 'All I could think at the time was thank God it wasn't me!'

Banks wasn't the only goalkeeper to be taken ill that summer. Having returned for pre-season training at Bellefield in July, Andy Rankin complained of severe stomach pain, which was later diagnosed as appendicitis, and required an emergency operation at Liverpool's Broadgreen Hospital. With Rankin ruled out of action for the next few weeks, his role as understudy to West was taken up by youth-team graduate Alex Clarke on the club's trip to Ireland. Ahead of the new season, the youngster also lined up opposite West in the final intra-squad friendly played at Goodison Park, unfortunately conceding seven goals in a heavy defeat for the second-string Ambers. After going on loan to Bristol Rovers and being linked with a move to Rochdale midway through the 1970/71 campaign, Clarke was released the following summer. An impressive spell at Runcorn resulted in a switch to Bangor City, for whom he kept a clean sheet and put in a man-of-the-match performance against Everton's reserves in a pre-season game in August 1972.

The 1970 title proved to be the final major piece of silverware of Gordon West's remarkable career, with Harry Catterick's talented side breaking up far too quickly. The following campaign was a difficult one for everyone concerned with the club. Four players – Brian Labone, Alan Ball, Keith Newton and Tommy Wright – returned from Mexico extremely jaded, resulting in the team getting off to a poor start that they never really recovered from. Against Icelandic outfit Keflavík in the European Cup in September, West's emotions got the better of him on what was a tough evening. Having conceded an unfortunate own goal and then received abuse from his own supporters for nearly losing control of a back pass, Everton's keeper replied with a V-sign and raced off the pitch as soon as the full time whistle was blown. Afterwards, he admitted, 'It was a stupid thing to do, hurrying off to the dressing room as I did. But I felt sick, shocked and shattered.'

Other than for a five-game spell in February, West played no further part in the 1970/71 campaign – with Catterick taking him out of the side for his own good. The manager told the *Liverpool Echo*, 'His confidence is shattered because he thinks every mistake he makes is going to cost a goal.' The next round of the European Cup paired Everton with German champions Borussia Mönchengladbach. The second leg at Goodison Park provided returning stopper Andy Rankin, back in the team after a three-year absence, with his most famous moment as Everton's goalkeeper. After both legs had finished 1-1, the European Cup's first penalty shoot-out was held at the Gwladys Street End, with Rankin saving the final spot kick before sudden death to win Everton the game. As a consequence, the Merseysider holds the distinction of being the first goalkeeper to save a penalty in a European Cup shoot-out.

Nonetheless, 12 months later, Rankin moved on to Watford, where he played for a decade, before finishing his career at Huddersfield, the club he was reported to have signed for in 1968. In total he made 105 appearances for Everton over an eight-year period. At Watford, he won the club's player of the year award twice in three seasons, and his fingertip save from Gordon McQueen's header in the Hornets' shock League Cup victory over Manchester United in 1978 was once described by Watford manager Graham Taylor as the greatest save he'd ever seen.

Although West would play in every game of 1971/72 and enjoy an extremely solid campaign between the sticks, his time at Goodison Park was also coming to an end. In one of his final games, away at Southampton in April 1972, he made a crucial penalty save from former team-mate Jimmy Gabriel that earned his beloved Blues a 1-0 victory. In the summer of 1973, aged just 30, he decided to retire from the game, only to be lured back by Tranmere Rovers, for whom he provided first-team cover and made 17 appearances between 1976 and 1979.

Following retirement, West fell on hard times and struggled with his physical health. Having ballooned in weight, he was helped back on to his feet by his old skipper Brian Labone and the Everton Former Players' Foundation. In his book *Everton Crazy*, Dr David France told the following heart-warming story, 'After the removal of the comfort blanket of professional football, life hadn't been kind to Gordon West. His loyal friend Brian Labone and I vowed to get him on to his feet. There was one obvious problem: the keeper had ballooned to a massive 20-odd stones and needed new togs. I recall that we had to drag the proud Yorkshireman to a big man's shop. As the salesman prepared to take the necessary measurements, I asked, "What size are you, Gordon?" The man with the tape-measure responded "58 regular". As quick as a flash, Brian retorted, "There's nothing regular about being 58 regular."

'Gordon was discombobulated. Reluctantly, he selected a suit plus a few white shirts, a couple of ties and handfuls of socks. I took care of the transaction, "How much do I owe you?" The salesman smiled, "Would you believe it? You're in luck. Today is our Football Legends Sale and there's an 80 per cent discount on every item. I'm a Red but my dad will be dead chuffed that I've taken care of the most expensive goalkeeper in the world. By the way, does he need a new handbag?" Anyone privileged to hear Gordon open his heart to his fellow Blues at the 2001 Hall of Fame dinner will testify to his appreciation of the work of the Foundation. It changed his life.'

Back on his feet, the gentle giant formed a wonderful comedic partnership on the after-dinner circuit with Labone, often under their stage names of 'Dolly' and 'Daisy'. According to the Cheshire Live website, 'The duo formed Goodison's very own Odd Couple – affectionately berating each other with mock banter. But each barb was always delivered with a glint in Brian's eye and a wink from Gordon. The pair clearly adored each other. Close friends say that Gordon never fully got over the death of his pal in 2006. They were team-mates for more than a decade, each other's best men at their respective weddings and remained firm friends after they had retired from the game.'

In many Evertonians' eyes, Gordon West sits second only to Neville Southall in the Goodison Park goalkeeping pecking order. Indeed, some Blues supporters of the 1960s claim he is the greatest stopper the club has ever had. BBC Sport's Phil McNulty, who caught the end of West's Everton career and grew up on stories of him at his peak, told me, 'Gordon West was a truly great goalkeeper. He was extremely flamboyant and, on some occasions, pure theatre. He had a tempestuous relationship with his own fans at times – even though they all loved him – and a wonderful relationship with the Kop. He could throw the ball more than half the length of the pitch and was such an interesting character. How could someone that good suffer so badly from nerves?'

A few years before his sad passing in 2012, the man who won two league titles and an FA Cup with the club, and made over

400 first-team appearances in the Everton goal between 1962 and 1973, had the following to say on the subject of the Blues' greatest goalkeeper, 'Neville was the best in colour, but Westy was the best in black and white.'

Very few Evertonians would disagree with him.

7

'Should've Signed Shilton' – The 1970s
and Issues between the Sticks

Although it would take Everton 14 years to win their next major
piece of silverware after clinching the 1969/70 First Division
title, the general feeling among match-going fans was that the
club was only a top-class goalkeeper away from glory at various
points during that period. Before the decade belonging to the likes
of ABBA, *The Godfather* and *Starsky & Hutch* was over, David
Lawson, Dai Davies, Drew Brand, George Wood and Martin
Hodge would all try, yet ultimately fail, to fill the sizeable void
left by Gordon West, though some of those men are remembered
more fondly than others by Evertonians.

In December 1970, Harry Catterick paid Swansea City
£25,000 to bring 22-year-old Welshman **David 'Dai' Davies**
to Goodison Park, despite the goalkeeper having played only
a handful of games for the west Wales club. Catterick told the
Liverpool Echo, 'David has only limited experience but possesses
a lot of potential. He is big, strong and cool-headed, and appears
to have what it takes to get to the top.' Towards the end of his
first season at the club, Davies, who had caught Catterick's eye
while playing for Wales under-23s against England at Wrexham,
was given his first Everton start, at Newcastle United, where he
suffered the embarrassment of scoring an own goal after Colin
Harvey's headed goal-line clearance hit him on the arm before
entering the net. Notwithstanding, he enjoyed a competent
debut, with journalist Michael Charters stating, 'Davies should
forget that unfortunate start to his league career with Everton.
He showed himself to be capable and sound in his handling,
making two brilliant saves from Gibb and Dyson. I predict he

will force himself into the first-team limelight regularly by next season.'

When Andy Rankin was sold to Watford in the autumn of 1971, it seemed to everyone on the outside that Davies would be the natural successor to West over the next couple of years. As it turned out, though, the Everton management team had different ideas; West was an ever-present throughout 1971/72, and, over the next three years, Davies disappeared from view as Everton explored an alternative option.

A decade after making West the most expensive goalkeeper in Britain, Catterick repeated the move when he snapped up **David Lawson** from Huddersfield Town for £80,000 in July 1972. Despite the Terriers suffering relegation to the Second Division in 1971/72, Lawson had attracted the attention of numerous suitors with a series of impressive top-flight displays, including a man-of-the-match performance in a 2-0 defeat at Liverpool, where he had knocked himself out when colliding with a post after making a series of incredible last-ditch saves. According to the *Liverpool Echo* reporter Chris James, Lawson came very close to earning his side a point, making seven superb stops and winning 'Anfield's hearts with a brave display ranking close to some of the great [goalkeeping] exhibitions seen there in the past'.

Courageous and agile, with cat-like reflexes, Lawson, who had played for Bradford Park Avenue and had an unsuccessful trial at Liverpool before signing for Huddersfield, was selected ahead of the ageing West at the start of Everton's 1972/73 campaign. Speaking ahead of the pre-season trip to Sweden, assistant manager Tommy Eggleston revealed, 'Lawson will start the season as first-team choice. Dai Davies is much younger than West and he will be given the opportunity to impress as well. I have been impressed with both of them in training but, of course, West has fought his way back into the first team before. He is the kind of character who could do it again.' The initial signs from Lawson were extremely encouraging; in his first nine games, Everton's new goalkeeper looked very confident. He conceded just five goals during that period and produced a match-saving performance against West Bromwich Albion at Goodison at the start of September – making a superb late save to preserve the points and earn the Blues a 1-0 victory. Even after making a mistake in the 2-1 win over Leicester seven days later – a win which saw Everton go top of the league – Lawson's apology was refused by forward Joe Royle, who was quoted in the *Liverpool Echo* as saying, 'You must be joking. One mistake in nine games – you're entitled to that!'

Indeed, Lawson's form had been so impressive that Catterick was willing to let either West or Davies head out on loan to Stoke City, who were suffering a goalkeeping crisis after Gordon Banks had been involved in a horrific car accident, which resulted in the England star losing vision in his right eye and having to retire from professional football at the age of 34. Although neither man ended up leaving for the Potteries, both had to be content with playing in the Central League team as Lawson was firmly established as the club's number one goalkeeper. There was, however, one goalkeeping departure that year. With Lawson, West and Davies all ahead of him, youngster Keith Williams, who sat on the bench for the second leg of the European Cup tie against Keflavík two years earlier, decided to leave the professional game and join the Liverpool police force. In November 1972, Williams was selected to play for the British Police against a Welsh Amateur XI at Stafford Rangers. He would go on to have an excellent career between the posts for several clubs in Wales.

Although Everton's form tailed off after that blistering start, Lawson's performances remained composed; Gordon West failed to make a first-team appearance that campaign until the final few weeks, only returning to the fold after Lawson suffered a groin injury at West Bromwich Albion, which kept him out of four of Everton's final five games (incidentally, Lawson was replaced in goal by centre-half Mick Lyons at The Hawthorns). At the end of Lawson's maiden Goodison campaign, it seemed as though the assessment of his ability provided by ex-Huddersfield team-mate Alan Jones ahead of the custodian's move to Everton ten months earlier was a fair one, 'He is a superb all-round goalkeeper and has the ability and courage to develop into an outstanding one.'

There was little to suggest otherwise throughout the following campaign. In the first half of 1973/74, Lawson conceded just 21 goals in 23 league games as new manager Billy Bingham's side ended the calendar year in fourth place – a huge improvement on the final position of 17th the previous season. Even in the disappointing Texaco Cup and FA Cup defeats to Hearts and West Bromwich Albion respectively, the ever-present Lawson performed tremendously, and though Bingham's team failed to maintain their impressive early season form, their defensive record remained strong, especially at home where they conceded just 14 goals in 21 games, a record bettered only by Ray Clemence and his backline across Stanley Park.

Sadly, Lawson's drop-off in form over the next three years was gargantuan and goes some way to highlight the fragile world of a top-flight goalkeeper – with both fitness and confidence levels dipping to such an extent that he would become a much-derided figure in Everton's history and unrecognisable from the player who had done so well in his first two years at the club. The summer of 1974 had been full of talk of Bingham making a move to bring Leicester City and England's Peter Shilton to Everton in a possible player-plus-cash swap deal involving Lawson. Nonetheless, despite Bingham admitting to the press that he had spoken to the Foxes about their goalkeeper and there being rumours of both Lawson and Joe Royle heading in the opposite direction, no deal could be struck. Bingham told the *Liverpool Echo* that no goalkeeper was worth the £325,000 Leicester wanted for Shilton, and that £200,000 was the maximum he would ever pay for a stopper. As a consequence, Lawson began 1974/75 as Everton's first choice, with Shilton eventually signing for Stoke for a world-record fee in November 1974. As he had done at Filbert Street seven years earlier, Shilton would take on the role of Gordon Banks's successor. At international level, over the next few years, he would compete with Clemence for the number one spot vacated by Banks following his England retirement.

After again starting the new season strongly, Lawson was hospitalised seven games into 1974/75, after sustaining a season-ending blow in the League Cup second-round replay exit to Aston Villa – a competition and opponent the luckless goalkeeper's name would become infamously synonymous with in Everton folklore. Although it was an infection of the kidneys that had done for him, figuratively, it was more like a kick to the guts he had received at

Goodison Park that evening as from that moment on, Lawson's career stalled before eventually hitting the rocks.

In his absence, Dai Davies, back after a brief loan stint at his old club Swansea City, returned to the fold. His 39-game spell that season was a microcosm of his whole Everton career, with terrific performances, like the one at Queens Park Rangers in September, being negated by misjudged crosses, indecisiveness and costly fumbles, leading to dropped points and cup exits against Chelsea and Fulham respectively. Nonetheless, with just five games of the season remaining, Everton sat top of the table, before a disastrous final month saw them pick up just four more points. At home to Sheffield United in the penultimate match, Davies gave an extremely poor display. After failing to hold on to a cross, the Welshman gifted the visitors an undeserved equaliser before Tony Currie completed the comeback and ended Everton's title hopes. In his entertaining autobiography, *Never Say Dai*, Davies recalled that traumatic afternoon, 'My terrible mistakes were the main reasons why Everton lost 3-2 and the defeat proved a turning point.'

Following his return to the first team from injury at the start of the 1975/76 season, Lawson would share goalkeeping duties with Davies for the next two years. During that period, both men failed to convince the club's management, their team-mates or the Goodison Park faithful that they were deserving of the position – on numerous occasions losing their places after not only sustaining niggling injuries but also committing high-profile errors, bordering on the ridiculous. Lawson's persistent thigh injury and Davies's broken thumb gave both keepers ample opportunities to stake their claims to be the club's outright number one that season – however, they were opportunities neither of them was able to take.

With Davies and Lawson sidelined through injury, 18-year-old **Drew Brand** was handed his debut against Leeds United in November 1975. At Elland Road, the Scot endured a torrid time; he was at fault for two goals and shipped five as Everton went down 5-2 to Jimmy Armfield's side. Although Brand also made several stunning stops that day, and was likened to the brilliant Pat Jennings in the *Liverpool Echo* by team-mate Dave Clements, he would play only one more game for the Blues – keeping a clean sheet in a 2-0 victory over Newcastle United on the final day of the 1976/77 season. By that point, any remaining faith in Davies, cruelly nicknamed 'Dai the Drop' by several wags on the Gwladys Street terraces, and Lawson – 'The Cat that gave his defence kittens every time he came for a cross' – had completely evaporated.

According to David Prentice, a match-going teenager during that period, Lawson may have come to Everton with a big reputation, but his physical appearance resulted in him being a goalkeeper who lacked any real presence. Prentice explained, 'Lawson came to the club as a British transfer record for a goalkeeper, but his sloped shoulders didn't instil confidence in many of us watching him that he could "boss his area" the way Shilton and Clemence did for their respective teams. The fact that Billy Bingham and then Gordon Lee would chop and change their last line of defence indicated that the managers we had during that time had very little faith in Lawson or Davies either.'

In his autobiography, *A Different Road*, forward Bob Latchford was no less forgiving in his assessment, 'The lack of a top-class goalkeeper was undoubtedly costly and although Dai Davies and David Lawson were reasonable keepers, they were not the sort of players to win you games. Individual mistakes – and both made them more frequently than they should have done – proved costly and also failed to build the trust of their defenders. This wasn't an irreconcilable problem. Remember: Peter Shilton left Leicester mid-season for Stoke. He would have been the difference between Everton being a team of nearly men and one of winners, not just for that season [1974/75] but throughout the 1970s.'

Perhaps a little unfairly considering his strong start at the club, Lawson is remembered mostly by Evertonians for his mistakes in the latter stages of the two domestic cup competitions in the 1976/77 campaign. Prentice recalled, 'I was around 13 years old at the time and our defeats to Aston Villa in the League Cup Final second replay at Old Trafford and then Liverpool in the FA Cup semi-final replay at Maine Road just weeks later broke my heart. On both occasions, we were so close to clinching silverware. Unfortunately, David Lawson was massively to blame on both occasions.'

Everton had clinched a place in their first League Cup Final after overcoming Bolton Wanderers 2-1 on aggregate in the semi-final. In the first leg of the last-four tie at Goodison Park, with just two minutes remaining and Everton leading 1-0, Lawson was punished for taking too many steps. From the resulting free kick, winger Willie Morgan tapped the ball to forward Neil Whatmore, who smashed it past the hapless goalkeeper to set up a tense second leg a month later. Fortunately, Latchford's winner at Burnden Park sent Everton, by then under Gordon Lee's management, to Wembley and temporarily spared Lawson's blushes. However, after performing well and saving bravely at Andy Gray's feet in the 0-0 draw at Wembley, the goalkeeper was beaten at his near post by John Deehan, whose prod towards goal was turned over his own line by Roger Kenyon in the replay at Hillsborough before Latchford came to Everton's rescue again – scoring with less than two minutes remaining to take the tie to a second replay.

At Old Trafford, Lawson's luck finally ran out. With Everton ten minutes away from victory, Villa centre-half Chris Nicholl let fly from 35 yards with a dipping strike that seemed to catch the goalkeeper completely by surprise. Before falling to his right in vain, Lawson was slow to shift his feet across and set himself for a diving save. Just 60 seconds later, and probably still smarting from being beaten by Nicholl's speculative strike, Lawson inexplicably came racing off his line for a ball he was never going to smother. From a tight angle, and with Lawson unnecessarily committed to the dive, midfielder Brian Little was able to slip the ball under him and turn the tie on its head. Two exceptionally poor pieces of goalkeeping within a minute of each other had cost Everton the League Cup.

Consequently, it was no surprise when Dai Davies was selected for the next two league fixtures. With both games finishing in victory, it was a huge shock to everyone when Lee recalled Lawson for the FA Cup semi-final against Liverpool, not least to the goalkeepers themselves. In *Never Say Dai*, Davies stated, 'As I played cards with some of the other players, I was called out by Lee and told that Dave Lawson would after all play in the game. It was quite a shock, but when I went back to the rest of the team and told Dave, his shock was just as great as mine.

"Shit! Shit! I haven't prepared" was his reaction.' Unfortunately for everyone of a blue persuasion, it most certainly showed. Terry McDermott's lob was voted as the BBC's Goal of the Season but Lawson's rogue positioning – more than six yards off his line for a strike from the edge of the box when it was clear that the opponent was not setting himself for a piledriver – played easily into the hands of McDermott, who was able to lift the ball over the goalkeeper for a clever yet simple finish. Alas, Lawson was also at fault for Liverpool's second goal – his weak punch from Steve Heighway's free kick did nothing more than tee Jimmy Case up for a header that the Liverpool man was able to send over both Lawson and covering defender Mick Lyons. Although the game finished 2-2, there was to be further replay heartbreak and errors from Lawson when Everton were trounced 3-0 at Maine Road just four days later in what turned out to be his final appearance for the club.

Within 48 hours of the defeat, Lee approached relegation-threatened Stoke about bringing Peter Shilton to Goodison Park. Although the *Liverpool Echo* revealed that 'England international Peter Shilton will almost certainly move to Everton during the summer', the transfer did not happen, with Shilton's wage demands – he was by far the highest-paid player in the country – being cited as the sticking problem. In September 1977, Brian Clough took Shilton to Nottingham Forest, where the two of them would win the league title, two League Cups and two European Cups within three years. According to David Prentice, the short-sightedness of the Everton board in failing to see the benefit of investing in a top-class goalkeeper cost Everton dearly, 'At a time when Italian clubs were spending fortunes on goalkeepers, it was really looked down upon in England. You spent fortunes on strikers and midfielders but it was always seen as a false economy with goalkeepers. The mindset was that they didn't win you games. Strikers did. Cloughie was ahead of the game there. I don't think the transfer fee for Peter Shilton was astronomical but his wages most certainly were. Nevertheless, Cloughie knew how important he could be for his team, which proved to be the case.'

Leeds United's out-of-favour Scottish international keeper David Harvey was the next to be linked with a move to Everton but after failing to agree terms with the player, Lee turned his attention to another Scot, Blackpool's George Wood, whose £150,000 transfer to the club spelled the end for both Dai Davies and David Lawson.

Just weeks after Wood's arrival, Davies moved to Wrexham, where he played the best football of his career and firmly established himself as his country's first-choice goalkeeper. After a stint back in the First Division with Swansea City and brief spells with Tranmere Rovers, Bangor City and Wrexham (again), he finally hung up his gloves for good in 1986. Following retirement from the game, the proud Welshman ran a natural healing centre in Llangollen and was reportedly made a druid in the Welsh Gorsedd of the Bards for his services to the Welsh language.

In February 2021, after the announcement of Davies's death from pancreatic cancer at the age of 72, Neville Southall told the *Liverpool Echo*, 'Dai had incredible mental strength and never let the odd mistake affect him. He just kept going. He won more than 50 caps and played loads of games at the top level and should be recognised as a top goalkeeper. His attitude was always spot on and he was a great guy as well, a really funny person.' Southall also took to Twitter to pay tribute to his predecessor in the Wales goal, 'RIP Dai Davies. My friend, a gentleman, an inspiration and a proper Welshman, a great mentor and a top keeper.'

Twelve months after Davies's Everton departure, David Lawson, having rejected an offer to stay at the club and play second fiddle to Wood, left for Luton Town, with the fee set at £15,000 on the completion of 20 first-team appearances for the Kenilworth Road outfit. However, after just five games for David Pleat's side and the arrival of new goalkeeper Jake Findlay from Aston Villa, Lawson moved to Fourth Division side Stockport County, where he retired in 1981, aged 34. In his final season as a professional footballer, Britain's one-time most expensive goalkeeper experienced further misfortune in the League Cup. Despite going on to make a succession of splendid saves in County's tie with Arsenal, Lawson gifted the Gunners their opening goal – palming John Hollins's long-range strike into the top of his net after just six minutes and badly damaging his left knee in the process.

On a more positive note, after being released by Everton in 1976, Liverpool-born Brian Parkinson, a product of the club's youth team, enjoyed an excellent five-year career in the American Soccer League. Earning the nickname 'Superstop' after some wonderful displays for Los Angeles Skyhawks, Parkinson played a significant part in the Skyhawks' 1976 ASL Championship victory, conceding, on average, less than one goal per game in the club's title-winning season and being named the league's leading goalkeeper. During his time in the USA, Parkinson also turned out for Santa Barbara Condors, Miami Americans and California Sunshine.

If there were a prize for the goalkeeper who engaged and connected most with their supporters, then **George Wood** would certainly have walked away a winner. Talk to any match-going Evertonian of the late 1970s and they will tell you stories of jovial interactions the Goodison crowd had with their new last line of defence. Though possessing nowhere near the ability of Gordon West, Wood, in the eyes of most fans, was a significant improvement on those who had followed West in the Everton goal. Nevertheless, he could not have got off to a worse start. On the opening day of the 1977/78 campaign, the new signing was at fault for all three of Nottingham Forest's goals as Brian Clough's side started as they meant to go on – winning 3-1 at Goodison Park. Wood's biggest clanger that day came when he failed to collect Tony Woodcock's high corner, which left John Robertson with an easy finish. The *Liverpool Echo* ran the headline 'The Expensive Flops', with Wood and winger Dave Thomas coming in for particularly harsh treatment.

However, if some home fans had started to worry that they had signed another keeper in the Lawson/Davies mould, then their fears were allayed just three days later, when Wood put on a stunning display at Highbury in a 1-0 defeat to Terry Neill's side. Reflecting on his first week at the club, Wood told the *Liverpool Echo*, 'I was pleased with my performance against Arsenal. The game also helped me to get a better understanding with the defence. Knowing what the players in front of you are going to do is 75 per cent of a goalkeeper's game and the sooner everything is settled here the better.' In the same interview with

The first kings of Anfield – David Jardine (fourth from the left on the back row) played a key role in Everton's 1891 title triumph.

The brilliant Billy Scott, an FA Cup winner in 1906 and recipient of 25 caps for Ireland. Courtesy of Brendan Connolly

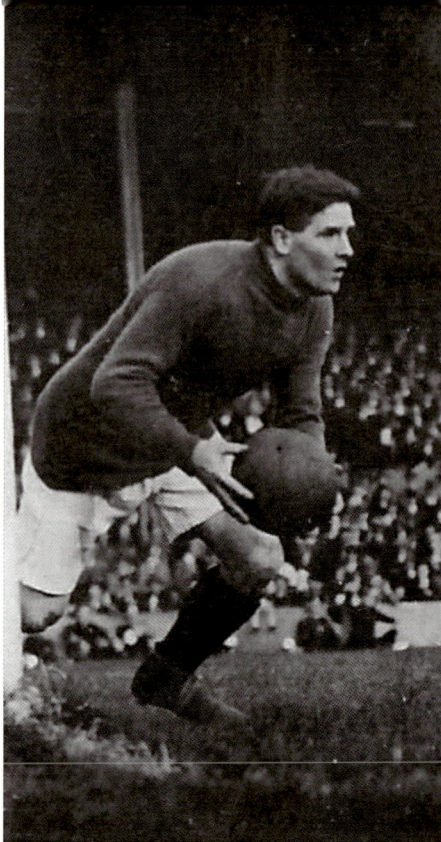

The evergreen Tommy Fern, a 1915 league title winner, who made 231 competitive first-team appearances for the club.
Courtesy of Brendan Connolly

Ted Sagar, Everton's first 'number one', collects a high ball at Wembley in Everton's 1933 FA Cup Final victory. Sagar won two league titles and an FA Cup in a 24-year Everton career that spanned both sides of the Second World War.

After Sagar's final appearance in the Everton goal, Irishman Jimmy O'Neill (right) receives advice from the retiring goalkeeper. O'Neill went on to make over 200 appearances for the club in the 1950s.

'The Bandit' – troubled goalkeeper Albert Dunlop makes a diving save at the Gwladys Street End.

The magnificent Gordon West holds on in Everton's FA Cup Final triumph over Sheffield Wednesday in 1966.

Handbags with the enemy. After blowing kisses to the Kop on an early visit, Westy often received a personalised new accessory on subsequent trips to Anfield. Mirrorpix

Andy Rankin – widely regarded as the best reserve keeper in England in the 1960s.

The luckless David Lawson had a number of unfortunate moments between the Everton posts.

Scotland international George Wood enjoyed a fabulous relationship with the Goodison Park supporters in the late 1970s.
Courtesy of Brendan Connolly

The safe and steady Jim Arnold, who played a significant role in Neville Southall's early development at Everton.

The world's greatest goalkeeper. Neville Southall poses with his Football Writers' Player of the Year award in 1985.

'Train heavy, play light.' Alan Kelly Senior with Southall and understudy Bobby Mimms at Everton's Bellefield training ground during the 1985/86 season.
Courtesy of Everton Football Club

Alex Goodman, Wood also mentioned how he had had very little time to prepare for the Forest game – as the move had only gone through a few days before – and how issues with confidence had been a problem for him in the past, 'One of my big faults before was a lack of confidence but I think I have overcome this now and of course playing in the First Division will help. The pace is quicker than in the Second and I think 80 per cent of shots are on target compared with about 60-65 per cent in the Second Division.'

Over the next 22 games, Wood and his team-mates would perform phenomenally, going unbeaten in the league, progressing in the League Cup and, bar a couple of high-scoring draws at Ipswich Town and at home to Newcastle United, conceding very few goals along the way (18 in total). On Christmas Day, the team sat second in the league and Wood continued to receive the plaudits. At Anfield, in a bruising autumn encounter, he was magnificent in a 0-0 draw, which had reporter Michael Charters stating Everton would have been well beaten had it not been for Wood – 'their finest goalkeeper since Gordon West'. Wood's colleagues were equally gushing with their praise. Ahead of the trip to Portman Road in November, Mick Lyons told the *Liverpool Echo*, 'George Wood usually pulls off great saves, and that makes us feel that we can go and win.'

Indeed, things were looking so good for Wood that he was being widely tipped for an international call-up. In his Inside Sport column in the *Liverpool Echo*, journalist Bill Bothwell told his readers, 'When Scotland go to the Argentine next year for the World Cup, they will take George Wood, the Everton goalkeeper, with them. That is my prediction after taking a look at the candidates on hand at this moment, and taking the view that Alan Rough, reckoned the best north of the border, doesn't measure up to the great Scottish keepers of the past.' Unfortunately for Everton's big custodian, Scotland boss Ally MacLeod chose to attend the wrong game – the aforementioned 4-4 draw with Newcastle at Goodison Park, where Wood, having accidentally bumped into MacLeod before kick-off, endured a traumatic afternoon – his old issues with confidence seeming to resurface.

Luckily for the Blues, he was quick to recover and just two days later, Wood was magnificent in a 2-1 win over Middlesbrough in the League Cup. After the game, he told the local press, 'After Saturday I knew there was going to be a lot of pressure on me. I put the Newcastle game right out of my mind and a couple of early saves at Ayresome Park gave me back a lot of confidence. Now I'll just have to wait and see if MacLeod comes to watch me again. But I still don't want to know when he comes to a game.'

Fortunately for Wood, MacLeod was too busy to attend the crushing 6-2 defeat to Manchester United on Boxing Day, Everton's first defeat in over four months. Unlike the majority of his team-mates, the goalkeeper actually came out of the game with a fair amount of credit, as indeed he did the next day at Elland Road, where he made a handful of excellent saves in a 3-1 loss. Having gone 22 games unbeaten, Gordon Lee's side had lost two games inside 24 hours, shipping nine goals in the process. Nonetheless, the Blues, aided by the goalscoring prowess of Bob Latchford, remained in the title hunt until the final month of the season, eventually finishing third behind Nottingham Forest and Liverpool. Much is rightly made of the attacking flair of that Everton side, who outscored both Forest and Liverpool that season, but the contribution of Wood and his backline should not be underplayed. A total of 19 league clean sheets was an impressive return for a team that had kept just ten and conceded 64 goals in the previous league campaign.

Wood's contribution had not gone unnoticed by legendary custodian Ted Sagar. In an article for the *Liverpool Echo* midway through the Scot's maiden season, Sagar stated, 'Everton have got a very good goalkeeper in George Wood. I thought he was very promising when he was with Blackpool, and I said then that if they wanted to buy a goalkeeper then George Wood was their man.' Although Peter Shilton walked away with a First Division winners' medal, a League Cup winners' medal and the PFA Players' Player of the Year award in 1977/78, the majority of Evertonians were more than happy with their own goalkeeper's performances that term.

Wood endeared himself further to the Goodison Park faithful in Harry Catterick's testimonial game, which took place days after the season had finished. With Everton leading 1-0 against an All-Stars XI, Wood swapped shirts with striker Jim Pearson and joined Bob Latchford in attack for the second half. By the end of the game, he had scored four goals as Everton trounced their opponents 5-1. At Runcorn just 24 hours later, he scored again in a testimonial for Alan King, and then banged five goals in at Wigan in another testimonial before the week was over. Ten goals in three matches was some record for any player, never mind a goalkeeper! Wood did have previous form in front of goal, however, having played, and scored, as a forward for East Stirlingshire early on in his career.

According to journalist and author Brian Viner, a match-going teenager during the 1970s, George Wood was a real character, who had a very special relationship with the Goodison Park crowd, 'There was something about Georgie Wood, even for an entirely heterosexual 16-year-old that was just incredibly beguiling and actually quite sexy. He was handsome and had this incredible head of blonde hair. I stood on the Gwladys Street terraces and he would respond to us whenever we asked him to give us a wave. My friends and I really worshipped him. He was physically the closest player to us at a game and to see him pull off a truly acrobatic save in front of us was incredible, really.

'The late 1970s was very much the time of fans' songs and chants. And Georgie Wood was a massive part of that. We'd all sing "Scotland's number one!" long before he had actually been capped. At that time, Ray Clemence and Peter Shilton were fighting it out to be England's outright number one goalkeeper. The Liverpool fans would all sing "We all agree that Clemence is better than Shilton" and on derby day our response would be "We all agree Shilton is better than Clemence and Georgie is better than Shilton". Deep down we all knew he wasn't, but he had a very winning mentality – and he was fearless, acrobatic and standing at 6ft 3in tall had a real presence about him. I bridle at the idea that we would have won the league had we signed Shilton as although Wood wasn't quite at Shilton's level, I thought he was a very, very good goalkeeper.'

Throughout the 1978/79 season, Wood and his team-mates again performed superbly for long periods. Just 40 goals were conceded in 42 league games as Everton again challenged for the title late into the campaign. As he had been the previous season, Wood was instrumental in helping Everton to secure a point at Anfield in March, making several tremendous saves that drew special praise from his opposite number Ray Clemence, who told the *Liverpool Echo*, 'George was brilliant. Without him, we could have been four or five up before they got back into it. Two or three saves were out of this world. For me his best save was from David Johnson's diving header just after half-time. It was the sign of a good goalkeeper that he didn't give up when all seemed lost.' Incidentally, two months earlier, on an ice rink of a pitch at Burnden Park, Wood was involved in an accidental collision with Bolton Wanderers' Peter Reid, which resulted in the future Everton title winner breaking his leg. At half-time, with the score at 1-1, referee Telford Mills abandoned the game. In his autobiography, Reid recalled, 'I slid in for a ball with George Wood at the Railway Embankment End and tried to stop myself but George came hurtling out at me, and the next thing I knew I was in a crumpled heap on the floor. There was a moment when one of the doctors said that I might not play again and asked me what I would do. I said I'd buy a gun and shoot George Wood – although my sister, Carol, did try and hit him after the game. I wasn't being serious, even though the situation was, because I know these things happen in football.'

A failure to turn draws into victories would ultimately cost the team, with Everton and Latchford finding goals much harder to come by in the league. At home games, Wood continued to enjoy his special relationship with the supporters. David Prentice recalled, 'I loved the affinity he had with the crowd. He always reacted to the chants before the games. And in quiet games for George, like the early rounds of the League Cup and against Finn Harps in the UEFA Cup, the Gwladys would chant "Georgie put the kettle on! Georgie put the kettle on!" and he would respond by mimicking the boiling of a kettle. I liked the camaraderie he had with us all. I get the impression that the relationship he had with those inside Goodison on matchdays was very similar to the one that Gordon West had enjoyed with the Everton supporters.'

A fortnight after the season had ended, Wood finally made his Scotland debut, in a 1-0 victory over Northern Ireland. He played twice more for his country that year, against England and Argentina. Although he was at fault for Steve Coppell's goal at Wembley and holds the dubious title of being the first goalkeeper Diego Maradona scored against in Argentina colours, Wood's international recognition was something that brought real pride to Viner, 'Me and my posse of Everton friends were so excited when Wood started getting into the Scotland squads that we avoided the scoreline all day for one international game and waited for the television highlights. Frustratingly, in scenes very similar to those in that famous episode of *Whatever Happened to the Likely Lads?* either the game ended up being postponed or he wasn't selected and we had to wait to see George make his international debut.'

In the 1979 close season, youngster Nick Banner departed the club. After short spells with Runcorn and Bangor City, Everton's 1976 FA Youth Cup runners-up goalkeeper agreed to join Stoke City, where he was expected to compete with Peter Fox for the number one jersey. However, following a change in management at the Potteries club, the deal fell through, resulting in Banner signing for non-league Altrincham instead. Sadly, after breaking his wrist, and then sustaining further injuries, Banner decided to turn his back on the game, having lost the confidence to play.

After two excellent campaigns, and with their goalkeeper having gained much-deserved international recognition, the drop-off in form of both Everton and George Wood in the 1979/80 season remains a mystery to many supporters. A shocking 4-2 home defeat to Norwich City on the opening day, Wood's 100th consecutive appearance, set the tone for the nine months that followed, as Everton struggled to climb out of the bottom half of the table and finished one place above the relegation zone. Things were no better in the cup competitions: although Wood had saved a penalty and been in fine form to help Everton get past Cardiff City in the League Cup, his performances in both legs of the UEFA Cup tie against Feyenoord, when he dived over the ball in the away leg before again being culpable at Goodison a fortnight later, drew criticism from Gordon Lee. After the second leg, when Wood was beaten by a swerving shot from distance, the manager proclaimed, 'You can't legislate for giving away goals like that. It was worse than the one in Rotterdam.'

From that point on, Wood's relationship with his manager seemed to break down. Having rejected a contract extension offer the previous summer, he told the *Liverpool Echo* in November 1979, 'When my contract is up, I know I can talk to other clubs unless I am offered a fairer deal. You are supposed to get out of football what you put in but in the case of myself and certain other players in football it doesn't work out that way. I told the boss that I wanted the same as two or three other players were getting and then I would be happy. I felt I had established myself in the Scotland squad and I thought that I deserved as much as the rest of the internationals in the team. But I didn't get it.'

Less than a week after the article was published, Wood found himself out of the team as Lee decided to put his faith in promising young keeper **Martin Hodge**, whom the club had signed from Plymouth Argyle for £135,000 four months earlier. Wood played just six more times for Everton before moving to Arsenal, where he kept the legendary Pat Jennings out of the side for almost a year. Although the Scotsman conceded just one goal in his final four matches for Everton and saved a penalty from Southampton's Mick Channon in his penultimate game in front of the home supporters, it was an extremely sad end to what had been an excellent Everton career.

After leaving Highbury in 1983, Wood moved across London to Crystal Palace, for whom he made over 200 appearances over a four-year period. He would later sign for Cardiff City, old club Blackpool on loan, Hereford United and Merthyr Tydfil, before both playing and managing at Inter Cardiff. In August 1994, at the age of 42, he lined up in goal for the League of Wales club's debut UEFA Cup preliminary-round tie against Polish outfit GKS Katowice.

In many Evertonians' eyes, Martin Hodge is one of the most underrated goalkeepers in the club's history. Born in Southport, he enjoyed two seasons at Home Park before making his way back up north in July 1979. According to David Prentice, Hodge's save from Billy Bonds in the 1980 FA Cup semi-final at Villa Park is one of the best he has seen at a game, 'It was voted third in the

BBC's very short-lived save of the season competition. When the West Ham corner came in, Bonds rose majestically and it was one of those headers that as soon as it leaves the player's head you think "God, we're 1-0 down" but Hodge somehow managed to react quickly to make an incredible reflex save and parry the ball away to safety. For me, he was a very talented goalkeeper who was disposed of a little too early.'

It is an opinion shared by many. Despite coming into a struggling side at just 20 years old, Hodge performed magnificently well, particularly at The Dell ten days before Christmas and at home to Nottingham Forest on New Year's Day, when he superbly tipped over Garry Birtles's deflected shot to earn his side a much-needed 1-0 victory. Even in the catastrophic 4-0 home defeat to Ipswich Town in the February, when cushions were thrown on to the pitch by disgruntled Evertonians sitting in the Main Stand, Hodge was again on top form, with the *Daily Mirror*'s journalist Chris James reporting, 'But for goalkeeper Martin Hodge, Ipswich would have scored many more. He must have felt like General Custer as Paul Mariner and his braves overran the Everton defence and besieged his goal. He made half a dozen outstanding saves.'

Speaking to the *Liverpool Echo* in February 1980, after a fine showing at Bristol City, Hodge stated that he was pretty much a no-fuss goalkeeper, who believed in getting the basics right – placing a huge emphasis on moving his feet quickly and not making things look overly spectacular. Journalist Charles Lambert's piece on Hodge was an extremely positive one and pointed to a bright future at the club for the unassuming youngster. However, after a horror performance at Spurs in April 1980, when Hodge dropped the ball at the feet of Ossie Ardiles and was then beaten from distance by Tony Galvin's hopeful effort, he was dropped for the final four games of the season.

Having allowed George Wood to move to Arsenal during the close season, the under-fire Gordon Lee decided he wanted to start the 1980/81 campaign with a more experienced keeper than the exceptionally modest and hard-working Hodge. As a consequence, 27-year-old **Jim McDonagh**, with almost 300 Football League appearances already to his name, was signed for £250,000 from relegated Bolton and came straight into the team. When Hodge sustained a nasty knee injury that ruled him out of all the club's pre-season games, Lee also signed Terry Gennoe on loan from Southampton as cover for McDonagh. Two years earlier, Gennoe had been in magnificent form against Everton, earning Southampton a share of the spoils after pulling off a series of fine saves, including one to deny Andy King from the spot, in a goalless encounter at Goodison Park. In a real goalkeeping merry-go-round that summer, Drew Brand exited the club – signing permanently for Hereford United, having previously gone on loan to Crewe Alexandra. Three years later, Brand left the game at the age of 26 to become a police officer in Cheshire.

Ahead of the new campaign, the *Liverpool Echo* reported that McDonagh's consistency at Bolton was what had persuaded Lee to sign him. The burly stopper's only season at Goodison Park started positively. At Christmas, Everton sat in fifth position, with McDonagh's form attracting the interest of Eire manager Eoin Hand, despite the goalkeeper having been born in Rotherham, Yorkshire. Having missed the FA Cup fourth-round victory over Liverpool with an ankle injury, and received a stern lecture from referee Clive Thomas for protesting against a decision given in Liverpool's favour from the Everton dugout that day, McDonagh returned to the side at Southampton in the next round. His heroics in the Valentine's Day clash at The Dell, where he saved smartly from Charlie George, Dave Watson and Malcolm Waldron, broke the hearts of the home supporters and earned Everton a replay following a goalless draw.

In a busy month for McDonagh, he also kept a clean sheet in the 1-0 replay victory, before making his debut for the Republic of Ireland, in a 3-1 defeat to Wales. Incidentally, Wales had tried to block McDonagh from playing in that game on the grounds of him having already represented England at youth level. Back on club duty four days later, in a 3-2 victory at bottom side Crystal Palace, McDonagh had to change his shirt at half-time, with the only spare jersey available emblazoned with the shirt sponsor HAFNIA. Consequently, in a bid to avoid falling foul of broadcast rules regarding advertisements, the *Match of the Day* cameras showed no close-up action in the Everton penalty area after the break.

McDonagh continued to perform steadily throughout the rest of the campaign, though his positional play for Paul Power's lobbed equaliser in the FA Cup quarter-final defeat to Manchester City was questioned by many Evertonians. Moreover, McDonagh blamed himself for City's first goal in the replay defeat, stating in the *Liverpool Echo*, 'If I hadn't touched it, then I think Billy Wright would have cleared.' In March 1981, the local newspaper ran with an article highlighting McDonagh's perceived consistency, in comparison to his predecessors, and his probable permanency in the Everton goal for years to come. However, following the cup defeat, the team went on a wretched run, winning just one of their final dozen matches, and, as soon as the season was over, Gordon Lee was relieved of his duties.

Incoming manager Howard Kendall would eventually change the fortunes of Everton, and one of the first big calls he decided to make was to overhaul the club's goalkeeping department. In the summer of 1981, Kendall shipped McDonagh back to Bolton in part-exchange for defender Mick Walsh, loaned Martin Hodge to Preston North End and signed two new men – one a relatively unknown stopper who had been around the non-league circuit in Wales before signing professionally for Bury; the other a sturdy presence who had done well for Kendall at his previous club. The former would go on to become the best goalkeeper in the world in the 1980s; the latter would most certainly help him to do so.

8

Neville Southall – The World's Greatest Goalkeeper

Among the many new faces Howard Kendall brought to Goodison Park during the summer of 1981 were two goalkeepers without a single First Division appearance between them. Although Mick Ferguson, Alan Biley, Alan Ainscow, Mickey Walsh and Mickey Thomas – the five outfielders from Kendall's ironically named 'Magnificent Seven' – failed to make any lasting impression in an Everton shirt, **Jim Arnold** and **Neville Southall** would turn out to be tremendous acquisitions for the club.

Over the next three years, Arnold would help Southall to develop into the greatest goalkeeper in world football – a position that the Welshman would arguably hold for over half a decade. In addition, Southall would become both the club's record appearance maker and most decorated player, winning two league titles, two FA Cups and a European Cup Winners' Cup during his 16-year tenure on Merseyside. On numerous occasions, during as well as after his extraordinary playing career, Everton's greatest goalkeeper would pay tribute to Arnold and express his gratitude for the role he played in his early development.

A latecomer to the professional game, Jim Arnold made his league debut for Blackburn Rovers at the age of 29 after being signed by Kendall from FA Trophy winners Stafford Rangers in June 1979. In his first season at Ewood Park, Arnold, a former local government accountant and England semi-professional international, helped his new side clinch promotion to the Second Division, keeping a club-record 19 clean sheets in 47 appearances for Blackburn that campaign. A year later, having narrowly missed out on a second consecutive promotion, Kendall and Arnold departed for Merseyside, with the new Everton manager paying his former club a reported £175,000 for their goalkeeper. On capturing his new stopper, Kendall told the *Liverpool Echo*, 'I believe he is one of the best keepers in the country and I rate him very highly. If Jim Arnold does what I think he is capable of, he will quickly become a crowd favourite. He will be a reliable and unspectacular keeper. In the last two years he has been very safe and beaten on few occasions.' In the same article, the modest Arnold gave a downplayed assessment of his game to his new supporters, 'I think I am average at stopping shots but my asset is that I am not bad at handling. I am better off my line than on it, and I think that a lot of my work is done preventing shots at goal and reaching through balls and crosses. I try to read the situation before it arises.'

Just a month earlier, Kendall had brought Neville Southall to the club from Third Division Bury, where the 22-year-old had won the Shakers' player of the year award in his sole season at Gigg Lane. Southall, who started playing in the Welsh men's leagues at the tender age of just 12, had endured a circuitous route to professional football, combining employment as a binman, hod carrier and chef with playing non-league football for the likes of Bangor City, Conwy United and Winsford United. In the foreword to Southall's autobiography, *The Binman Chronicles*, Kendall told the story of how Neville first came to his attention, 'I first got a whisper about Neville Southall in 1980 from a very good friend of mine called Norman Jones, who had a public house in Llandudno. I was player-manager of Blackburn Rovers at the time and Neville was playing for Winsford United in the Cheshire League. Norman said, "I think you should come down and see this young goalkeeper at Winsford United and have a look at him. His father drinks in my pub as well." I asked him what the pub was called, and he said it was The Nevill. I knew then that we were fated. I went down to Cheshire to see Neville play. It's very rare that you see a goalkeeper that you're impressed with so much when watching them for the first time. I was fortunate this particular night; he was coming out for crosses, he was shot stopping, his kicking was good, his positional play was a little raw – but that was to be expected. In short, he had all the qualities you love to see in a goalkeeper. So I contacted my chairman and told them that I'd found a goalkeeper. But the £6,000 fee was too much for Blackburn at a time when the club already had two senior keepers, and Bury snapped him up instead. A year later I had moved back to Everton and was looking for another goalkeeper and thought of Neville straight away. He had done well in his year at Gigg Lane and his price was a bit higher too. But at £150,000 he proved one of the best bargains ever.'

After both keepers enjoyed strong pre-seasons, Everton went into Kendall's first campaign in charge with Arnold in possession of the first-team jersey. He made his debut in the 3-1 home victory over Birmingham City and a week later received the *Liverpool Echo*'s man of the match award for his performance in the 1-0 defeat to Southampton at The Dell, where, according to reporter Ken Rogers, he made 'three tremendous saves in the last seven minutes that kept Everton's hopes alive until the final whistle'. A month later, Arnold again won the newspaper's award, for his breathtaking display in the 1-1 draw with West Ham United, when he made 'at least a dozen good saves, the pick of them being a wonderful acrobatic dive to catch a thunderbolt from Trevor Brooking'. However, for Everton's next game, a 2-1 win at home to Ipswich Town, Arnold was ruled out with a hip injury and Southall made the first of his 751 appearances for the club. Speaking afterwards, defender Mick Lyons paid tribute to the debutant, 'At no time did the defence feel nervous because we had a new keeper. Neville had impressed us all with his ability in training and when it came to the crunch that ability was there along with the right temperament. He came through a test with flying colours.'

Although Arnold returned for ten matches after recovering from injury, a week before Christmas he was dropped for the visit of Aston Villa. Ahead of the game, Kendall told the *Liverpool Echo*, 'I just feel that Jim has been on edge for the last couple of games and I think the rest will probably do him good.' For the remainder of the campaign, Southall guarded the Everton posts. In the FA Cup third-round defeat at West Ham in early January, he was in superb form, with Ken Rogers describing his saves from Trevor Brooking and Geoff Pike as 'stunning' and 'unbelievable'. Less than a week later, after another excellent Southall performance, this time at Old Trafford in a battling 1-1 draw, Kendall told the *Liverpool Echo*, 'I think our goalkeeper is one of the best in the First Division outside the Big Three [Ray Clemence, Peter Shilton and Joe Corrigan] and he will be one of the Big Three in a couple of years.' The following month, Southall kept three clean sheets in a row as a shot-shy Everton ground out consecutive goalless draws with Stoke City, West Bromwich Albion and West Ham. Even a night in hospital after sustaining an injury in the final minute of the home draw with Manchester United – when Mick Lyons took over in goal – could not spoil a promising maiden campaign for the Llandudno-born stopper, whose impressive performances had helped him to gain a place in the Wales squad. In May 1982, Southall made his international debut, keeping a clean sheet in a 3-0 victory over Northern Ireland.

Unfortunately for him, however, the 1982/83 campaign started in an inauspicious manner. In the opening-day defeat at Watford, Southall was booked after arguing with the match officials following the award of Watford's second goal. Adamant that he had not stepped backwards after catching Pat Rice's sliced 40-yard free kick on his goal line, Southall became incensed when referee Ken Baker pointed to the centre circle. Worse was to follow. Against Liverpool in November, Everton were humiliated at home 5-0, with Southall's Wales team-mate Ian Rush bagging four goals on a chastening day for the blue half of Merseyside.

After the game, Southall spent three days in hospital, where doctors cut apart the swollen ulcerated toes that he had played with for over 12 months – a procedure that would rule him out of action for over a fortnight. Upon his return, he found himself dropped for Arnold, whose form in several big games following his recall from a loan spell at Preston North End would be of the very highest quality. In the January, Arnold pulled off a magnificent last-minute penalty save from Norwich City's John Deehan at Carrow Road to earn the Blues a hard-fought 1-0 victory. A few weeks earlier, having been unable to force his way back into the team, Southall had headed out on loan to Fourth Division club Port Vale, before returning to the Everton first team for the last four games of the season following a thigh injury sustained by Arnold at Birmingham City.

Two of Arnold's greatest performances during the 1982/83 campaign came just seven days apart in March – the first at Old Trafford in the 1-0 FA Cup quarter-final defeat and the second in a goalless draw at Anfield. Despite being on the losing side against Ron Atkinson's Manchester United side, Arnold was given the man of the match award in the *Sunday Mirror*, whose reporter Vince Wilson described his save from Steve Coppell and two stops from Norman Whiteside as 'astonishing'. In the derby the following weekend, Arnold was even busier, making several impressive courageous blocks, even after appearing to be knocked unconscious following a collision with Craig Johnston. Arnold's post-match interview stuck with David Prentice, who gave the following appraisal of the brave goalkeeper over 40 years after his performance at Anfield, 'I will always remember Jim saying that he'd had his tooth kicked out but pronouncing it "tough". He was incredible that day, as he had been at Old Trafford the previous week, and had two really excellent seasons with Everton. Undoubtedly, Jim Arnold gave Neville Southall the opportunity to breathe, and both his calmness and experience really helped Neville during his formative years.'

It is an opinion shared by centre-back Kevin Ratcliffe, who later became Southall's skipper at club and international level, 'Jim was a big plus for Nev. They had a similar background and he gave Nev the breathing space he needed to become the goalkeeper he turned out to be.' Ratcliffe also cites Southall's loan spell at Vale Park as being crucial to his development, 'When Neville first arrived from Bury, he was nothing like he is today. He was very quiet and reserved. But after the Port Vale loan, he came back a different man. He was a better goalkeeper and a far more confident individual. It was at that point that we started to see this incredible transition in him, where he would change from being a man off the pitch to being this absolute monster on it.'

That summer, Martin Hodge finally left Everton on a permanent basis, joining Sheffield Wednesday for £50,000, having spent the previous campaign on loan at Oldham, Gillingham and Preston. Although Arnold started Everton's first seven games of 1983/84, Southall would soon establish himself as the club's number one stopper. But not before a crisis. After a poor run of results in the autumn and early winter, which had seen the Blues drop perilously close to the relegation zone, Kendall asked both his goalkeepers ahead of the home game with Coventry City on New Year's Eve whether they could guarantee him a clean sheet. With neither being able to answer 'yes', Kendall opted to stick with Southall. It proved to be the correct decision as Southall started to regularly put in the kind of outstanding performances that would prove his manager had been right two years earlier when predicting that he would become one of the country's leading goalkeepers. In the FA Cup fourth-round replay at Gillingham at the end of January, he kept Everton in the competition with a string of fine saves, including one from Tony Cascarino deep into extra time, when he stood up for as long as possible before blocking the forward's low effort with his legs.

After the game, Gillingham manager Keith Peacock described Southall as being 'a very special goalkeeper'. In the *Liverpool Echo*, Jimmy O'Neill was also full of praise, 'Neville has come on amazingly. A year or so ago it was Jim Arnold who was attracting attention for the way he played against Manchester United, but now Neville has claimed the place on merit. He's growing in confidence all the time and I'm sure he will continue to improve because a goalkeeper rarely reaches his peak until his late 20s. He combines good goalkeeping with common sense. When he comes out, he spreads himself right across the goal, just like Pat Jennings, and he's liable to save with his elbow or his head. That's not luck though, just good anticipation.'

Following the heartbreaking League Cup Final replay defeat to Liverpool, Scottish midfielder Graeme Souness, who scored the only goal of the tie past Southall at Maine Road, also paid tribute in the *Liverpool Echo*, 'Everton will be a difficult side to beat in the FA Cup. Their keeper Neville Southall is possibly better than anyone in the country at the moment.'

In the FA Cup semi-final at Highbury against Southampton, who had Peter Shilton between the posts, Southall put in his strongest performance of the season, denying forwards Danny Wallace, Frank Worthington and Steve Moran before Adrian

Heath's headed goal won the game late in extra time. At Wembley in May, he enjoyed a much quieter day, though still had to be on his mettle to make two smart stops from Watford's John Barnes that helped Everton to clinch their first piece of silverware in 14 years. It had been some turnaround in less than five months for manager Kendall, whose exciting young side was beginning to come of age.

Incidentally, that same month, Everton tasted success in the FA Youth Cup for only the second time in their history, with England under-18 international goalkeeper Stephen Hall excelling in both legs of the final against Stoke City. A year earlier, keeper Ken Hughes and his Everton team-mates had narrowly missed out on lifting the same trophy, losing 1-0 to Norwich City in a replay after the two-legged final had finished 5-5 on aggregate. En route to the 1983 final, Welshman Hughes kept six consecutive clean sheets, including one at Vale Park in the third-round replay win over Port Vale. Sitting with Hughes's dad in the stands that evening was Neville Southall, who was midway through his loan spell with the Valiants. Following his release from Everton and a brief spell back in his homeland with Porthmadog, Hughes signed for Crystal Palace, where he acted as backup to George Wood, and later made appearances in the Football League for Wrexham and Shrewsbury Town. Maghull-born Hall, highly rated by everyone at the club and a Central League debutant at just 17 years old, remained at Everton for a further 12 months but departed in the summer of 1985, having opted to take up a study place across the Atlantic at the prestigious Harvard University in Cambridge, Massachusetts.

The 1984/85 campaign would turn out to be the most successful in the Blues' history, with silverware being lifted on the domestic front and in Europe. Having amassed a club-record points total of 90, Everton were able to wrestle the First Division title away from Liverpool; moreover, the European Cup Winners' Cup also found its way into the club's trophy cabinet after a 3-1 victory over Rapid Vienna in Rotterdam, where Southall courted controversy for wearing a red shirt against the green and white-clad Austrians. Indeed, only Norman Whiteside's extra-time winner in the FA Cup Final prevented Everton from retaining the trophy and completing a historic treble. Considering the team was so dominant that season and contained such a wealth of talent, including the attacking flair of Kevin Sheedy, Trevor Steven and Graeme Sharp, and the midfield guile and industry of Paul Bracewell and Peter Reid, it is testament to Southall and his performances that he was voted the Football Writers' Association's (FWA) Footballer of the Year in 1985. The previous goalkeeper to receive the award was Southall's idol Pat Jennings, who later described the Welshman as 'a goalkeeper without a weakness'. In an ever-present campaign, Southall kept a club-record 31 clean sheets in 63 matches.

The two Southall saves made during the run-in that have stuck with many Evertonians are those from Tottenham's Marc Falco and Sheffield Wednesday's Imre Varadi. On 3 April 1985, with just a dozen league games of the season remaining, Everton travelled to White Hart Lane and went into the game neck and neck with their opponents. With Everton leading 2-1 and just minutes remaining, Falco powered in a header from six yards out that Southall somehow managed to turn over the bar. In the *Daily Express,* the save, which had brought generous applause from opposing goalkeeper Ray Clemence, who had slumped to his knees in both despair and disbelief, was likened to Gordon Banks's miraculous stop from Pelé in the 1970 World Cup. Southall's typically modest reaction to all of the fuss was that the forward had headed it straight at him. In Ken Rogers's book *Everton Greats*, Southall stated, 'Everyone went on about it but it was more or less straight at me. When you're going for a title and it's an important game, things sometimes look better than they are. People overlook the unorthodox saves you make with your legs or your knees. I don't think about particular incidents too much. The time to look back is when your youngster is old enough to sit on your knee and ask you about it.'

According to skipper Kevin Ratcliffe, his compatriot's save from their old team-mate Varadi was even better, 'I joked at the time that he should've held the Falco one and not given away a corner as we were right under the cosh, but it was a brilliant save – a title-winning save. Nonetheless, the stop from Varadi was on a different level. How he managed to get down so quickly and generate enough power to turn the ball around the post only he will know. But that was Nev. He was performing at such a high level every week that the manager used to tell us not to risk giving a penalty away or getting sent off if the striker had beaten us and was clean through on goal as they still had to beat the big man. His standards were ridiculously high, and he hated praise as he was easily embarrassed. Before the 1984 FA Cup Final, comedian Freddie Starr spent some time with the players and at one point was just gazing into Neville's eyes saying, "You're incredible! You're amazing!" Neville hated it and told him in no uncertain terms where to go! He would never comment on his saves and was the first to say that he was just doing his job. He focused far more on any errors he made and then worked his backside off in training in a bid not to make them again. By some distance, he was the hardest trainer at the club.'

In the extended version of Rob Sloman's 2019 documentary *Howard's Way*, Ratcliffe's view of the goalkeeper and his bid for perfection is supported. In the film, Southall states that he was never interested in any save of the season awards, and that he would much prefer to be shown a goal of the season, as he would then try to come up with a way of keeping out such a strike.

At the end of the successful 1984/85 campaign, former Preston North End goalkeeper and manager Alan Kelly started working as Everton's goalkeeping coach and reserve-team manager. That summer, Kelly, who gained 47 caps for the Republic of Ireland between 1956 and 1973, told the *Liverpool Echo* that he couldn't wait to start working with Southall, 'Neville was named Footballer of the Year last season, but he still wants to work twice as hard and improve his game. He's one of the best around and in one against one situations is fantastic. Clearly the staff at Bellefield have looked after him well and given him the right attitude.'

Kelly's 17-year-old son, Alan Kelly Junior, who would later enjoy an outstanding playing and coaching career of his own, was a regular attendee at Everton's Bellefield training ground that summer. He explained how he was often left dumbstruck by Southall's work ethic and the saves he pulled off from some of the country's leading players, 'Dad was a hard taskmaster. He believed that you trained heavy and played light, which Neville really liked and totally bought into. I remember being five yards from the action at Bellefield, completely fixated on Neville, thinking, "Wow! This fella's absolutely amazing!" I was totally captivated. All these years later I can still visualise the A-frame of the goal, the square netting and Neville effortlessly keeping out rockets from Graeme Sharp, Adrian Heath and Kevin Sheedy.'

In his autobiography, *So Good I Did It Twice*, winger Sheedy described how difficult it was to beat Southall in training, 'I would choose Neville Southall, in his pomp probably the best goalkeeper in the world, as the greatest professional during my time at Everton. You had to be good to put a shot past him in training. You had to stick the ball into one of the corners of the net to have any chance of beating him and if you ever chipped the ball over him you'd better look out! He hated being beaten in training as much as he did in matches. Alan Kelly used to throw a medicine ball into Nev's stomach to toughen his muscles and he had "no hands" stints in training, when he would make saves just with his body. He demanded so much of himself and his team-mates. He never settled for second best. In games where he had little to do his concentration level never dipped and he'd be switched on to make that one often crucial save.'

In the summer of 1985, after making 59 appearances over four years between the Everton posts, Jim Arnold exited the club and joined Port Vale. In his one full season at Vale Park, he was voted their player of the season. A year later, at the age of 36, he won the FA Trophy with Kidderminster Harriers, saving a penalty in the 2-1 final replay victory over Burton Albion at The Hawthorns. In his 2020 book *Mind Games: The Ups and Downs of Life and Football*, Southall paid tribute to his goalkeeping ally, 'I learned a lot from Jim Arnold. He got a groin strain but wanted to get fit, so he did nothing for the entire week and was passed fit for the Saturday, when he played really well. I was amazed at the mental strength that it took for him to avoid doing anything all week, when he was itching to train, and then be able to play that well at the weekend. I was totally different. I was an awful patient at the start of my career, going stir crazy. But Jim taught me to see things differently, to rest for good reason and trust the healing process.'

Sadly for Southall, rest was the order of the day the following March after he was badly injured while away on international duty against the Republic of Ireland. Having landed awkwardly following a collision with John Aldridge, he sustained severe dislocation of the ankle and damage to the ligaments, which resulted in a frustrating seven-month spell on the sidelines. It was a devastating blow to player and club as he had been in tremendous form and instrumental in the team heading the table with fewer than ten league games remaining.

Less than a month before sustaining the injury, Southall had been a colossus in a 2-0 victory at Anfield, denying old adversary Ian Rush on multiple occasions, with the pick of the saves being a persistent smother at the forward's feet when it looked as though the Liverpool man had got the better of him on three separate occasions. Indeed, Kendall had told the *Liverpool Echo* that Southall was playing better than ever, thanks largely to the expertise of Alan Kelly's training methods, 'We all know what a great goalkeeper Neville Southall was last season. I feel Alan has got a little bit more out of him, and that was never clearer than in Saturday's derby. Alan is bringing out the best in him. Neville certainly responds to hard work. He hates missing training.'

Although stand-in goalkeeper Bobby Mimms did very little wrong in Southall's absence (see the next chapter for Mimms's story), the Blues ultimately had to settle for second place in the league and FA Cup that season as Liverpool finished the campaign extremely strongly. According to assistant manager Colin Harvey's frank assessment, Everton's first-choice stopper was sorely missed at the business end of the campaign, 'Bobby Mimms didn't do too badly, but there's a difference between a good keeper and a world-class keeper. Neville won games for you. Bobby didn't.'

On 25 October 1986, Southall made his long-awaited return to the first team at home to Watford. By then Gordon Banks had replaced Kelly as Everton's goalkeeping coach – with the ex-Preston man teaming up with former team-mate Alan Spavin to run a football camp in Maryland, in the USA. Phil McNulty recalled a save Southall made from another Marc Falco header, 'It was right up there with the save at White Hart Lane

18 months earlier. The whole ground rose and gave Neville a standing ovation. It was complete and utter relief on the terraces. We all knew at that point that we had our world-class goalkeeper back.'

After a huge upturn in form in the new year, and some terrific performances from their keeper, who conceded just six goals in the final 12 league contests, Everton won the title back from Liverpool – finishing six points ahead of their rivals. In Southall's eyes, helping Everton to win their second championship in three seasons was more satisfying and a greater achievement than winning it in 1985. In his autobiography, he stated, 'It was so easy first time around; we just won games for fun. 1987 was more of a struggle, or rather a series of battles. It was all incredibly fulfilling.' Incidentally, in the Full Members' Cup quarter-final defeat to Charlton Athletic in the March that season, Southall scored in a penalty shoot-out held at the Gwladys Street End of the ground but couldn't prevent the Blues from exiting the competition.

Unfortunately for everyone at Goodison Park, everything was about to change for the worse. With no European football available for English clubs following the implementation of the Heysel ban, Everton's talented squad began to break up. In the summer of 1987, Howard Kendall left to manage Athletic Bilbao and, within two years, numerous key players, including Gary Stevens, Trevor Steven, Paul Bracewell, Kevin Ratcliffe and Peter Reid, had either moved on to play in European competitions (for Scottish giants Rangers) or been replaced having suffered several persistent injuries. During his three years in charge, in a desperate attempt to find a winning formula, new manager Colin Harvey invested heavily in new additions, many of whom, including record-signing Tony Cottee, came in on big contracts, which reportedly caused friction in the squad and a clear division between many of the old guard and the new players. In his autobiography, *The Real McCall*, midfielder Stuart McCall, a summer signing from Bradford City in 1988, claimed that the bad feeling between the two 'camps' severely affected team morale, with both sides being guilty of throwing accusations at each other and failing to take responsibility for their own poor form on the pitch. McCall went on to state that it was no coincidence that the only two players outside the cliques were the club's two star performers during that period – defender Dave Watson and Neville Southall.

Although Everton were in decline, it could be argued that Southall played the greatest football of his career in Harvey's struggling side. After conceding just 25 goals in 34 league matches during Harvey's inaugural campaign, he put in possibly the performance of his career in a smash-and-grab 1-0 victory at Highfield Road in the second game of the 1988/89 season. In making the perfect hat-trick of saves that day, Southall denied Brian Kilcline from the spot with a tremendous spring to his right, then foiled Gary Bannister from six yards with a lightning-quick push over the bar, before going full length to his left to deny full-back Greg Downs, whose powerful drive from distance had been heading for the top corner. That October, in a 1-1 home draw with Manchester United in front of the ITV cameras, Southall was named man of the match after a stunning double save denied the forward pair Brian McClair and Mark Hughes at the Gwladys Street End. Only weeks earlier, Dutchman Ruud Gullit had called Southall the greatest goalkeeper in world football after the Wales stopper's superb performance in his country's World Cup qualifier defeat to the Netherlands. Playing in struggling sides at club and international level, Southall was given ample opportunities to showcase his unbelievable talent.

During Harvey's time in charge, Southall was put through his paces by goalkeeping coach Jim Barron, who often incorporated hurdles and medicine balls into his gruelling sessions. In a 2012 interview with the Everton fan website The Executioner's Bong, Southall stated, 'Jim Barron was probably my best coach; he got me the fittest I've ever been with his military sessions.' A fine example of the combining of Southall's incredible bravery, technique and fitness came in the home Merseyside derby of 1988/89, when he dived low to his left to keep out Peter Beardsley's arrowed strike from the edge of the box before getting himself up as quickly as possible to deny the onrushing John Aldridge. It was the kind of save that he had worked hard on the training ground to perfect with Barron, who only had positive things to say about the workaholic, 'Neville was great fun and worked really hard in everything we did because he could see the reasons behind what we were doing. He was at his happiest when diving around like a pig in shit and had tremendous agility. Around that time, the balls were beginning to change a bit so we worked on how to get enough power into a parry to knock the ball away if you weren't able to hold on to it. That's why we brought the medicine balls in – with the reasoning being if you could knock one of those out of harm's way then you'd have no problem with the footballs! The harder he worked, the better he got and on his day he was virtually unbeatable. He had this aura about him. You meet a lot of very odd and selfish people in football, who, quite frankly, aren't worth the time of day. Neville was different. It was my pleasure to work with him. It was never an ordeal and I used to look forward to my commute from Cheltenham to Liverpool, knowing that I was in the presence of greatness.'

Despite another fantastic performance at Wembley in May, Southall ended up on the losing side in the 1989 FA Cup Final, with Everton going down 3-2 after extra time to Liverpool in an emotional all-Merseyside affair a month after the tragedy of Hillsborough. The game was nowhere near as close as the scoreline would suggest; only Southall's brilliance that day kept Everton in with a shout of lifting the trophy. At full time, crouched by his right-hand goalpost, he cut a forlorn and frustrated figure.

The following April, Everton took a team to Cheltenham Town for a joint testimonial game for players Nick Jordan and Ray Baverstock. That night, Southall played for the opposition and was in magnificent form, denying his usual team-mates Tony Cottee, Dave Watson, John Ebbrell and Norman Whiteside with a string of stunning saves before setting up an unlikely winner for home forward Simon Brain. In another extremely frustrating season for Southall, who once again swept the board at the club's player of the year awards evening and made the PFA First Division Team of the Year for a fourth consecutive campaign, it was a rare evening of light relief. Despite Colin Harvey's best efforts, Everton finished the season 20 points behind champions Liverpool and after the home game with Aston Villa on the final day, Southall threw his kit into the crowd – an action which many interpreted as him saying goodbye to the supporters.

That summer, having submitted several transfer requests, he was constantly linked with a move away, with Manchester United looking the most likely destination, though transfers abroad, to Italian side Torino and Spanish giants Barcelona and Real Madrid, were also mooted in the press. Fearful of losing their number one asset, Everton insisted he was not for sale but took the precautionary step of taking Ahmed Shobair on trial after his splendid performances in the 1990 World Cup in Italy, though they opted against signing the Egyptian after being told he would only be granted a work permit if he were installed as the club's undisputed first-choice goalkeeper.

On the opening day of the 1990/91 season, a clearly unhappy Southall was still an Everton player. With his team 2-0 down to newly promoted Leeds United at half-time, he bizarrely decided to leave the home changing room and enter the field of play, sitting by his post at the Park End throughout the interval, an action which both shocked and angered thousands of Evertonians, who interpreted his 'sit-in' as a protest against the board and manager Harvey. In the coming weeks, hate mail, including death threats, would come the way of Southall, who, to this day, remains insistent that he was doing nothing other than trying to clear his head after a poor first-half performance, 'It was shit. We were shit. At half-time I needed to get out of the dressing room and get my head together, so I left and went and sat down in the goalmouth. People went on about it and said it was a protest, but it wasn't at all. At worst it was badly timed, coming around the same time as my transfer request. I certainly wasn't protesting against Colin, who didn't even know about it until the evening.'

After a dismal run of results that autumn, Harvey was relieved of his managerial duties and Howard Kendall re-instated – with Kendall quickly installing the outgoing manager as his right-hand man. In the February, Southall, seemingly settled once more, was at his best in the trilogy of FA Cup fifth-round games against Liverpool, making crucial saves in the 0-0 draw at Anfield and the tremendously entertaining 4-4 draw at Goodison Park, before putting in a man-of-the-match performance in the second replay at Goodison, which Everton won 1-0. Afterwards, Ian Rush called his international team-mate the 'best in the business; number one in the world', while opposing keeper Bruce Grobbelaar described Southall as 'an inspiration'. Nonetheless, Kendall's side was knocked out of the competition in the next round at West Ham and although they reached the Full Members' Cup Final that season, a heavy defeat to Crystal Palace after extra time resulted in Southall refusing to collect his runners-up medal. Less than a month after the end of the 1990/91 campaign, he then put in probably the best performance of his international career, making several excellent saves from Jürgen Klinsmann, Matthias Sammer and Stefan Reuter in Wales's 1-0 victory over world champions Germany.

Sadly for Evertonians, in Kendall's second spell in charge, which coincided with the birth of the Premier League and the ruling that goalkeepers could no longer pick up balls played back to them by their team-mates, the manager could not replicate the successes of the mid-1980s and the club began to fall further behind its traditional rivals. With Jim Barron having taken the assistant manager's position at Aston Villa, Southall was coached by Mark Wallington for a short time during the early 90s. According to Southall, the pair would often clash or disagree about matters on the training pitch, 'I was very fortunate with the coaches that I got to work with: Gordon Banks, Peter Bonetti, Jim Barron, Alan Kelly and Alan Hodgkinson – they all brought different things to the table. They were all good goalkeeping coaches, but of course some suited me better than others – that's the nature of things. I worked with Bob Wilson at Wales, and sometimes if a coach is too nice, as with Bob, I didn't like it. That was no fault on his part. He was a lovely guy, but I'd sometimes worry that he might avoid criticising me or finding fault with my game. I also worked with Mark Wallington for a while, who had been at Leicester City and competed with Peter Shilton for a first-team place. He would tell me that "Shilton did this" and "Shilton did that" or that "Shilton would never let a shot in in training". But I didn't care. I only cared about performing between 3pm and 5pm on a Saturday, and telling me about another goalkeeper was never going to have an impact on me.'

After bottom-half finishes in the final season of the old First Division and the inaugural campaign of the Premier League, a disillusioned Kendall resigned midway through the 1993/94 season. In the October, at Spurs, Southall – wearing the all-black Lev Yashin-esque kit he favoured in the first few years of the Premier League era – made a phenomenal flying save to his right from Teddy Sheringham's header that was at least equal to the one he had made in the same goal from Mark Falco in 1985 in terms of difficulty. However, in a game typical of that frustrating period, Everton threw away a 2-1 lead, conceding two late goals, with Darren Caskey drilling home the winner in added time after Southall had initially saved well again from Sheringham. A month after Kendall's departure, the club employed Norwich manager Mike Walker, a former Wales under-23 international goalkeeper, with whom Southall struggled to see eye to eye. Following a disastrous run of results from March onwards, only a dramatic final-day victory over Wimbledon would preserve Everton's top-flight status.

According to captain Dave Watson, Walker was a manager who could really get to Southall, 'Mike Walker tried his best, but he never showed a great desire to get the best out of the lads and he was intimidated by the bigger characters. He found it difficult to tell Neville what to do and there were days when he would have you scratching your head as the training fell way short of the required standard. Things got sloppy and this infuriated Neville as he was a workaholic – he was always the first into Bellefield and the last out – so to have somebody putting on sessions that weren't up to scratch was difficult for him to take.'

After a shocking 3-0 loss at Elland Road on the penultimate weekend of the season, Everton went into their final game knowing they had to beat Wimbledon to remain in the Premier League. Within 20 minutes, they were 2-0 down after conceding a penalty and an own goal in tragi-comical circumstances. However, just five minutes later, they were given a lifeline when Sweden winger Anders Limpar won his side a penalty. With nobody looking like they fancied it, Southall left his goal and picked up the ball with the intent of taking the spot kick himself, only for Graham Stuart to eventually step up. Stuart's goal sparked the unlikeliest of comebacks and Everton just about survived. Nonetheless, Watson has no doubt that Southall would also have scored had he ended up taking the penalty, 'He was a big-game player – a huge personality who just wanted the best for the club. He would definitely have converted the penalty had he taken it that day.'

Although Walker started 1994/95 in the manager's hot seat, the board decided to dispose of his services after the Blues made their worst start to a season – at the beginning of November, Everton sat bottom of the league with a pitiful eight points, having won just one of their opening 14 matches. In an interview with *Goal* magazine in 1996, Southall admitted to feeling the pressure during the difficult mid-90s period, 'When you're young it doesn't matter. You don't care as long as you're playing. In the last few years, we've nearly gone down twice and it's been a worrying time. I still enjoy playing but in a different sort of way. There's a lot of pressure because you know what the people expect of you, and you don't want to let them down.'

In new manager Joe Royle's first game in charge – a Goodison derby under the lights in front of the Sky Sports cameras – Southall made a crucial save from Steve McManaman low to his right before goals by Duncan Ferguson and Paul Rideout got the former Oldham boss's tenure off to a perfect start. At Chelsea the following week, Southall, who had been heavily criticised by fans and press alike earlier in the campaign, was in inspired form as Everton snatched an unlikely 1-0 victory. Keeping seven successive league clean sheets that winter – a new club record – Royle's men began to inch themselves away from the foot of the table, and in the new year made progress in the FA Cup, thanks in no small part to Southall, who made a series of fine saves in the narrow victories over Derby County and Bristol City. In the next round, Everton demolished Norwich 5-0 before a tremendous display from Southall and a headed finish from Dave Watson helped them to overcome Newcastle United in the quarter-finals and set up a semi-final clash with Tottenham Hotspur.

The award of a contentious penalty, given against Watson for a soft push in the box on Jürgen Klinsmann, resulted in Southall finally conceding a goal in the competition but it mattered little as Royle's spirited side, affectionately nicknamed 'The Dogs of War', overpowered the north London favourites 4-1 at Elland Road. Everton, having got themselves safe with some resilient displays (six clean sheets were kept in the concluding seven league matches that campaign) and strong work from set pieces, would face Manchester United in the FA Cup Final – a decade after the Red Devils had denied Southall and his 1985 team-mates a treble.

At Wembley, it was a case of the old guard once again coming to Everton's rescue. Although Paul Rideout scored the only goal of the game, Everton's real heroes were the wily duo of Watson and Southall. The skipper put in a colossal display in front of his goalkeeper, who made several fine stops in the second half, especially from youngster Paul Scholes, who was twice denied in quick succession. However, Southall's most impressive work that day came in the last minute, when a high ball was launched more in hope than judgement into the Everton box. More than 12 yards out from his goal line, the veteran came through a body of players to claim it one-handedly. Looking at his masterful best, and with the presence and aura about him that so many had mentioned previously, Southall gave the impression that he could have played all weekend and not conceded a goal.

The victory at Wembley was one in the eye for Southall's many doubters in the media, who had written him off earlier in the season and cruelly depicted him as a shadow of his former self: a sullen, ageing figure of a man seemingly forever rocking on his heels and berating his backline after conceding yet another goal. Instead of attending the post-match banquet, he drove home to his family in Llandudno, and even stopped to help a couple of Manchester United supporters, whose car had broken down on the motorway, along the way. As he had done all his career, the idiosyncratic stopper continued to do things in his own inimitable manner.

That summer, a month shy of his 37th birthday, the stalwart was granted a testimonial game against Celtic at Goodison Park. In the matchday programme, many of the great and good of Merseyside football, including old rivals Ian Rush and Bruce Grobbelaar, paid tribute to the man who Joe Royle nicknamed the 'King of Keepers'. Rush stated that he would have beaten Dixie Dean's goalscoring record in derby matches long before he did had it not been for his compatriot's 'tremendous skill', while Grobbelaar wrote the following about his old friend, 'Neville

Southall is a goalkeeper of exceptional courage, ability and authority. He has been a saviour to Evertonians and I believe he has kept them in the Premier League over the last three seasons. We have a strong mutual bond between us on and off the field and I have applauded his fantastic saves more than any other keeper.'

Although Southall was awarded an MBE for his services to football that year and played in every game of the 1995/96 campaign – keeping 15 clean sheets in a side that finished sixth in the Premier League and missed out on UEFA Cup qualification only on the final day of the season – it became increasingly clear that his time at Goodison Park would soon be coming to an end. After a public falling-out with Joe Royle the following season, regarding failed moves to Wolves and Chelsea, and then a disastrous start to Howard Kendall's third spell in charge of the club, the 39-year-old made his final appearance for Everton at home to Tottenham Hotspur in November 1997. His 92-cap international career also came to an end that season, when he was ignominiously hauled off at half-time in Wales's 6-4 defeat to Turkey by under-fire manager Bobby Gould. Ten months earlier, behind a porous backline, Southall had made over a dozen fine saves in an embarrassing 7-1 defeat to the Netherlands. Before retiring from the professional game, Southall made appearances lower down the pyramid for Southend United, Stoke City, Doncaster Rovers and Torquay United, as well as one more Premier League appearance, at the age of 41, for Bradford City. After Gould's departure, Southall and Mark Hughes took charge of Wales for a match against Denmark.

During the final two seasons of Southall's Everton career, Alan Myers was employed as the club's press officer and formed a close friendship with Everton's record appearance holder, especially on away trips. Myers told me, 'I'd been a huge fan of Neville Southall throughout his career so to end up working with him and become his friend was quite bizarre. He was this international icon of the game but would rather get to the grounds early from the hotel with me, the kit man Jimmy Martin, the masseuse Jimmy Comer and our coach driver "Bluey" to help us put out the kit. Nev used to love the camaraderie. That's how he would relax and get his head away from the game. He was the biggest wind-up merchant ever! Neville is very outspoken and has said things that haven't always gone down well with the club's hierarchy, but he has only ever spoken from the heart. He's a winner, a mentality monster and the greatest keeper there has ever been.'

It is an opinion shared by the club's two main captains during his time on Merseyside. According to Dave Watson, 'Everyone absolutely loved him. He was headstrong and believed in what he did and there was no doubting his ability or desire. He had everything going for him but was really modest about it all.' The final word goes to Kevin Ratcliffe, his skipper during the club's glory years and a one-time emergency goalkeeping replacement following Southall's dismissal at Stamford Bridge in October 1985 for receiving two yellow cards, the second of which he was given for handling the ball outside his box, 'Nev never got to show it at a World Cup or European Championship, but there is no doubt that he was the greatest. He was hugely important in the club's successes, and, in my mind, is comfortably the greatest player to have ever worn an Everton shirt. I've always been hugely critical of keepers, including Jordan Pickford at times, because I played with the best there's ever been for over a decade. He saw off so many keepers – a load of them didn't even get to play one game for us – and goalkeeping coaches – the likes of Gordon Banks, Peter Bonetti and Mark Wallington – because they couldn't teach him stuff. He was too good!'

In his 16-year Everton first-team career, Neville Southall evolved from being an extremely shy individual with incredible raw ability into the world's greatest goalkeeper. In doing so, he saw off several challengers to his position at Goodison Park. However, his commitment, work ethic and search for perfection helped many of those keepers forge excellent careers for themselves away from the club.

The next chapter, titled 'Backup Plans', is dedicated to the many understudies during the Southall era.

9

Backup Plans

When Jim Arnold left Everton to join Port Vale at the end of the 1984/85 season, Howard Kendall moved quickly to secure the services of promising young goalkeeper **Bobby Mimms** from Rotherham United for £150,000.

Already an England under-21 international, having replaced David Seaman in a couple of friendlies for Dave Sexton's side earlier in the year, Mimms moved to Goodison Park as understudy to Neville Southall, the recently crowned FWA Footballer of the Year, after spending three and a half years at the Third Division South Yorkshire club.

Mimms explained to me how the move to Goodison came about, 'I'd been a near-ever-present at Rotherham for two years after Emlyn Hughes signed me from Halifax. I was doing well with the England under-21s and there were rumours that Liverpool were interested in me, but Everton were the first to make contact. Howard Kendall reached me while I was away with the under-21s in Finland. I flew back into Luton and then travelled up to Liverpool the next day with Paul Bracewell, who had been with me with the under-21s, to meet Howard and sign the contract. It was a few days after the 1985 FA Cup Final and Everton were playing Liverpool that night, so I stayed to watch the game with my wife to be, Karen. We were getting married the following Saturday and were supposed to be having our stag and hen parties, but they got cancelled so that I could finalise my move to Everton. I got married on the Saturday, was in for training on the Monday and then went off for the summer break a week or so later.'

When asked what his thinking was behind joining the champions of England, Mimms said, 'I knew it was going to be very difficult to go in and shift Nev from the team. He had just had a brilliant season and I knew he wasn't going anywhere soon, but I saw the move as the next progression in my career. It was an opportunity to come in and learn from the best, get some games in the top division under my belt and then move on. Rotherham had been a step up from Halifax and now Everton was the next step in my career.'

Training at Bellefield was on a different level from the fitness-heavy sessions Mimms had been used to at Halifax and Rotherham, 'Everything we did at Everton was game orientated. There were loads of possession-based drills and small-sided games. The spirit in the camp was terrific, though Colin Harvey was the sorest loser on the planet, and he really gave you both barrels if you were ever on his side and made a mistake in the head tennis competitions we had on a Friday! Obviously working with Neville in the goalkeeper sessions helped to bring my game on too.'

Under the tutelage of goalkeeping coach Alan Kelly Senior, Mimms witnessed first-hand how hard Southall worked at Bellefield in perfecting his craft, and the two quickly built up an extremely strong bond. Mimms stated, 'As a goalkeeper, he was top drawer and he had everything in his armoury. He's certainly the best I've had the pleasure to work with. Sometimes, he would go days without conceding a goal in training and would often dive with his hands behind his back to give the forwards a chance. His footwork was so fast that he would get in line with the ball so quickly that he wouldn't need to use his hands to make the save! All I could do was go in and try and help the side win points when he wasn't in the team.'

In March 1986, Mimms was given that opportunity. Having been sent out on loan to Notts County to gain regular first-team action at the start of the month, he was recalled by Everton after just three games for the Third Division side following a sickening injury sustained by Southall while away on international duty.

Playing for Wales against Ireland at Lansdowne Road, not long after the rugby union Five Nations Championship fixture between Ireland and Scotland had been played there, Southall went up for a routine high ball with John Aldridge, only to come down and get his foot caught in a pothole in the mud-bath of a pitch. Although there was no break, Southall had dislocated his ankle and torn all his ligaments, and was initially told he would be out until Christmas, at the very earliest. Mimms recalled, 'I was playing at Maine Road for England under-21s when news came through about Nev's injury. Colin Harvey was at my game and told me I'd be coming back to Everton straight away. It was such a critical stage of the season and Nev must have been absolutely gutted inside to be missing games, but he never let it show. He didn't moan or groan. He just came in, got on with his rehabilitation work and was extremely encouraging towards me.'

With Everton sitting top of the table with just nine games remaining, Mimms, whose only Blues appearance hitherto had come in a 1-1 draw with Manchester City in late October, when Southall served a one-match suspension following his dismissal at Chelsea, made his Goodison debut in a 1-0 win over Newcastle United on 29 March 1986, and would perform extremely well, keeping clean sheets in his first six league outings and helping his team book their place in the FA Cup Final, overcoming Sheffield Wednesday – and former Toffee Martin Hodge – after extra time at Villa Park. He added, 'Although I knew how important all the games were at that time, I wouldn't say I felt nervous. In many ways, it was easy. I was going into a good team and at that age, I was 22 at the time, you feel as though you are the best anyway. Some players go missing when they're out there in front of the big crowds but, for me, the bigger the game, the better the experience.' However, following the infamous midweek 1-0 loss to relegation-threatened Oxford United, when Gary Lineker missed a host of chances after famously forgetting to pack his lucky goalscoring boots that evening, the Blues dropped to third in the league, behind Liverpool and West Ham. Despite winning their final two games handsomely, beating Southampton 6-1 and West Ham 3-1, Mimms and the rest of the squad finished the season as runners-up, two points behind their fiercest rivals.

Worse was to come for Everton. Less than seven days after completing their league programme, Everton were beaten 3-1 in the FA Cup Final by Liverpool, despite taking the lead through Lineker. An Ian Rush brace and a strike from Craig Johnston settled the game and the Blues had the ignominy of heading back to Merseyside on the same plane as their victors. Ahead of the Wembley showdown, Mimms roomed with legendary goalkeeper Pat Jennings, whom Howard Kendall had signed as emergency cover as the club was facing a potential keeper crisis.

In early April, with Southall ruled out for the rest of the season, Kendall, who had released first-year professional Neil Deamer just four months earlier – ironically, citing an embarrassment of riches in the goalkeeping department as the reason for letting the teenager go – signed Fred Barber from Third Division Darlington as cover for Mimms, only to find out that he was ineligible to play in the FA Cup having already played in the competition that season. Youngster Mike Stowell, signed by Alan Kelly Senior in November 1985 after impressing for Leyland Motors, was also ruled out of playing in any FA Cup ties as he had played in the preliminary stages, meaning there was nobody to cover Mimms should he become unavailable.

Jennings, having been tracked down by Kendall at Heathrow Airport after an international fixture for Northern Ireland, agreed to sign a short-term deal, on the understanding of only being used in a genuine emergency. After sitting next to Southall at Wembley and making a then-record 116th international appearance during the five weeks that he was registered as an Everton player, Jennings left the Toffees to prepare for the World Cup finals that summer. In Mexico, on his 41st birthday, the Ulsterman played the final game of his professional career, a 3-0 defeat to Brazil in their last match of the group stage. Barber, an unused substitute in the 1986 Charity Shield draw with Liverpool, also left Merseyside without making a first-team appearance, joining Walsall that autumn, where he began a 13-year circuit of the lower leagues. Your archetypal crazy keeper, Barber is fondly remembered by Peterborough United supporters in particular, for whom he often carried out his pre-match warm-up while wearing a rubber mask bearing the face of an old-aged pensioner. After retiring from playing at Kidderminster Harriers, Barber moved into coaching – finding employment as a goalkeeping coach at a host of English league clubs, as well as on the international front with Northern Ireland during Nigel Worthington's spell in charge between 2007 and 2012.

Such is the reverence that Southall is held in, many Evertonians believe that his injury cost Everton the double in 1986. On reflection, though, that seems extremely unfair on Mimms, who conceded just three goals in nine league games in the spring of 1986 and finished on the losing side only once in that run. Typically, Southall had nothing but positive words to say about how his understudy had fared in his absence, 'I thought he was different class; nobody missed me, and that is the biggest thing I could say about him because he played so well. He came in and there was not too much fuss; he made some decent saves and the lads trusted him. That's the highest praise you could give him; to have the trust of players of that calibre was no mean feat.'

Mimms's impressive club form, coupled with an outstanding performance for England under-21s against Italy in the second leg of the European Championship semi-final, resulted in talk of him being part of Bobby Robson's England World Cup squad that summer. As Gary Bailey was struggling with the knee injury that would curtail his top-flight career, a goalkeeper slot was seemingly up for grabs in the squad, with Robson apparently torn between selecting Martin Hodge, who'd had a fabulous campaign at Sheffield Wednesday having built his career back up after his own horrendous injury issues, and Mimms. In the end, Bailey made the squad, only to break down again that summer. Mimms recalled, 'I had a very good game against Italy at Swindon's County Ground even though Howard had told Dave Sexton not to pick me as he was worried about me getting injured. I made four or five really good saves that night and it looked as though we were going to make it through until Italy scored late on. Howard wasn't too happy when I reported back for training at Everton. In fact, he went ballistic at me! Maybe that performance came a little bit too late for me to be seriously selected for Mexico. I probably needed to oust Dave Seaman from the under-21s starting XI a little earlier than I did, but there were definitely rumours about me going to the World Cup finals that summer.'

With Southall still sidelined, Mimms, now being coached at Bellefield by World Cup winner Gordon Banks, started the first 16 games of the 1986/87 campaign. He again performed extremely well before losing his place to the returning Southall in the autumn. Upset at finding himself out of the team for the game with Watford on 25 October 1986, Mimms, having conceded just 12 goals in the first 11 league games, slapped in a transfer request the following Monday, which, on the advice of Howard Kendall, was rejected by the directors. The boss went on record saying, 'Mimms is one of the best goalkeepers in the First Division. It just happens that until he was injured I had the best in the business in Southall.' Before the turn of the year, Mimms went on loan to Sunderland and then spent January with Blackburn Rovers before returning to Everton to collect a championship winners' medal, just rewards for his solid displays early on in the campaign behind a much-changed backline from that which had played the previous season.

Speaking about his decision to ask for a transfer, Mimms told me, 'I never really wanted to leave Everton as I was enjoying my football and loved the environment of the club. But in the back of my mind I always knew that Nev was on his way back and I just wanted to play. When I went to see Howard, he ripped up my transfer request and told me that I would leave when it was right for the club to move me on.'

It was a similar story at the beginning of the 1987/88 campaign. Another injury to Southall saw Mimms start the opening six games of Colin Harvey's first season in charge, and the plaudits were forthcoming after a breathtaking display in a 0-0 draw at Nottingham Forest. The *Liverpool Echo* reporter Ian Hargreaves called it 'Bobby's dazzling show' and gave him the newspaper's man of the match award for 'three outstanding saves that earned Everton a point' at the City Ground. Goalkeeping coach Gordon Banks told the same newspaper, 'Bobby was tremendous and once again showed that he is worth a regular place in the First Division. From Everton's point of view, it is a great pity that he is so keen to move on, but you can understand how frustrating it must be to understudy Southall, who is probably the best goalkeeper in Britain.' Although Mimms was quickly recalled from a loan spell at Manchester City in October, when Southall missed two more games through injury, it was clear that he needed to leave Everton if he wanted to play first-team football.

Mimms explained, 'I knew I needed to go. Derby County had been interested the previous summer as they had just been promoted back to the First Division, but Arthur Cox then went and signed Peter Shilton while I was on holiday. By that point, I was near enough just marking my time at Everton. Again, I didn't really want to leave but, for the sake of my career, knew I had to move on.'

In February 1988, he made the move to Tottenham Hotspur, who were looking for a new goalkeeper following an injury to Ray Clemence. Mimms's £325,000 transfer to the capital came about after Southall had recommended him to Doug Livermore, who was Mike Smith's assistant manager for Wales and also the reserve-team manager at Spurs during that period. Unfortunately, it never really worked out for Mimms at White Hart Lane and within two years he moved back up to the north-west when Kenny Dalglish signed him for Blackburn. He recalled, 'It was a bad move going to Spurs when I did. In hindsight, I should have stayed until the end of the season at Everton and then done a proper pre-season at my new club. Spurs were a mess at the time. I had gone from such a tight-knit club, where the fans were appreciative of everything you were doing for them, to a really fractured environment, where supporters had such high expectations without any real foundation. Terry Venables had come in and inherited a number of older players; then there was the group of lairy younger Cockneys, if you like, and the new signings – the likes of myself, Paul Walsh, Terry Fenwick and a bit later down the line Paul Stewart. There were three or four cliques within the changing room.

'I started really well. We beat Manchester United 3-1 on my debut, and I went full length and took a catch in the top right-hand corner. After the game, one of the lads came up to me and said, "That was a bit risky, wasn't it?" I remember thinking, "Jesus, is this what I am going to be up against?" After that, my form dropped off massively. It wasn't easy following Ray Clemence, who officially retired a few months after I got there, and Tony Parks was a bit of a fans' favourite, rightly so, after his heroics in Europe a few years earlier. I should have been taken out of the team far earlier than I was, but Venables had an issue with Parksy so he kept me in the side and left me to struggle, in all honesty.'

The switch to Ewood Park was a far more positive experience, 'I'd gone to Blackburn on loan a few years previously and really enjoyed my time there, playing for Howard's old captain from his spell as Rovers manager, ironically another Tony Parkes! So going back just felt really easy. I knew Kenny rated me and it was the perfect opportunity to start all over again. We were an excellent side with some really top defenders, the likes of Colin Hendry and Kevin Moran, and were pretty much ready for top-flight football.'

Mimms was a big part of the club's promotion push to the newly formed Premier League in 1992 and kept the most clean sheets of any keeper in the competition's inaugural campaign. Nonetheless, aided by Sir Jack Walker's chequebook, Dalglish began to build a side that could challenge for the title and in 1993 broke the British transfer record for a goalkeeper when he signed Tim Flowers from Southampton for a reported £2.4m.

Mimms added, 'It does rankle with me a bit how my time at Blackburn ended. Don't get me wrong, Tim Flowers did brilliantly both for the club and for England, but I had been playing well. I had kept 19 clean sheets the previous season and then kept another five in the first two months of the new campaign. In many ways, I was a victim of circumstances. Jack had all his money and Liverpool were sniffing around Tim. Kenny was never going to let him go there so maybe brought him in a little earlier than he would have otherwise done. Tim came straight into the team and though I stuck around for another two years and was part of the title-winning squad in 1995, I knew my time was up there.'

Following short spells at Crystal Palace, Preston North End and then both back at Rotherham and with hometown club York City, Mimms retired at the end of the 2000/01 campaign, having spent his final season with Mansfield Town. He then went on to have a hugely successful career as a goalkeeping coach, in England and also overseas. He told me, 'I have obviously taken a lot from the sessions I had with Neville at Everton and the coaches I worked with during my career, particularly Kells [Alan Kelly Senior] and Terry Gennoe at Blackburn. I still use a lot of their drills today, but what I really took from them was their delivery. They did what they did to bring the very best out of you, and not just force it out of you.'

According to Southall, Mimms was the strongest of all his goalkeeping understudies. Southall also believes that Mimms's relaxed nature and casual approach was probably his greatest strength and biggest weakness, 'I don't think Bob was ever fazed coming in to replace me. If he had been a different sort of personality, it might have been hard, but being so laid-back it didn't bother him, but he could have been an even better goalkeeper had he worked harder on the training ground. He was the complete opposite of me: completely laid-back, not bothered about training in the slightest.'

In July 1987, with Mimms having been expected to depart Merseyside that summer, Alec Chamberlain became Colin Harvey's first signing as Everton manager. A year later, he sold Chamberlain to Luton Town for £150,000 – making a tidy profit of £70,000 on the young goalkeeper he had signed from Fourth Division Colchester United.

After sitting on the bench against Coventry City in the Charity Shield, Chamberlain spent three months of his only season on Everton's books on loan at nearby Tranmere Rovers, where he proved himself to be a goalkeeper with excellent temperament and technique, catching the eye of Luton boss Ray Harford, who needed to find cover for the experienced Les Sealey. Chamberlain broke into the first team at Kenilworth Road towards the end of his first season there and remained the Hatters' first choice for the next three seasons. Hugely popular with the Luton fans, he was named player of the year in his first full season with the club, before moving to Sunderland in 1993, where he helped the club gain promotion to the Premier League. After a short loan spell at Anfield in 1995, where he failed to make a single appearance but did collect a League Cup winners' medal after being named as an unused substitute for the final against Bolton Wanderers at Wembley, Chamberlain moved to Watford, where he played a huge part in their promotion back to the top flight. In 2007, having spent over a decade at Vicarage Road making over 200 appearances for the Hornets, he came off the bench in the last minute against Newcastle United at the age of 42, making him one of the oldest players to play in the Premier League.

Like Mimms and Barber, and many of Southall's other understudies, Chamberlain carved out an excellent coaching career for himself after retiring from playing, and was hugely influential in the early development of England international Ben Foster. Speaking ahead of the League Cup Final in 1995, Chamberlain told the *Liverpool Echo*, 'Neville was a great help to me. Even after I left Everton, I'd speak to him a lot and he was always encouraging me. He's been an inspiration all the way through my career.' Incidentally, Chamberlain's brief loan spell at Liverpool came about after the Reds' usual reserve keeper, Michael Stensgaard, who had been on trial at Everton two years earlier, dislocated his shoulder while using an ironing board. The Dane, once dubbed 'the next Peter Schmeichel', failed to fully recover from the freak injury and retired from the game aged just 26.

Following the departures of Mimms and Chamberlain in 1988, Preston-born stopper **Mike Stowell** found himself elevated to second in the Goodison goalkeeping pecking order. The former BT technician had spent the majority of the 1987/88 season away from the club, on loan at Chester City, York City and Manchester City. After a two-month spell at Port Vale in the autumn of 1988, he returned to Goodison to make his sole appearance for Everton, keeping a clean sheet in a 2-0 victory over Millwall in the much-maligned Full Members' Cup. Just 3,703 supporters turned up for the game, and their ambivalence towards the competition (and others, such as the Screen Sport Super Cup, played in 1986/87) was seemingly matched by everyone bar Southall, who would have been extremely disappointed to have missed out on playing in that game, as, regardless of the competition, he always wanted to be on the pitch. In his autobiography, Southall stated, 'I absolutely loved it. I loved it because the manager – particularly when Howard was there – didn't want to have anything to do with these competitions. I'm sure he tried to pick a team to get knocked out and so picked all the kids. I also loved the responsibility of being an elder member of the team and helping young players to develop. It was good for them, good grounding. Not that I ever wanted to relinquish my position in the team. Why would you ever want to rest a goalie? It's pointless.'

Southall played in all the other games that season (including the 4-3 Full Members' Cup Final defeat at Wembley to Nottingham Forest) and Stowell spent the final two months on loan at Wolverhampton Wanderers, where he made an indelible impression on manager Graham Turner, who made his move permanent the following summer. Stowell went on to play a full decade in goal for the Molineux club and became a true fans' favourite before winding down his career at Bristol City. Following retirement, he also moved into coaching, and between 2007 and 2023 was Leicester City's caretaker manager on no fewer than six different occasions.

The aforementioned Full Members' Cup tie against Millwall in December 1988 was the only game Southall missed between returning from injury on 24 October 1987 and 12 January 1993, when a one-match suspension following his sending off for handling the ball outside his penalty area against Queens Park Rangers brought an end to an impressive run of 215 consecutive appearances. At Loftus Road, Southall, seemingly concerned that skipper Dave Watson's headed back pass wasn't going to reach him, ventured into the D of his 18-yard box and instinctively picked the ball up, with old foe Les Ferdinand lurking in close proximity. Straight away, Southall knew what was coming from referee Gerald Ashby and appeared to apologise to the official, who, under the new FA legislation, had no option other than to show the red card. As Southall trudged off the pitch, a trio of opponents, including old friend Alan McDonald, sympathised with the disconsolate goalkeeper, who had made two stupendous saves from deflected efforts in the opening moments of the game to keep the score at 0-0.

With clubs now permitted to name a substitute goalkeeper for every league game, rookie **Jason Kearton** took his place between the sticks following Southall's dismissal and produced a splendid save from the resulting free kick, diving smartly to his right to repel David Bardsley's fierce strike. It was some way for the Australian, who had joined the club from Brisbane Lions four years previously and been on loan at Stoke City and Blackpool in 1991/92, to mark his start to life as an Everton goalkeeper. Minutes later, the debutant produced an even better save, clawing out Simon Barker's powerful header, only for Andy Sinton to sweep home the rebound from close range. In the second half, Kearton was beaten on three more occasions (twice more by Sinton) as nine-man Everton, who also had Paul Rideout sent off, went down 4-2 in the capital. Speaking after the game, Howard Kendall told the *Liverpool Echo*, 'The lad is an outstanding prospect and did himself proud. He was asking after the game how many games Neville would be missing for. He was disappointed when we said just one. They have got a tremendous respect for each other and it's nice to see.'

Bizarrely, it was a similar story just six weeks later, with Southall learning the hard way when it came to the new laws surrounding punishment for handling outside the box. Having pulled off two fantastic reflex saves only for the opposition to convert both the rebounds within a minute of each other, Southall and Everton found themselves 2-0 down after just 17 minutes at Sheffield Wednesday. Soon after, the Welshman, who according to *Match of the Day* summariser Clive Tyldesley 'must have stepped under a dozen ladders en route to Hillsborough' that afternoon, came racing off his line, again instinctively handling the ball a yard or so outside his area. In almost identical scenes to those at Loftus Road, he saw red and watched on as stand-in Kearton dealt with the resulting free kick brilliantly before being beaten in the second half by Chris Waddle's follow-up effort after initially making a smart diving save to his left.

A second suspension of the season for Southall paved the way for Kearton, who had made his Goodison Park debut, and been at fault for John Fashanu's opening strike, in the disappointing home FA Cup third-round replay defeat to Wimbledon in January, to make two more starts in early 1993. In both games he was beaten twice as Everton went down 2-1 at Villa Park and drew 2-2 at home to Oldham Athletic. The 23-year-old also played just under half an hour of Everton's final game of the campaign at Manchester City, much to the disgust of Southall, whose desire to play every minute of every match had not diminished, despite him now being in his mid-30s and having earlier strained a lower back muscle in the Maine Road encounter – incidentally, the first top-flight competitive game in which both teams brought on their substitute goalkeepers.

The only time Southall's run of 215 consecutive appearances had looked in any real danger of being halted prior to his suspension came a year before his dismissal at Loftus Road. On Boxing Day 1991, Howard Kendall took the unusual step of naming experienced keeper Gerry Peyton as one of his two substitutes for the clash with Sheffield Wednesday at Goodison Park. Throughout the Christmas period, Southall struggled with an ankle injury. Although he came through the game unscathed, he was a serious doubt for the Merseyside derby just two days later and did little more than watch Peyton being put through his paces in the pre-match warm-up. Nonetheless, Southall was deemed fit enough to play, and Peyton, who had signed from Bournemouth the previous summer, had to make do with a seat in the stands as Everton came from a goal behind to take a share of the spoils.

The following month, Southall paid tribute to his new understudy in the *Liverpool Echo*, 'Gerry has been great for me this season. We talk about goalkeeping a lot. He knows the kind of preparation I want and he is ready to help me. If I'm feeling fed up, he lifts me with his enthusiasm. I know how desperate he is to play and it makes me realise that I should be just as keen.'

In the same article, the number one explained how he and Peyton were keen to pass on their wealth of experience to the younger keepers at the club, 'Players might not make it here, but they might go on to do a job elsewhere. Both Gerry and I are very keen to do some specialised coaching. We've got over 100 caps between us yet we don't get the chance to pass anything on, which is quite sad.'

However, in the second half of that campaign, Peyton, who had gone to the World Cup in Italy as Pat Bonner's understudy in Jack Charlton's Republic of Ireland squad 18 months earlier, went on loan to Bolton Wanderers and Norwich City. Interestingly, on the final day of the 1991/92 season, he was again named as a substitute for a top-flight fixture – taking his place on the bench at Elland Road for the Canaries' trip to face First Division champions Leeds United. Peyton explained, 'The regular goalkeeper was OK but if Norwich lost by a big margin, it was possible that they could still go down. Their thinking was that the keeper could be sent off for a professional foul or he might get injured. In their position, they felt the risk, no matter how small, wasn't worth taking. By putting me on the bench, they covered everything so they weren't going to get hammered.'

Throughout the following season, when the newly formed Premier League introduced the naming of substitute goalkeepers, Jason Kearton was consistently Kendall's choice of understudy for Southall, despite Peyton having added three more international caps to his collection that summer (taking his total to 34) and the manager often stating that he liked to put his faith in experienced keepers as, in his words, so much of goalkeeping was about know-how gained through playing matches. Unable to break into the matchday squad, Peyton spent time on loan at Brentford and Chelsea, before moving to Griffin Park on a free transfer in March 1993. After a short spell with West Ham United, the Irishman retired from playing the following year. He would later enjoy an excellent career as a goalkeeping coach, including a 15-year spell at Arsenal as part of Arsène Wenger's backroom staff.

Liverpudlian Ray Newland is another of Southall's short-term training partners from that period who carved out a successful coaching career for himself after hanging up his gloves. In the summer of 1992, the 21-year-old left Everton and signed for Peter Shilton's Plymouth Argyle, after Southall had recommended him for a trial at Home Park towards the end of the 1991/92 campaign. Over the next seven years, Newland enjoyed a nomadic career in the lower leagues before retiring through injury at the age of 28. In 1998, he established Just4Keepers, a goalkeeper training schools company, and later launched his own glove brand. At his wedding in 2014, the former Chester City trainee had 147 best men, all of whom were his goalkeeper students at the time.

Following Peyton's departure, Stephen Reeves was elevated to the role of third-choice keeper, having seen off the challenge of John Carridge, the Formby-born youth-team graduate who was released at the end of the 1992/93 season. Although Reeves never made a first-team appearance for Everton, the Dagenham-born stopper did play for a Merseyside XI in Graeme Sharp's testimonial against a Manchester XI in 1992 and did make the bench 16 times during his 30 months as a Goodison professional. At St James' Park, on a freezing Wednesday evening in February

1995, Reeves was told to warm up after Southall took a knock while making a brave save at the feet of Newcastle United's Lee Clark. Southall, however, managed to soldier on and complete the full 90 minutes. In Reeves's words, 'Nev would have played on, even with a broken leg!' Nevertheless, in an ill-tempered contest, with Everton already down to nine men after Earl Barrett and Barry Horne had received their marching orders within 60 seconds of each other, Southall was somewhat fortunate not to see red himself, having berated referee David Elleray and kicked the ball off the penalty spot in disgust following the award of a contentious spot kick to Kevin Keegan's side.

Along with Jason Kearton and youngsters Richard Moore and James Speare, Reeves appeared in Southall's goalkeeping coaching manual *In Search of Perfection*, which was published in 1995. Following his release from the club in the same year, Reeves signed for Chelsea but failed to break into the team at Stamford Bridge. He departed for Oxford United a year later, before retiring from the professional game with persistent knee injuries not long afterwards.

Throughout the dramatic 1993/94 campaign, Kearton was again a regular on the bench. He also made a first-team appearance in the first leg of the League Cup tie at Lincoln City, where Everton ran out 4-3 winners in a topsy-turvy encounter. Three days earlier, Southall had been in fine form in the 2-0 Goodison derby victory, a game remembered fondly by many Blues for Bruce Grobbelaar's angry exchange with team-mate Steve McManaman, after the winger's poor clearance of Andy Hinchcliffe's inswinging corner had inadvertently set up Mark Ward to fire Everton ahead at the Gwladys Street End. Much to the delight of the Evertonians behind that goal, the Zimbabwean went ballistic at McManaman, waving his fingers aggressively at him before screaming in his face and grabbing him by the neck. As Martin Tyler stated on commentary duty that day, 'That's what it means to lose a goal in a Merseyside derby!' In the second half, Liverpool came out with far more attacking intent, and Southall had to be on his mettle to keep out a close-range effort directed towards goal by Ian Rush before springing to his right to repel a piledriver sent in by Julian Dicks from distance. However, after the game, Kendall told the *Liverpool Echo* that his goalkeeper had injured himself in the opening seconds of the first half, after colliding with Rush, and needed a pain-killing injection at half-time to get through the second period, 'It [the game at Lincoln] will be the first time we've called on Jason Kearton because of injury to Neville. In the past he's always been suspended.'

Midway through the 1994/95 season, Kearton was handed a rare Premier League start, when Southall was away on international duty. The Australian kept a clean sheet in a goalless draw at Villa Park in early December, thus playing his part in Everton setting a new club record of seven consecutive clean sheets in league matches. In the new year, he spent time on loan at Howard Kendall's Notts County, where he was put through his paces by goalkeeping coach Mark Harrison, who had worked with Kearton and Southall in a similar position at Bellefield the previous season. Kearton ended the campaign with an FA Cup winners' medal, having sat on the bench for the 1-0 victory over Manchester United at Wembley. Somewhat cruelly, the 25-year-old had been denied the opportunity to play at Wembley himself a few weeks before the FA Cup Final, after Everton, lacking goalkeeping cover options for Southall, recalled Kearton early from his spell at Meadow Lane. The call-back came only four days before he was expected to line up for County in the Anglo-Italian Cup Final against Serie B outfit Ascoli. In the all-English semi-final victory over Stoke City, Everton's on-loan keeper had been the Magpies' hero – denying Paul Allen and Vince Overson from the spot in the penalty shoot-out after both legs had finished goalless.

As soon as Joe Royle took charge in November 1994, it was rumoured that the new manager wanted a changing of the guard in the goalkeeping position. As he had worked so closely with the highly rated former England under-21 goalkeeper Paul Gerrard at Oldham Athletic, it seemed only a matter of time before Royle would bring the Heywood-born stopper to Goodison Park to work alongside Southall, before taking his place in the team. As a consequence, it was clear that Jason Kearton needed a new challenge. After failing to get a look-in at all during the 1995/96 season, and with the club having completed the signing of Gerrard in July 1996, Kearton moved to Crewe Alexandra, where he won promotion from the Second Division in his first season at Gresty Road. For the next four years, Kearton was the Railwaymen's first choice and is fondly remembered by their fanbase, especially for his incredible performance against Blackburn Rovers in 2000, when he made no fewer than ten tremendous saves in front of the Sky cameras in a smash-and-grab 1-0 victory at Ewood Park. Kearton returned to Australia in 2001 and, after spells with Brisbane Strikers, Queensland Lions and Brisbane Roar, he set up his own goalkeeping coaching company. Like Bobby Mimms, Kearton is another of Southall's understudies that the number one seemed to have a lot of time for. In his book *Everton Blues: Diary of a Season*, Southall stated, 'Jason is a nice lad and I am delighted he went on to enjoy success at Crewe Alexandra. He needed a break in his career because he didn't really get a chance to prove himself at Everton.'

On the 1994 goalkeeping coaching video *Great Save: The Essential Guide to Brilliant Goalkeeping*, the connection between Southall and Kearton is clearly evident. Giving viewers an insight into the drills that professional keepers carry out on a daily basis, the video shows the two men, under the guidance of former Chelsea and England keeper Peter Bonetti on the Bellefield training ground, being extremely relaxed around each other and vociferous in their encouragement and praise of each other's high-quality performances. Interestingly, though, Southall is on record as saying that he would have never forced advice on a fellow professional goalkeeper. In *In Search of Perfection*, he wrote, 'Jason has a lot of talent and can develop into a top-class player. But I won't force any information on him. Sure, if I spot something I will tell him. It's just that nobody ever told me what I was doing wrong – I had to find out myself. And I think that's one of the best ways of learning. It's got nothing at all to do with the fact that we are rivals. On the contrary. I don't want to tell him to be doing this or that because he's at the stage where I want him to do what comes naturally rather than filling his head with too much talk.'

Gerrard's arrival also spelled the end of the road for Richard Moore and James Speare at Goodison. Following their releases, Moore moved to Blyth Spartans, and Speare, after a brief spell at Darlington, signed for Irish club Sligo Rovers. From there, he went on to enjoy a six-year stint as Accrington Stanley's number one before moving on to Lancaster City, Southport, Barrow and Colwyn Bay. Talking about the heartbreak of leaving Everton, Speare, who sat on the first-team bench 11 times between 1994 and 1997, told the *Ipswich Star*, 'Joe Royle paid over £1m for Paul Gerrard, so the writing was on the wall and within a week or two he told me it would be best if I moved on. Joe explained that I would be doing well to play in the reserves, never mind the first team, so I didn't really have much choice.'

Even though Southall started the 1996/97 and 1997/98 seasons as the first choice, Kearton's departure in the summer of 1996 was the final time a main understudy of his would leave the club – the Australian was the final entrant into what Joe Royle had called in the *Liverpool Echo* 'Neville's personal graveyard' of goalkeepers. That year, a seismic shift was taking place in the goalkeeping department: for over ten years, all the keepers the club had brought in were given the thankless task of playing understudy to the world's greatest, learning lots through working alongside Southall every day, but never really standing a chance of taking his place in the team. In 1996, Everton were no longer in the market for a backup for Southall. They were looking for somebody to replace him.

Although top goalkeepers such as Alan Kelly Junior, Nigel Martyn and Andy Goram had been constantly linked with a move to Everton earlier that year, none of the deals involving those players came to fruition, and the Blues would have to wait another seven years before finding an adequate replacement for Southall. For many seemingly competent keepers, a description based on their performances and careers either side of their time at Goodison Park, following Neville Southall proved to be the Impossible Job.

Paul Gerrard would be the first to try his hand.

10

The Impossible Job – Following Southall

According to Phil McNulty, BBC Sport's chief football writer and former reporter at the *Liverpool Echo*, **Paul Gerrard** was 'a goalkeeper capable of very good days but not really a goalkeeper of the highest quality, as he also had far too many bad moments in an Everton shirt. You would put him in the same bracket as a lot of the other keepers who came into the club at around that time – goalkeepers blighted by inconsistency to the extent that it severely undermined the team and, to be frank, goalkeepers who were nowhere near good enough to replace the legendary Neville Southall.'

Gerrard had done exceptionally well for Joe Royle at Oldham Athletic and had been a regular in the England under-21 set-up after making his Premier League debut for the Latics at just 19 years old. As Royle had been linked with a host of goalkeepers over the previous 18 months and missed out on signing Crystal Palace's England international Nigel Martyn earlier that summer (more on that later!), it was no real surprise when he returned to Boundary Park with a cheque for £1.2m to bring the highly rated 23-year-old stopper to Merseyside in July 1996.

In his autobiography, Royle dedicated a chapter to what he called 'The Southall Factor' and the difficulties he had replacing the Welshman, 'As soon as I walked through the door at Bellefield, people were telling me that Neville had "gone" and, though that was too severe a criticism, I soon made up my mind that his goalkeeping was changing. He was starting to struggle to control his weight and was losing the spring in his leap, which is so crucial for a goalkeeper, and was relying more on his vast experience to tell him where to be at the right moment. Despite my misgivings, and in recognition of his service to the club, I had given him a new contract shortly after I took over [in November 1994], a deal that took him well into his 30s. But my conviction that Neville was past his peak drove me to search for new talent.'

The relationship between Royle and Southall was beginning to break down. In his book *Everton Blues: A Premier League Diary*, Southall claimed that, just days after Gerrard arrived at the club, Royle told the veteran that he was free to speak to Wolverhampton Wanderers 'because they're desperate to sign you'. However, after a less-than-convincing display by Gerrard in a 4-3 friendly win over Wrexham at the Racecourse Ground, Royle began to have doubts that his new signing was ready for the first team and so Southall began the 1996/97 campaign as Everton's first-choice goalkeeper.

Gerrard's only appearance in the first half of the season came as a second-half substitute in the 7-1 thrashing of Southampton in November, but, after an embarrassing home FA Cup fourth-round defeat to Bradford City at the end of January, when Chris Waddle scored from more than 35 yards, Royle decided to bring his patient protégé into the side, 'I made up my mind after that match that it was time to give Paul Gerrard his chance. All I can say is that you could have put a stopwatch on Neville as he tried to get back to Waddle's chip. The fact is he was having weight problems and he simply wasn't agile enough to get there.'

In Everton's next fixture, away at Newcastle United, Gerrard was beaten four times, though, according to Southall, his replacement was not at fault for the heavy defeat, 'Paul Gerrard can't be blamed for any of the goals. I take no pleasure in seeing balls fly into our net, even though I wish it was me out there.' In his next two outings, Gerrard fared much better – keeping clean sheets in a win over Nottingham Forest and in a draw at Coventry City, where he saved bravely at the feet of Darren Huckerby to earn his side a share of the spoils – before a groin injury ruled him out of the next three games. Injuries had been a massive issue for Gerrard throughout his time at Oldham, so much so in fact that he'd often worn knee supports in matches for the Latics. Just four matches into his Everton career, fitness doubts were already beginning to surface.

Prior to the draw at Highfield Road, Royle had tried to sign Mark Schwarzer, who had been outstanding for Bradford City at Goodison the previous month, but missed out when the Australian, unimpressed by what the club had offered him, joined Bryan Robson's Middlesbrough instead.

Just five games later, after a horror show by the returning Gerrard at home to Manchester United, when he let Ole Gunnar Solskjær's tame effort slip through his hands and then dropped David Beckham's cross at the feet of Eric Cantona, Royle's time in charge of Everton came to an unexpected end. Feeling the pressure and hugely frustrated by the sale of star player Andrei Kanchelskis to Fiorentina and the club's failure to sign both Schwarzer and forward Tore André Flo, Royle left the club by 'mutual consent' after a bizarre meeting with chairman Peter Johnson, which, for long periods, seemed to be going nowhere. In Royle's words, he became 'a victim of the sacking that never was and the resignation that never was'.

With his old mentor gone, Gerrard's future at Goodison also lay in the balance, especially when caretaker manager Dave Watson recalled Southall for the remaining seven games. Everton, once again, were embroiled in a relegation dogfight. Watson recalled, 'When I was given the caretaker role, I immediately brought Neville back into the team. I needed his presence – something Paul Gerrard didn't really have – to try to get a bit more out of the players around him. Although he was a very decent keeper, there was a question mark over whether Paul could deal with the big occasions and also over his physicality when coming for crosses. There was a bit of doubt there – and if there's a bit of a doubt with a goalkeeper, it doesn't half affect the team. It can spread panic when defending set plays. We needed strong characters. Neville came back in and, with a good win at home to Spurs, followed by a draw with Liverpool and a point on the road at West Ham, where Nev saved a penalty, we managed to get the job done.'

Watson had been handed the temporary manager's role after Peter Johnson selected him over Southall. Alan Myers told me, 'After meeting Peter Johnson at the training ground, I asked the chairman what we were doing there. He used to confide in me a lot did the chairman and he told me, "We've got to pick a temporary manager and I am thinking either Neville Southall or Dave Watson, and because he won't have as much to worry about, being a goalkeeper, I'm leaning towards Neville Southall." As we were talking, this big Volvo parked up close to where we were standing. Neville got out and shouted, "All right Myers, you fat bastard!" He may have used a stronger word! As he said that, Peter Johnson looked at me, sternly, and said, "It's down to one – I am going with Watson." And that was Neville's chance to become Everton manager gone.'

It also looked as though Gerrard's chance of becoming Everton's regular goalkeeper had passed when Howard Kendall, back for a third spell in charge, started the 1997/98 season with Southall in goal and then signed Norwegian **Thomas Myhre** from Viking Stavanger halfway through what turned out to be yet another torturous and tumultuous campaign.

With Everton sitting bottom of the table in early December, Kendall made the decision to call time on Southall's first-team career at the club – offering him the position of goalkeeping coach, which the Welshman turned down. Southall told the *Liverpool Echo*, 'I want to continue my playing career for as long as possible. I also want a broader responsibility at a club when I finally move into coaching and not be pigeon-holed as a goalkeeping coach.' The position would instead be taken up by former West Ham United and Leeds United keeper Mervyn Day, who had recently left his post as manager of Carlisle United.

Unconvinced by Gerrard, who had struggled in the 4-1 League Cup exit to Coventry two months earlier, Kendall brought Myhre into the side for the trip to Leeds United. The new stopper was in majestic form at Elland Road, earning his side a point in a 0-0 draw after making stunning saves to deny Rod Wallace and Harry Kewell. In his next two games, he kept further clean sheets, against Wimbledon and Leicester City, before performing well but being beaten twice on Boxing Day at Manchester United. Leading the plaudits was centre-half Slaven Bilić, who, in his weekly column in the *Liverpool Echo*, stated, 'Thomas Myhre has done remarkably well since coming here from Norway. It's always difficult for foreign players to settle quickly, but he has enjoyed some good performances, which obviously helps.'

Incidentally, the presence of Myhre and Southall in the matchday squads came at the expense of young goalkeeper John O'Toole, who had sat on the bench for four of Everton's matches in November and appeared on Southall's coaching video, *Great Save: The Essential Guide to Brilliant Goalkeeping*, as a young teen some four years earlier. O'Toole was released at the end of the season having not made a first-team appearance.

A huge factor in helping Myhre to settle quickly at Everton was the man he had replaced in the team. Speaking towards the end of his first season in English football, the Norwegian told the *Weekly News*, 'I was well aware of Neville before I arrived. He has always been a great keeper. Now I know he is a great person as well. Neville was great to me when I first arrived. He knew the club was going to buy a new keeper and that there wasn't anything personal in it. We talked a lot and he passed on advice about what I would face. He backed me up all the time.'

Similar comments had been made by Gerrard during the previous campaign. He had told the same publication, 'When I came to the club, I didn't know how Neville would react to having me here. It was obvious that I'd been bought to replace him at some stage, but he has been brilliant with me. He said to me that he would be cheating himself if he didn't help me settle in and eventually succeed him. Replacing Neville is like asking somebody to go to Manchester United and replace Bryan Robson. Nev has warned me that people will make comparisons between us and he has said it will be hard for me, but I will have to cope with it.'

Despite a dreadful error against Coventry on the final day of the 1997/98 season, when, again, Everton did just enough to preserve their top-flight status, Myhre, who let Dion Dublin's looping header slip through his hands at Goodison Park, could reflect on an excellent maiden campaign. Speaking about his first season in England and near-fatal final-day mistake, he told the *Liverpool Echo*, 'I'd made a decent start at Everton but had no break after a long season in Norway. I'd played 56 or 57 league games plus cup matches on the trot and at the end I was tired and wasn't playing well. The Dion Dublin header was an easy save and I basically dropped it in the goal. If I could have found the biggest digging machine to open the fucking ground, I would have done it.'

Alan Myers told me, 'Thomas came in when the team was going through a really difficult patch and did very well. I remember a game away at Barnsley when we were just outside the relegation zone and he lost one of his contact lenses. God knows how but one of the backroom staff found it on the pitch, wiped it on his shirt and put it back in Thomas's eye. Howard Kendall was obviously under a lot of pressure at the time, and I remember him turning to the others on the bench and screaming, "Nobody told me we'd signed a goalkeeper who needs fucking glasses!" It was a brilliant line during an exceptionally stressful period.'

According to David Prentice, Myhre was an interesting character, who took his craft very seriously, 'Thomas was an extremely intense guy. He usually had the space under his top lip stuffed with tobacco as he used "snus", an oral tobacco product used by a lot of Scandinavian players at the time for calming purposes, and, after conceding an awful goal at West Ham, when he flapped at a cross, he shaved all his hair off as some form of penance. He made a few mistakes in that first season and really beat himself up about them, but, on the whole, his Everton career started very well.'

Although the first-team squad had endured another difficult campaign, in May 1998 Everton's youngsters lifted the FA Youth Cup for only the second time in the club's history. Despite goalkeeper Dean Delany failing to make the grade at Goodison Park, the Dubliner enjoyed a solid career on both sides of the Irish Sea following his release, making 37 appearances for Port Vale between 2000 and 2004 before serving Shelbourne, Waterford and Bohemians with distinction over a 15-year period. He was also capped at under-21 level.

The following season, with Walter Smith in charge following the sacking of Kendall, Myhre was an ever-present in the league, conceding just 12 goals in 19 games at home, where Everton played out seven dour goalless draws. His excellent form in Smith's struggling side brought him much-deserved international recognition and led to him being linked with a move to treble winners Manchester United, who were in the market for a new goalkeeper following the departure of their own legendary stopper, Peter Schmeichel. At Newcastle in April, Myhre was in inspired form, making a string of fine saves, including one from an Alan Shearer penalty, to earn his side a vital three points. However, a broken right leg sustained while training with the Norway team in the close season, followed by a break to his left leg after a freak bathroom accident at home, cruelly brought a halt to a run of 60 consecutive league appearances and allowed Paul Gerrard, who had done well on loan at second-tier outfit Oxford United that spring, an unlikely opportunity to again stake his claim to be the club's first-choice goalkeeper ahead of the new campaign.

It was an opportunity which, in the short term at least, Gerrard grasped with both hands. In the opening-day draw with Manchester United, he was magnificent behind the centre-back pairing of Dave Watson and Richard Gough, who, at a combined age of 74 years old, were colossal and used every ounce of their experience to protect their keeper from United's exciting front three of Ole Gunnar Solskjær, Andy Cole and Dwight Yorke. On the few occasions the backline was breached, the Red Devils' attack found Gerrard in splendid form, making fine saves from Scholes and Yorke before going full length to keep out a vicious strike from Roy Keane in the second half. In the *Liverpool Echo*, David Prentice, making reference to Gerrard's horror show two years earlier against Alex Ferguson's side, wrote, 'Paul Gerrard had some personal demons to exorcise – and he did so splendidly. If the goalkeeper is prone to nerves, he settled them very early on with a superb block when Paul Scholes had waltzed into a goalscoring position.' After the game, Graeme Sharp, who had briefly managed Gerrard at Boundary Park, wrote in his column in the same newspaper, 'Paul Gerrard has never lacked ability, merely confidence. He worries too much about his game and worries too much about what other people think of him, instead of simply getting on with it. He has had a lot of criticism, but this is a lad who needs to play on confidence and he was full of it after a great early save from Paul Scholes.'

Gerrard was voted man of the match at Tottenham Hotspur the following week and, along with the rest of his team-mates, was terrific at Liverpool less than a month later, making a superb late plunging save from Eric Meijer's deflected volley to help Everton record an unlikely victory, courtesy of the late Kevin Campbell's early strike in front of the Kop. Even after a heavy defeat at Arsenal in mid-October, the *Liverpool Echo* was full of praise for the seemingly redeemed Gerrard, calling his display against Arsène Wenger's side 'breathtaking'. In the same newspaper, his performance at Middlesbrough a fortnight later was described as 'another astonishing display of shot-stopping'. Gerrard's Everton revival appeared complete when the club rewarded him for his outstanding form and resilience with an improved four-and-a-half-year contract. Speaking to the *Liverpool Echo*'s Phil McNulty, Walter Smith said, 'He has done well for us this season. It is well known he had a bit of a rocky spell early in his career at Everton, but I am really pleased in the manner he has gone about his work.' To many match-going Evertonians, the ex-Glasgow Rangers trio of manager Smith, defender Gough and goalkeeping coach Chris Woods appeared to have instilled a previously unseen confidence in the Heywood-born stopper.

Even when the old injury issues resurfaced and he had to spend time on the sidelines after limping off against Southampton in January 2000, Gerrard's position as Everton's first choice was not thrown into doubt. Although England under-21 international **Steve Simonsen**, signed from Tranmere Rovers at the start of the previous campaign, had replaced Gerrard in the 2-0 loss at Southampton, Thomas Myhre, back in the fold after recovering from injury and spending time on loan at Rangers, played in the next six games. Unfortunately for the big Norwegian, he looked a shadow of the goalkeeper who had played so well in his first two seasons. A shocking performance in the FA Cup quarter-final exit to Aston Villa, when he was partly to blame for both goals conceded that day, angered Smith, who dropped Myhre as soon as Gerrard was fit again, and then loaned him to Birmingham City soon after.

It was a similar story halfway through the following season. When Gerrard collapsed at Goodison after his knee had given way against West Ham United, in an incident that has since gone down in Goodison folklore after Hammers forward Paolo Di Canio caught the ball and stopped play instead of prodding it home in a tremendous act of sportsmanship, it was Simonsen who again came on from the bench, but Myhre who would play the next eight games in Gerrard's absence. Again, he looked shaky, and the embarrassing 3-0 home defeat to Tranmere Rovers in the FA Cup proved to be his penultimate game for the club. A public war of words with Smith then took place, with Myhre claiming that there was 'bad chemistry' between the two of them. As it had been for Georgie Wood more than two decades earlier, it was an extremely sad way for a talented goalkeeper's Everton career to finish. After a year in Turkey with Beşiktaş, Myhre returned to England to play for Sunderland, Crystal Palace and Charlton Athletic. On 2 January 2006, in his second game back at Goodison Park as an opposing player, he saved a penalty from James Beattie but could not prevent the rebound from being converted or his Charlton side from slipping to a 3-1 defeat.

After a very consistent 18-month period, Gerrard also started to struggle towards the end of the 2000/01 campaign. With injuries beginning to creep back in and punctuate his runs in the team, and with Gough and Watson no longer in front of him, he looked far less confident when coming for crosses and less decisive in his actions. On Easter Monday, he conceded a ridiculous goal in the last minute of the Goodison derby after being caught woefully out of position for Gary McAllister's 45-yard free kick. McAllister told the *Liverpool Echo*, 'Prior to taking the free kick that we would score the goal from, we had a free kick in the exact same spot literally a minute before. I deliver it, float it up to the far post and I think it's Sami Hyypiä who flashes a header wide. A minute goes past and we're into stoppage time. Because I'm signalling that I'm going to replicate the free kick, I can see Paul Gerrard thinking he was going to kill the game and just take the cross. If you see a goalie making an early decision and going early you have got that split-second to change your mind.' It was an awful error of judgement that he would not be allowed to forget. From that moment on, Gerrard's confidence seemed to plummet further.

Although Gerrard started the 2001/02 season in the team, his Goodison Park career was all but over after a catastrophic mix-up with defender Abel Xavier outside his box in the 3-1 loss to Newcastle just 11 games in. Having already had one attempted clearance charged down by Craig Bellamy in the opening minutes, Gerrard again came racing off his line midway through the first half, this time completely missing the ball and clattering into Xavier, to leave Bellamy with a simple finish. With Smith's patience having finally run out, Gerrard found himself axed from the team. An Everton career that had started horrendously before showing great promise was ending the way it had begun. Alan Myers recalled, 'Paul was a good keeper and a really loveable fella who suffered badly in the big moments. He put way too much pressure on himself but you could understand why – it could not have been easy for him coming in after Neville Southall, especially into a struggling team. Those two components made it a "perfect storm" and very difficult for him to succeed.'

Because of Gerrard's poor form, Steve Simonsen was finally given an extended run in the team. Simonsen had joined in the summer of 1998 after impressing at nearby Tranmere, where he had set a club record of seven consecutive clean sheets and kept 18 shut-outs in 35 league games after forcing his way into John Aldridge's team at the age of 17. In the *Daily Mirror*, journalist David Maddock reported that the deal Everton had struck with the Prenton Park outfit would make the highly rated Simonsen the 'most expensive goalkeeper in the world' at £3.5m. However, the actual breakdown of the transfer, which saw youngster Graham Allen head in the opposite direction, was as follows: a player exchange deal involving Allen, who was valued at £300,000; a £500,000 initial payment; a further £500,000 payment at the end of his first season; a payment of £1.5m after 150 appearances for Everton; £500,000 if he were to play for England. As Simonsen would go on to make only 35 starts in a disappointing six-year spell at the club, and fail to get anywhere near the England squad, the fee that Everton actually ended up paying for him was a much cooler £1m, plus the value of the departing Graham Allen.

According to Dave Watson, 'There were lots of promises when Steve Simonsen came in that he was going to be the next

England goalkeeper and achieve this and that in the game. He definitely had a bit more of a presence about him than the other keepers at the club at that time did. He was a big lad and looked the part at least, but I think, if you make a mistake, especially at Goodison, where the fans can get on your back when things aren't going too well, and where the supporters had been used to the ridiculously high standards of Neville Southall, it can be really hard. Once he'd made a few mistakes, it got to the point where the supporters started to think, "Oh no, he's not in goal again, is he?" We were all guilty of doing it – comparing goalkeepers to Neville – which was unfair, really.'

In his early appearances for the club, in the two-legged League Cup defeat to Oxford United in 1999 and when coming on for the injured Gerrard at Southampton in January 2000, Simonsen looked extremely nervy. Indeed, in many quarters, he was blamed for both the goals that Everton conceded at Southampton on his Premier League debut, especially Jo Tessem's opening strike, to which he seemed very slow to react. Following Gerrard's howler against Newcastle in October 2001, Simonsen, who had been linked with a move to Wigan Athletic in a swap deal for Northern Ireland's promising young keeper Roy Carroll earlier that year and a key figure in the Blues' FA Premier Reserve League North title the previous season, played 29 consecutive games for Everton – the only time in his six years at the club that he put any kind of run in the first team together. In some of those matches, such as the goalless draws with Chelsea and Leicester City, he showed glimpses of the goalkeeper Everton thought they had signed. In both matches he made impressive match-saving stops, denying Gianfranco Zola with a brilliant fingertip save in the dying moments of a drab encounter at Goodison before doing the same to stop Jamie Scowcroft from winning the game for the Foxes at Filbert Street six days later.

In March 2002, after a dreadful run of results in the league and a dismal defeat to Middlesbrough in the FA Cup quarter-final, Walter Smith was relieved of his managerial duties. Having steered the club to safety with three wins in his first four games in charge, new manager David Moyes decided to give Simonsen and Gerrard the opportunity to impress him in the final five fixtures of the season. However, neither man managed to convince the ambitious Scot that they were the goalkeeper he wanted for his first full campaign in charge – Everton's 100th in the top division of English football. As a consequence, though both remained on Everton's books for a further two years (joining Nottingham Forest and Stoke City respectively in 2004), they played only five more games between them. In the summer of 2002, Everton were once again in the market for a new first-team goalkeeper. Incidentally, Andrew Pettinger, who had sat on the bench alongside fellow FA Youth Cup finalist Wayne Rooney for two of the club's Premier League games towards the end of the 2001/02 season, was released around that time too – returning to his native Lincolnshire, where he signed for Grimsby Town, before dropping into non-league football. Tragically, Alex Cole, Pettinger's backup during the FA Youth Cup run, would lose his life in a road accident in 2004 after his car careered off the M53 exit slip road, hit a lamppost and overturned.

According to David Prentice, 'Thomas Myhre was probably the goalkeeper who came closest to succeeding in those few years after Neville Southall's departure. But he, like all the rest of the goalkeepers we had at that time, just was not consistent enough. That was the real issue during those years – we frequently saw our goalkeepers go through spells when they'd look very good, only for them to then spoil that run by dropping a real clanger. Paul Gerrard, Steve Simonsen and Thomas Myhre – they all had their good days, but had some real stinkers too. It could have all been very different if Walter Smith had been allowed to bring Petr Čech to the club from Sparta Prague for less than half the price that he ended up going to Chelsea for a couple of years later. Of course, Čech went on to become an outstanding goalkeeper, who challenges Schmeichel for the title of the Premier League's greatest-ever goalkeeper.'

Prentice continued, '**Richard Wright**, the goalkeeper who did come in next, was very similar to the ones who preceded him. He too would have spells where he'd look incredible and make fabulous reflex saves, but he was also capable of making mad, catastrophic errors. It was hardly a classic era for Everton goalkeepers.'

Wright was signed from Arsenal for a reported £4.5m, just 12 months after Arsène Wenger had taken him to Highbury from Ipswich Town. At Portman Road, Wright had established himself as one of the country's leading young goalkeepers, making his international debut and helping his hometown club gain promotion to the top flight in 2000. In his first start for England, away in Malta, he scored an own goal and gave away two penalties (one of which he saved), in a performance which typified the wild, frantic, out-of-control nature of much of his career. Capable of the brilliant, he had been signed by Wenger, who was looking for a long-term successor to the ageing David Seaman; however, in his only season with the Gunners, the Suffolk-born custodian was less than convincing – after punching the ball into his own net against Charlton, he was at fault for Gus Poyet's late equaliser in the north London derby a fortnight later. As the season progressed, Wright dropped down the Highbury pecking order, with Wenger often opting to select youngster Stuart Taylor as Seaman's understudy.

As Phil McNulty explained, 'The alarm bells should have been ringing when Arsène Wenger soon realised he had made a mistake signing Wright and decided to move him on. Everton had been linked with a move for Estonia goalkeeper Mart Poom of Derby County that summer but, when nothing happened there, David Moyes decided to go for Wright. In his first year at Everton, although the club finished seventh, he was very inconsistent. He gave off no air of confidence at all and the supporters were always worried that something terrible was going to happen.'

It very often did. On his home debut against Spurs, Wright was at fault for both goals in a 2-2 draw. Then the following week, at Sunderland, he put in one of those frenetic performances that never seemed to be too far away. Having made a wonderful reflex save to deny Kevin Phillips, Wright then completely misjudged a harmless-looking crossed ball that sailed into the net before being incorrectly ruled out for offside. Further chaos was to follow when he gave away a penalty for ludicrously grappling with Niall Quinn, which he then superbly saved – diving athletically to his right to repel Phillips's fierce strike with a strong left hand before collecting the ball, almost in slow motion, on his goal line. In all the madness up on Wearside, Wright had injured himself, which resulted in Simonsen and then Gerrard coming in for two games each. In the 3-1 away defeat to Manchester City on the final day of August, Simonsen became the first Premier League goalkeeper to wear an outfield kit – sporting Everton's black third strip in the fixture as the club's sky-blue goalkeeper shirt clashed with their opponents' kit.

After returning to the side in late September, Wright enjoyed some excellent moments over the next three months. He made a crucial save from ex-Everton forward Nick Barmby in the Blues' first league win at Leeds in over 50 years and was part of a strong defensive unit that went five league games without conceding a goal that autumn. He also kept a clean sheet at Liverpool in a goalless draw just three days before Christmas and repeated the feat at home to Bolton Wanderers less than a week later as Everton finished the calendar year in fourth position.

In the new year, Wright and his team-mates found shutouts harder to come by (keeping just two in 18 games) and he was part of the Everton side that was humiliated at Gay Meadow by Kevin Ratcliffe's fourth-tier Shrewsbury Town in the FA Cup third round. Although a seventh-placed finish was a huge improvement on the relegation dogfights of the previous few seasons, there was to be final-day disappointment when Everton missed out on European qualification after a 2-1 defeat to Manchester United – with many questioning Wright's positioning for David Beckham's floated free kick.

Wright made 35 league appearances in the 2002/03 campaign, which was 25 more than he had managed at Arsenal the previous year. Indeed, after returning to the side after injury in September, he missed only one game until the end of the season – a 4-3 loss at Spurs, where **Espen Baardsen** endured a torrid afternoon against his old club. After Wright injured his knee in the pre-match warm-up, and with both Gerrard and Simonsen unavailable, Baardsen, signed on a short-term deal from Watford, was press-ganged into action at his old stomping ground. Unfortunately for Everton, the California-born Norwegian international looked unfit on a frustrating afternoon for the club. It proved to be the final game of his professional career. Bored with the life of a professional footballer, Baardsen retired at the age of 25. After a period of travelling, he entered the world of finance. 'I got bored of football,' he told *The Guardian*. 'Once you've played in the Premier League and been to the World Cup, you've seen it and done it. It was dictating what I could do and when. I wanted to travel the world. I had finished with Watford, been on loan at Everton and had just started at Sheffield United. I had been living out of hotels and suitcases for months. I felt unsatisfied intellectually.'

It would not be long before Evertonians became dissatisfied and infuriated by the actions of their first-choice goalkeeper. Having performed adequately overall – at times both erratically and brilliantly – in his maiden campaign at Goodison Park, Wright fell out of his parents' loft in the close season, damaging his shoulder in a freak accident. Further ridiculous incidents, on as well as off the pitch, would follow over the next three years, including him tripping over a 'Not In Use' sign placed in one of the goalmouths ahead of an FA Cup tie at Stamford Bridge in 2006, which resulted in another spell on the sidelines for the calamitous custodian.

By that point, David Moyes had long come to realise that Wright was not the answer to Everton's continuous goalkeeping problem. Thankfully, his next signing was. If Wright proved to be Moyes's costliest transfer error, then his next main goalkeeping purchase would arguably turn out to be his shrewdest piece of business.

It would take Everton over half a decade to find a goalkeeper capable of filling the void left by Neville Southall. Paradoxically, the man they eventually found to replace the Welshman was the same stopper they had inexplicably let slip through their grasp over seven years previously. During his three seasons at Goodison Park, Nigel Martyn's calming presence would prove to be invaluable at both ends of the Premier League table.

11

Nigel Martyn – One in a Million

There are very few men who can lay claim to being the greatest stopper of the Premier League era at two different clubs, let alone three, yet England international **Nigel Martyn** – Britain's first million-pound goalkeeper – is certainly in the running for that title at all three of the clubs at which he played top-flight football. Despite making fewer than 100 starts for Everton, and joining the club in the twilight of his career, the likeable Cornishman made a significant impact during his three-year spell on Merseyside at both ends of the Premier League table, which resulted in manager David Moyes describing him as his best signing for the Blues, and many Everton supporters describing him as the club's 'best since Neville Southall'.

Like Southall, Martyn entered professional football at a relatively late age. Having found employment in a plastics factory and for a coal merchant in his native Cornwall, the South Western League starlet's big break came in 1987, when Gordon Rowlands, the owner of a carpet shop in St Blazey, rang his friend Vi Harris – the Bristol Rovers tea lady – to tell her that the Third Division club should come and have a look at Martyn. After a two-day trial with the Pirates and impressing in a game against Gillingham the following weekend, Martyn was offered a 12-month contract – worth £10 a week more than what he was earning back in Cornwall. On capturing his new keeper, manager Gerry Francis told the *Bristol Evening Post*, 'The fact Nigel plays in Cornwall and has only been around a couple of seasons meant he had not yet come to the notice of many clubs. That would soon have changed had we not acted quickly. Nigel has an ideal build, and is very confident and agile. His handling of crosses is particularly impressive.'

With first-choice stopper Tim Carter sidelined through injury, Martyn went straight into the team at Twerton Park and made his debut in a 3-1 opening-day victory over Rotherham United, just days after celebrating his 21st birthday. Having been unable to dislodge Martyn, England youth international Carter submitted a written transfer request later that month and sealed a move to Sunderland before the year was out – as Martyn's fine early season form firmly established him as the club's number one. Over the next ten months, his mainly excellent performances resulted in Francis recommending him to the England under-21 boss Dave Sexton. After keeping a hugely impressive 12 clean sheets in the final 13 fixtures of his first campaign in the Football League, Martyn made his England under-21 debut against Switzerland in May 1988, coming on for Crystal Palace's Perry Suckling in a 1-1 draw. That summer, he was a key member of the squad that reached the last four of the Toulon tournament, starring in particular in the 1-0 victories over Morocco and the Soviet Union, which led to him being voted Goalkeeper of the Tournament.

Although Martyn's rise had been a meteoric one, there were, of course, some huge learning moments in his maiden campaign. After a dip in form in the autumn, he was taken out of the side for a short spell and then, against Wigan Athletic in February, Francis came out in defence of his goalkeeper after Martyn had been caught out by an inswinging corner from Paul Cook that sailed over him and into the far corner of the net. Francis told the *Western Daily Press*, 'It was an error of judgement by Nigel. He has done exceptionally well this season but people tend to forget that his background is in minor non-league football. He has a great future in the game and this goal was a pity.'

Following Martyn's heroics in Toulon, Francis again went public with his praise and told the *Bristol Evening Post* that he would resign if the club ever sold his goalkeeper for anything less than £1m – a price that had hitherto never been paid for a keeper by a British club. Just over 12 months later, First Division newcomers Crystal Palace met Francis's valuation, paying the seven-figure fee for a goalkeeper with only two seasons of Third Division football behind him.

Martyn arrived at Selhurst Park in November 1989, days after making his England B debut against Italy. He immediately replaced the unfortunate Perry Suckling – who had conceded five in the League Cup a fortnight earlier and been beaten nine times at Anfield in September – in the Palace starting XI. Unfazed by the hefty price tag, Martyn told the *Bristol Evening Post*, 'I am very excited about what has happened to me this early in my career and feel honoured to be the most expensive goalkeeper. But I don't think the pressure is on me as much as it is on the club. They are the ones who have valued me at that and have paid the money.'

Interestingly, the two managers involved in the deal had differing views on the fee paid. Crystal Palace boss Steve Coppell told the *Daily Mirror*, 'It is a lot of money to pay for a goalkeeper, but we had to do something. I am confident Nigel will become one of the top four goalkeepers in the country.' In contrast, Gerry Francis felt that Bristol Rovers had sold Martyn on the cheap. Speaking to the *Bristol Evening Post*, he said, 'If Nigel had stayed with us until the summer, we could have got £1.5m – and he would probably have gone to a bigger club. Nigel's valuation might start to drop with Palace because he will be playing behind a bad defence. At Rovers, everything was well organised in front of him.'

Although the bustling London lifestyle initially came as a bit of a shock to Martyn and his wife Amanda, with the couple reportedly struggling to settle in their new surroundings at first, on the pitch he quickly adapted to life as a First Division footballer and was instrumental in Palace's unbeaten run during December, when the Eagles defeated Manchester United and Charlton Athletic on the road and beat Norwich City and drew with Chelsea at Selhurst Park. At Old Trafford, in particular, Martyn was in wonderful form – making two lightning-quick reflex saves to his right from Russell Beardsmore and Brian McClair in a 2-1 victory. Five months later, he was in equally fine form in the dramatic 4-3 FA Cup semi-final victory over Liverpool at Villa Park, where he made several brave saves to help the Eagles exact revenge for their early season thrashing at Anfield and set up a final date with Manchester United. At Wembley, after drawing the initial game 3-3, Martyn and his team-mates were defeated 1-0 in the midweek replay, a game mainly remembered for the contrasting fortunes of their opponents' two goalkeepers, following Alex Ferguson's ruthless decision to select Les Sealey and axe Jim Leighton after several unconvincing displays by the Scotland international.

The following May, Martyn was back at Wembley and this time picked up a winners' medal after the Eagles' victory over Everton in the Full Members' Cup Final. With the game locked at 1-1, he made a vital save from Poland international Robert Warzycha to take the game to extra time. A goal from John Salako and a brace by Ian Wright in the additional 30 minutes handed Palace the silverware and rounded off an excellent season for the Eagles, who finished third in the First Division, having conceded just 41 league goals – 25 fewer than in the previous league campaign.

Martyn's club form had not gone unnoticed by England manager Graham Taylor and in April 1992 he gained his first full international cap after coming on as a substitute against the CIS (the Commonwealth of Independent States) in Moscow. That summer, he headed to Sweden after being named as Chris Woods's backup in England's European Championship squad.

After losing strike partners Ian Wright and Mark Bright in the space of a year, to Arsenal and Sheffield Wednesday respectively, Palace struggled to emulate their 1990/91 form and were relegated at the end of the inaugural Premier League season in May 1993. Despite returning to the top flight at the first time of asking, the club would yo-yo between the two divisions over the next few years, resulting in many of their key players, including Martyn, requesting transfers away from Selhurst Park. In Martyn's case, it was essential for his international career that he was playing regularly at an established Premier League club. Although Woods's England career had long come to an end by 1996, David Seaman, Tim Flowers and Ian Walker had all moved ahead of Martyn in the goalkeeping pecking order by then, resulting in the Cornishman missing out on a place in the squad for the European Championship held on home soil that summer.

Ahead of the 1996/97 season, Martyn completed a £2.25m move to Leeds United, but only after a bizarre set of events on

Merseyside resulted in him not signing for Everton that summer. According to manager Joe Royle, a deal had already been agreed between the two clubs, and Martyn had intimated to his agent Phil Graham that he wanted to sign for Everton ahead of the pair travelling up north to meet with Royle and complete the move to Merseyside. Unfortunately, Royle's wife Janet was taken ill on the morning of the proposed meeting and with chairman Peter Johnson also unavailable, it was left to club director Clifford Finch to finalise the signing.

In his autobiography, Royle re-told the story of when a panicked Finch left a voice message asking him to call him back straight away that day, 'I had a sense that something was amiss and that was borne out when I was told that Martyn had walked into the meeting and immediately announced that he wasn't going to sign that day because Howard Wilkinson, at Leeds United, wanted to speak to him. To the dismay of the chairman, Martyn drove to Elland Road without giving him any assurances, and despite Clifford Finch reminding him that his agent had given us every reason to believe that he was coming to sign on the dotted line. Phil Graham told Johnson that a fee had also been agreed between Leeds and Palace and that they wanted to talk terms with Leeds too. They did that all right – and signed for Leeds the following day. I had been powerless to intervene because of Janet's pressing medical condition, and to say I was angry with Phil Graham is an understatement.'

In a story that has since gone down in Everton folklore, a clearly flustered Finch unintentionally assisted Leeds with the signing of Martyn. In a 2005 interview with the *Daily Telegraph*, Martyn recalled how Finch had told him and his agent, 'If you're going to speak to Leeds, you probably need to get a move on, because you need to get back through the Mersey tunnel and pick up signs for the M62, because it does start getting busy around this time.'

It has since been claimed that Martyn reneged on the Everton deal after hearing that Neville Southall planned to stick around and fight for the first-team place, but he was keen to put the record straight on that score in a 2021 interview with the Everton fan website Royal Blue Mersey, 'It had been mooted I went to Leeds because I was frightened because Nev wanted to play another season, but I hold him in as high an esteem as any Evertonian. He was a hero of mine growing up, so I don't think there'd have been any problems in that department at all. But when I came across to Leeds, they made it really clear how desperate they were to get me. We just felt we were really wanted over there.'

Martyn endured a tough start to his time in West Yorkshire. After a heavy defeat at home to Manchester United in September, Howard Wilkinson was replaced by former Arsenal manager George Graham, whose success at Highbury had been built on making his teams difficult to score against. Although things would get worse before they got better at Elland Road – at the end of October, Leeds were just above the relegation zone and no team had conceded more goals in the Premier League – Graham's efficient methods began to bear fruit soon after. In the lead-up to Christmas, the Whites kept a club-record five successive clean sheets, including a shut-out in a drab encounter at Goodison Park, where Martyn was booed every time he touched the ball for choosing his new employers over Everton.

Less than a month later, he broke the hearts of his old supporters back at Selhurst Park, when he saved a last-minute penalty in the 2-2 FA Cup third-round draw – a feat he would achieve again the following December when denying Gary Speed from the spot in another goalless draw with Everton, which saw Thomas Myhre make his debut for the Blues. At the end of his second campaign at Elland Road, Martyn was voted into the PFA Premier League Team of the Year – an achievement that would be repeated at the end of the following two campaigns as Leeds began to challenge for the Champions League places and Martyn enjoyed the best spell of his career.

His form saw him make a much-deserved return to the international fold and, in May 1997, he made his first appearance for England in four years in the 2-1 friendly win over team-mate Lucas Radebe's South Africa at Old Trafford. The following season, he added three more caps to his tally before heading off to France as part of Glenn Hoddle's World Cup squad, providing backup to Arsenal's David Seaman. It was a role that Martyn would frequently take up over the next four years – making just one appearance in a finals competition for England, the 3-2 defeat to Romania in England's last group game of Euro 2000. Although many supporters, not just those of Leeds, believed that he should have been given more of an opportunity to wrestle the starting position away from Seaman, Martyn has always remained philosophical about his role as deputy on the international front. He told the City of Leeds YouTube channel, 'David Seaman always seemed to play well for England. At times, I was probably playing better at club level than he was, but when it came to England he always did well and the managers really liked him, which I totally respected. However much I wanted to get ahead of him, I never once thought that he shouldn't have been playing. It never stopped me from trying, of course, but I always understood what the hierarchy was.'

In March 2000, Martyn put in the performance of his career away at AS Roma in the fourth round of the UEFA Cup, making numerous incredible saves in what felt like, at times, a personal duel with Italian midfielder Francesco Totti. In typically modest fashion, Martyn, awarded a ten by the *Yorkshire Evening Post* for his display that evening, played down his performance, telling the newspaper, 'They were always going to put us under pressure. We managed to ride out our luck. They've got a lot of quality. They'll have to be watched in the return leg. It's a long way from being done. It might even be harder because they'll look to hit us on the break.'

European adventures would become the norm for Leeds, by that stage managed by David O'Leary, over the next few years – with Martyn singling out the 1-0 home victory over AC Milan in September 2000 in the first group stage of the Champions League as being one of the greatest atmospheres he ever played in. However, after sustaining a groin injury against Charlton Athletic less than a month later, he was replaced in the team by youngster Paul Robinson, who would enjoy his own special Champions League night under the lights at Elland Road, pulling off several terrific saves in the 1-1 draw with Barcelona that autumn.

Although Martyn returned as good as ever later that campaign and was an ever-present in the Premier League the following season, conceding just 37 goals in 38 games, his time as Leeds' first choice came to a sorry end after he asked for a few days' extra holiday following his return from the 2002 World Cup in South Korea and Japan. Incoming manager Terry Venables refused his request and installed the emerging Robinson as his new number one.

After spending a season sitting on the bench, having turned down a move to Chelsea as backup to Italian keeper Carlo Cudicini, Martyn finally made the move to Goodison Park, seven years later than originally planned – a transfer that did not sit well with former Toffee Peter Reid, who had replaced Venables in the Elland Road hot seat after a woeful campaign by the then cash-strapped club. In his autobiography, Reid stated, 'The financial pressure we were under meant that we couldn't keep two top-class keepers on the books. I thought Martyn was slightly better than Robinson, so wanted to retain him. David O'Leary was in charge of Aston Villa and he came in for Robinson, with a £3m fee being agreed, but personal terms proved an issue and the deal was in jeopardy. Knowing we needed to bring funds in if I was able to make any kind of impression in the transfer market, I suggested to [the chairman] Professor McKenzie that we should use £500,000 of the fee to make up the shortfall in Robinson's wages because we would still be banking £2.5m, but that idea was rejected. Nigel, who wanted first-team football, ended up joining Everton, where he did really well.'

The move came about when Everton goalkeeping coach Chris Woods contacted the Cornishman about signing, as Richard Wright was struggling with a persistent knee injury and looked likely to need an operation. Martyn told the club's official website in 2024, 'I came across and spoke to David Moyes and he backed that [Woods's statement] up completely by just saying that if Richard is out for quite a few weeks and you come in and do really well, then you'll force me to keep you in the team.'

In the first game following Martyn's arrival, Wright limped off in the draw with Newcastle, and a fortnight later Martyn kept his first league clean sheet for Everton, in the 4-0 demolition of former side Leeds United at Goodison Park. However, despite the goal glut that day, the Toffees struggled badly at the top end of the pitch throughout a difficult 2003/04 campaign, and their goalkeeper's performances in many tight games that season, including in five 0-0 draws, proved to be crucial in preserving the club's top-flight status.

In one of those goalless draws, at Liverpool in January, Martyn was in majestic form, pulling off fine reflex stops from Dietmar Hamann and Jamie Carragher, and twice denying Reds captain Steven Gerrard with acrobatic saves that belied his veteran years. After the game, he was keen to devote his maiden derby display to manager Moyes, who, in Martyn's words, 'had given me my footballing dignity back and given me a chance to carry on. I remember saying to the gaffer, "That performance is for you." That's what it felt like. It was nice to repay him with that.'

On his first return to Elland Road, in a real relegation six-pointer in April, Martyn was in equally brilliant form. Under the lights in West Yorkshire, the home side laid siege to Everton's goal either side of the break, but Martyn's wonderful one-handed stop from James Milner's curling effort and smart reflex saves to deny Mark Viduka and Alan Smith helped his side earn another point on the road and, more importantly, prevented his old club from narrowing the gap at the foot of the table.

Reflecting on his first season on Merseyside, Martyn told the Blues' official website, 'I hadn't played for over 12 months in the Premier League, so I think my form got better and better as the season went on. We ended up staying up and Leeds got relegated. I didn't necessarily want them to get relegated, but it kind of showed to me that if they'd have stuck with me then maybe it would have been the other way around.'

His tremendous performances that term saw him named Everton's player of the year and resulted in there being calls for him to be selected for England's Euro 2004 squad that summer, which Martyn shut down, stating how it would have been detrimental at his age not to have a break and referencing how exhausted he was after coming home from the World Cup two years previously.

Having just survived the drop the previous term, and about to lose their prodigious teenager Wayne Rooney to Manchester United following his sparkling displays for England in the Euros, Everton started the 2004/05 campaign as many pundits' favourites for the drop. A 4-1 opening-day loss at home to Arsenal did little to lift the gloom around Goodison Park and many supporters readied themselves for another exhausting relegation dogfight. Certainly, nobody saw the run the club would go on that autumn coming – with Moyes's well-organised side winning 12 of their next 18 matches, and Martyn keeping an impressive nine clean sheets during that run. According to Phil McNulty, he exuded confidence and brought some much-needed stability to the Everton backline, 'Martyn had this cool, calm Cornish demeanour and never became flustered. Quite simply, he had everything you want your goalkeeper to have – with his quality and calmness resulting in the people in front of him having no concerns. He had real presence and was different from all the others who had come into the side post-Southall. His team-mates completely trusted him as he was capable of great saves and didn't mess up when it came to making routine saves.'

Scotland international David Weir was a mainstay of the Everton backline during Martyn's time at Goodison. In his autobiography, *Extra Time*, Weir supported McNulty's high opinion of the custodian, 'He was an excellent keeper, probably the best I played with. He was a down-to-earth Cornishman and very genuine and normal. Not a flash footballer, but a consistent one who didn't do daft things. Nigel would make difficult saves look easy or his positioning would be such that he didn't have to make a difficult save.'

A fortnight before Christmas, Martyn was again in tremendous form in the 1-0 home derby victory that sent Everton soaring to second place in the Premier League table, but an injury away at Charlton over the festive period resulted in Martyn missing the next six games, including the 5-2 New Year's Day mauling at Spurs, where his presence was severely missed by the Everton backline.

After returning to the side for the 1-0 victory over Norwich City in February, Martyn saved his best performance of the season for a special evening at Goodison Park in April, when Duncan Ferguson's diving header and a goalkeeping masterclass secured all three points against Manchester United as Everton closed in on the most unlikely of Champions League qualification places.

Everton writer Lou Reed Foster, author of *Fear and Loathing at Goodison Park*, remembered the evening vividly, 'Everton's 1-0 win over Manchester United in April 2005 is best remembered as one of Duncan Ferguson's last great Goodison Park performances, and while the Big Man's totemic display grabbed the headlines, Nigel Martyn's individual brilliance in that game has always stood out in my mind. Despite being 38 years old, Martyn's consistent capacity for saving the practically unsavable prompted comparisons to Neville Southall and his performance against United was a standout display during his short time at the Blues. Saving a powerful effort early in the first half from a teenage Wayne Rooney – on only his second return to Goodison – Martyn was equal to every attempt on his goal, plucking a Cristiano Ronaldo drive out the air just before the break. However, the pick of the bunch was a point-blank save from a Paul Scholes effort early in the second half, with the United midfielder's attempt little match for Martyn's goalkeeping prowess.

'As the Blues went 1-0 up, United pressed for an equaliser and Ronaldo was once again denied by the Everton veteran with 20 minutes remaining, adding yet another to his collection of saves against an increasingly frustrated opposition. Easily one of the most electric Goodison Park atmospheres in living memory, Nigel Martyn's contribution to this classic encounter was outstanding, and it is easy to see why David Moyes believed him to be his best signing during his time as Everton manager. It's only a shame we didn't sign him ten years earlier.'

Champions League qualification was confirmed just over a fortnight later, with a 2-0 victory at home to Newcastle, when Martyn again pulled off several excellent saves, most notably from former Leeds team-mate James Milner, whose rasping drive was superbly tipped over the bar. Having almost single-handedly kept the Blues in the Premier League the previous season, the veteran stopper had been just as big a factor in Everton clinching a place in the qualifying stages of club football's elite cup competition.

For the final two games of 2004/05, Martyn was given a much-deserved rest. His calming presence was again hugely missed, with Everton conceding ten goals in those two matches

– including seven at Highbury on an embarrassing evening for the returning ex-Gunner Richard Wright.

Sadly, despite the optimism around Goodison Park ahead of the club's first adventure in the Champions League, Everton endured a miserable opening few months of 2005/06. By the end of October they sat bottom of the Premier League table and had exited the Champions League and then the UEFA Cup. The Champions League third qualifying-round draw had been extremely unkind, pairing Everton with eventual semi-finalists Villarreal – a tie Martyn later admitted that the players were a little 'undercooked for' as the first leg had taken place in early August, four days before the start of the Premier League season.

After aggravating an old groin injury against Blackburn Rovers in early December, Martyn had to be replaced by Richard Wright at half-time at Ewood Park, and then missed the next three games in the build-up to the busy festive period. Far worse news regarding the Cornishman was to come Everton supporters' way just a month after his return to the team, when it was decided that an operation for a long-term ankle injury could not be put off any longer, bringing an abrupt end to his season and, sadly, resulting in Martyn calling time on his outstanding career. It was later revealed that the operation should have taken place far earlier in the season, but, with Everton struggling at the wrong end of the table, Moyes needed his goalkeeper to play through the pain barrier for as long as he possibly could that winter.

Martyn told the Royal Blue Mersey website, 'My ankle injury probably started in November. Playing those games in pain wasn't ideal; kicking the ball was extremely painful, as you can imagine. You'd want to say I wouldn't have done it if I'd have known, but we were in such deep shit. The threat of relegation was hanging over us and as a player, you want to be involved and play in those games. The manager just said "Can you play this one?" and "Can you play this one?" We won at Sunderland 1-0 and beat Arsenal at home 1-0, and he said, "Play the cup game on Saturday and then go and get your ankle sorted. Whatever it is, if it takes you a couple of months, we'll get you sorted and get you back in the team." It felt as though I was quite important to him. The season finished, and I've got my foot in a boot because I've just had an operation to mean I can carry on walking, and I'm walking around the pitch knowing I'm finished.'

Fittingly, Martyn's final appearance for Everton was his 100th in total for the club (he made 99 starts and one substitute appearance) and again finished with him being voted man of the match. Having made a series of outstanding saves in the FA Cup fourth-round tie with Chelsea, Martyn earned his side a replay following a 1-1 draw at Goodison Park.

When people talk about Nigel Martyn's time at Everton, the words 'calmness' and 'presence' often enter the conversations. The man who earned 23 England caps and was voted into Crystal Palace's Centenary XI in 2005 and Leeds United's greatest team in 2006, is, in the eyes of many Evertonians, right up there when it comes to the club's goalkeeping greats. According to David Prentice, 'Nigel Martyn is probably second only to Neville Southall in the post-West era. For consistency, he was unmatched. He had a huge presence and was always really calm. We nicked many games 1-0 while he was here, and it was often down to him keeping things tight at the back.'

With Martyn unavailable for the Stamford Bridge replay and Wright out of action after falling over a sign placed in the penalty area telling keepers not to warm up there, youngster **Iain Turner**, a £50,000 signing from Stirling Albion in 2003, made his Everton bow on a tough night in west London, when Everton exited the competition after a 4-1 loss to José Mourinho's expensively assembled side. Three days later, Turner made his Goodison debut but lasted less than ten minutes as he was sent off by referee Peter Walton for handling centre-half Alan Stubbs's headed back pass outside his box in the early exchanges of the 1-0 victory over Blackburn Rovers.

Following Turner's dismissal, David Moyes brought on teenage keeper **John Ruddy** for his only appearance in the first team – meaning the Toffees had used all four of their named goalkeepers across the two games with Blackburn that season. The former Cambridge United stopper made a big save from Sergio Peter's deflected long-range drive after the break to preserve a clean sheet and help Everton gain all three points inside an electric Goodison Park. Nonetheless, before the next game, away at Newcastle, Moyes felt as though he needed to go with a more experienced figure and drafted in ex-Liverpool custodian **Sander Westerveld** from Portsmouth on a short-term loan, after failing to secure a deal for Arsenal's Estonia international Mart Poom.

Ahead of the trip to St James' Park, Moyes told Sky Sports News, 'John Ruddy came on against Blackburn and did brilliantly well for us, but no matter whether we were going to play John or not we needed to get a keeper in just to sit on the bench. We thought, if that was the case, we might as well get one in who could go above John just now, someone with experience. There are not many goalkeepers sitting around who teams are just going to give you, so you have to try and get what you can and fortunately Sander has some experience and can hopefully help us in the months ahead.'

In an Everton career that lasted just two matches, both played away from Goodison Park, there is very little to comment on when it comes to Westerveld's time between the sticks for the blue half of the city. Indeed, as David Prentice stated, 'Undoubtedly, Sander Westerveld is remembered more by Evertonians for his performances against the Blues in Merseyside derbies than he is for anything he did for the club. In the "Kevin Campbell derby" at Anfield in 1999, he had a stand-up scrap with Franny Jeffers that resulted in both players receiving their marching orders, and then at Goodison in the return game in April he most certainly got away with one when he smashed a free kick against the back of Don Hutchison and the ball rolled into the net at the Gwladys Street End, only for referee Graham Poll to ridiculously disallow the goal on the grounds he'd already blown for full time.'

Having returned to the side in early March and enjoyed an eight-game run, Richard Wright again pulled up injured, away at Middlesbrough in Everton's penultimate match of the season. Iain Turner came off the bench and kept a clean sheet in a game that Everton won thanks to a last-minute strike from James McFadden. Turner also played in the final game of the season – an emotional 2-2 draw with West Bromwich Albion at Goodison Park, when the retiring Duncan Ferguson fired home at the second attempt in stoppage time, having had his spot kick saved by Poland stopper Tomasz Kuszczak, who enjoyed an inspired afternoon on Merseyside.

Although Turner remained on Everton's books until 2011, the Scotland B international made just two more appearances, both in the 2006/07 campaign. Alas, in his final game, his unfortunate fumble of a routine catch of a corner sparked a second-half Manchester United comeback, with John O'Shea poking the ball home from six yards to score the first of the visitors' four goals having been 2-0 down that day. In total, Turner played six times for Everton and had eight loan spells away from Goodison Park before exiting permanently for Preston North End. Incredibly, John Ruddy had even more loans (nine in total) before signing permanently for Norwich City in 2010. Ruddy's excellent form at Carrow Road was rewarded with full international honours – he received an England cap in 2012 after coming on at half-time in the 2-1 friendly victory over Italy. After seven years in East Anglia, Ruddy moved to the Midlands, where he helped Wolverhampton Wanderers gain promotion to the Premier League in 2018, before moving to Birmingham City in 2022 and then Newcastle two years later.

On 8 June 2006, Nigel Martyn formally announced his retirement from professional football. He told the Blues' official website, 'I've loved every minute of my time at Everton and have a lot to be thankful for. I had a follow-up CT scan to see if the crack in the bone had healed but it clearly showed no healing. It means I will have to have another operation to pin the bones back together. It was a decision based on being able to live a normal sort of life afterwards – that was the primary concern because it is a nasty bone to have a problem in.'

Less than a month after Martyn's announcement, the club confirmed the season-long loan signing of Manchester United's USA international goalkeeper Tim Howard, who had fallen out of favour at Old Trafford. What would start as a temporary relationship of convenience for both parties would turn into an endearing love affair, with Howard falling head over heels at Goodison Park and publicly stating his affection for Everton on countless occasions, during and after his decade between the sticks on Merseyside.

12

Tim Howard –
The Secretary of Defence

'If Manchester United is the biggest football club in the world, then Everton without doubt is the greatest. Everton is one of the best things that ever happened to me in my life. I am so very proud to be an Evertonian and what that means and how much of the fabric of the club that I am. David Moyes is the greatest manager I ever played for. I stand before you today to tell you that if he asked me to run through the gates of hell seven days a week, I would smash through them every single day, because that's how great he was. He instilled in me leadership, accountability, responsibility. He taught me to be mature. I grew up into the person I always hoped I'd be playing for David Moyes.'

In May 2024, **Tim Howard** gave the above impassioned speech about how much Everton and the manager who brought him to the club mean to him. Eight years earlier, ahead of his final appearance at Goodison Park, he wrote the most emotional of goodbye letters to the Everton faithful, in which he laid bare just how much affection he had for several of the players he had shared a changing room with during his ten-year spell at the club, and told the fans how he would depart 'with love in my heart for the greatest of football clubs, the people's club, Everton FC'. It is fair to say that no goalkeeper in the club's history has ever been so overt about their feelings for Everton Football Club as New Brunswick's Timothy Matthew Howard.

Having made his international debut the previous year, Howard moved to England in 2003. On the recommendation of goalkeeping coach Tony Coton, Manchester United paid around £3m to MLS side New York MetroStars for Howard's services.

On his debut, he saved the decisive spot kick from Robert Pires in the penalty shoot-out victory over Arsenal at Wembley in the Community Shield, and ended his first season in England with an FA Cup winners' medal and a place in the Premier League Team of the Year. However, after a costly error against José Mourinho's FC Porto in the Champions League and several high-profile mistakes at the start of the 2004/05 season, he found himself 'playing goalkeeping musical chairs' with Roy Carroll throughout the whole of his second campaign at Old Trafford. Not convinced by either option, Sir Alex Ferguson signed Edwin van der Sar from Fulham for a reported fee of £2m in June 2005. After a year of playing second fiddle to the experienced Dutchman, Howard signed a season-long loan deal with Everton in the summer of 2006.

At Goodison, in only his second home game, Howard experienced his first Merseyside derby atmosphere and was outstanding in an emphatic 3-0 victory. His main takeaway from the game was the passion of the supporters, describing them in his autobiography, *The Keeper*, as 'roll-up-your-sleeve, blue-collar fighters who'd had to scrap for everything they had'. That season, he played 36 league games and conceded just 29 goals. Tellingly, in the two games he missed – against parent club Manchester United, which he was ineligible to play in – the team conceded seven goals. Howard had enjoyed an excellent first campaign on Merseyside and was desperate to make the move away from Manchester United a full time one. Although the transfer would not officially be made permanent until the close season, somewhat fittingly, considering the affection Howard has shown for the club over the last two decades, the deal was actually struck on Valentine's Day 2007.

He again posted excellent records at the end of the following campaign. In the 36 league games Howard played in during 2007/08, just 30 goals were conceded as Everton went on to finish fifth in the Premier League. In the winter, he began to develop an excellent understanding with summer signing Phil Jagielka. Along with Howard, the new centre-half would become one of Moyes's trusted lieutenants over the next six seasons and go on to skipper the side before leaving in 2019. After the 1-0 victory over Reading in February, when Jagielka scored the winner and made two vital blocks in front of his goalkeeper, Howard told the *Liverpool Echo*, 'When you have Jags back there, you know exactly what you are going to get from him, game in and game out. He just plays well all the time and he's been a big positive for us. We are delighted for him. He's a great guy. He works hard all the time and gets along with the boys. He never has a bad word to say, he never takes a day off and he is the type of guy who epitomises what an Everton player should be about. He's been fantastic.'

With Richard Wright having departed, John Ruddy out on loan and Iain Turner out of action after injuring his back during the pre-season tour of the US, Howard's understudy during the 2007/08 campaign was **Stefan Wessels**, who joined the club from Bundesliga outfit 1. FC Köln, having previously been backup to Oliver Kahn at Bayern Munich. Despite making only seven appearances for Everton, Wessels managed to play in all four competitions Everton were involved in during his sole season on Merseyside. After Howard sustained a nasty hand injury in September, he came into the side for the league games against Manchester United and Aston Villa, and the UEFA Cup first leg against Ukrainian outfit Metalist Kharkiv at Goodison Park and the League Cup tie at Sheffield Wednesday. At Hillsborough, the German kept Everton's first clean sheet of the season and went on to keep another shut-out in the following round against Luton Town in October. Wessels also played in the entertaining 3-2 victory over AZ Alkmaar on a freezing night in the Netherlands in the group stage of the UEFA Cup.

Perhaps a little unfairly, Wessels is probably best remembered for being in goal for Everton's embarrassing home defeat to Oldham Athletic in the third round of the FA Cup in January, when he was beaten from distance by Gary McDonald's looping shot at the Gwladys Street End. At the end of the season, he returned to Germany and signed for VfL Osnabrück. He later had spells in Switzerland with FC Basel and in Denmark with Odense, where he replaced Howard's old Manchester United rival Roy Carroll. Another goalkeeper who departed the club in the 2008 close season was teenager Jamie Jones, who went on to have an excellent career in the lower divisions, most notably with Leyton Orient and Wigan Athletic. Almost a decade after his Everton exit, the Kirkby-born keeper made the 2017/18 League One Team of the Year after an outstanding maiden campaign with the Latics.

In 2008/09, Howard was an ever-present as Everton again finished fifth in the league, keeping 17 clean sheets – at the time of writing, still a club Premier League record. The Blues also came very close to winning their first piece of silverware in 14 years, losing to Chelsea in the FA Cup Final having defeated Liverpool and Manchester United en route to the final. In the tricky third-round tie at League Two side Macclesfield Town, Howard made a vital save in stoppage time to secure the victory. He was again in fine form in the next round at Anfield, when Everton did enough to earn themselves a replay following a 1-1 draw. Ten days later, on a magical night under the lights at Goodison Park, Howard's clean sheet and Dan Gosling's extra-time winner secured a 1-0 victory. After Aston Villa and Middlesbrough were dispatched at Goodison Park in subsequent rounds, Howard's former employers awaited in the semi-final.

With neither side able to break the deadlock, the game went to penalties, which gave Howard the opportunity to show his former manager that he had been wrong, not only for letting him leave Old Trafford but also for not bringing him on ahead of Manchester United's FA Cup Final penalty shoot-out defeat to Arsenal in 2005 (despite Ferguson telling Howard to warm up and be ready to make the difference). Against his old club, he did not disappoint – making saves from Dimitar Berbatov and Rio Ferdinand to clinch his side's place in the final.

In his autobiography, Howard told the story of how he broke down in tears after that game, 'I tossed my towel over my head to wipe the sweat from my face. But instead of removing the towel, I left it there. I sat for a moment in the dark, amid all the cheers and whoops of my celebrating team-mates. And before I understood what was happening, I clutched the towel to my face and began sobbing. I didn't care that my team-mates could see my shoulders shake. Didn't worry if my cries could be heard over their sounds of laughter.'

In the same book, Howard made reference to how his penalty heroics had 'slain the dragon' that day, though it is unclear whether the 'dragon' he referred to was in fact Ferguson, who once told Howard he would send him straight back to the MLS if he did not think he was up to it, his own self-doubt following his negative Old Trafford experience, or his old coach Tony Coton, who Howard believed did very little to support him during his difficult spell at Manchester United and then blanked him once Edwin van der Sar arrived at the club. In *The Keeper*, Howard implied that Coton had blamed his dip in form on him having Tourette's syndrome – a neurodivergent condition that causes a person to make involuntary sounds and movements. Howard also recalled the time his coach coldly informed him that he had made the Premier League Team of the Year at the end of his first season at Old Trafford, 'He simply informed me I was getting the award, and then bizarrely he walked away. A few months earlier he had paraded me around and patted himself on the back for discovering me. Now it was like he was embarrassed that I would be representing Manchester United at the awards banquet.'

Unsurprisingly, in his own autobiography, *There to be Shot at*, Coton remembered the events differently. He dedicated a whole chapter to his one-time protégé, titled 'Tim Coward', showing just how much their relationship had broken down, 'I don't want to come across as bitter, but in my view Howard told a pack of lies in his book in an attempt to make me look like a complete idiot. If he wants someone to blame for failing at Manchester United then he should take a long, hard look in the mirror.'

At Everton, Howard found a manager and a goalkeeping coach who both completely trusted him, and, perhaps more importantly in the case of the latter, in whom he had complete trust. In their first meeting in 2006, David Moyes assured Howard that he would not be dropped after a couple of mistakes – that he in fact expected him to make a few errors and that he would become a better goalkeeper for doing so as he would learn from them. With goalkeeping coach Chris Woods, Howard built up an instant rapport. He said that the ex-England international 'let me be my own man from the start. He was taking me to the next level. Yet he was comfortable enough in his own skin that he didn't need to micromanage me.' It became a relationship that would work on both the domestic and international fronts, with Howard requesting Woods as his goalkeeping coach for the US national team in 2011.

Such is a goalkeeper's lot, though, it was not all plain sailing. In many quarters, Howard was blamed for allowing Frank Lampard's winner to beat him in the 2009 FA Cup Final defeat to Chelsea, with a great number of supporters and journalists believing he should have got stronger hands to the England midfielder's long-range strike in the second half. Nonetheless, with the full support of his manager and coach, Howard was once again an ever-present in the league throughout the next campaign. At home to Tottenham in December, he made a stunning last-minute penalty save from Jermain Defoe to earn the Blues a share of the points and the following weekend captained the team in Phil Neville's absence at Chelsea, becoming the first Everton goalkeeper since Neville Southall in the 1996/97 season to wear the armband. Indeed, the only game Howard missed in the whole of the 2009/10 campaign was the UEFA Europa League dead rubber against FC BATE Borisov, played in arctic conditions at Goodison Park in December, when the veteran **Carlo Nash**, who had signed from Wigan Athletic in September 2008, took his place between the posts for his one and only appearance in an Everton shirt.

Having dropped out of the academy system at Manchester United in his early teens, boyhood Evertonian Nash took the nomadic and circuitous route to top-flight football. After spells with non-league outfits Rossendale United and Clitheroe, the Bolton-born stopper joined Crystal Palace in May 1996, replacing Leeds United-bound Nigel Martyn ahead of the new season. Having starred in the Eagles' promotion campaign back to the Premier League and kept a clean sheet at Wembley in their play-off final victory over Sheffield United, Nash was surprisingly replaced in the first team by Kevin Miller ahead of the 1997/98 campaign. After a season of sitting on the bench, he returned to Lancashire in June 1998 and signed for Stockport County, where his fine form over the next three seasons brought him to the attention of Manchester City. Signed by Joe Royle, Nash spent two and a half years with the club and played in the 2002/03 derby draw with Manchester United – a game remembered by many for Roy Keane's infamous revenge tackle on Alf Inge Haaland – after an injury to Peter Schmeichel ruled the Dane out of the game against his former side.

In the close season, Nash moved on to Middlesbrough, but, in 2005, having failed to get any real opportunity at the Riverside, he again returned to the north-west, spending three seasons at Preston North End before moving to Wigan as backup to Mike Pollitt and Chris Kirkland. Having spent time on loan at Stoke City and having helped them gain promotion to the Premier League with some stunning performances towards the end of the 2007/08 campaign, Nash reported back for pre-season training at Wigan in the summer of 2008, much to the surprise of the Latics manager Steve Bruce, who had told him he had expected him to stay in the Potteries. Recalling the incident following his move to Everton, a bemused Nash told the *Liverpool Echo*, 'I felt like I was wasting my time at Wigan. Then Moyes's goalkeeping coach Chris Woods called. I knew Chris and he was someone I liked. He rang me and said, "This is the situation, you're going to come in. It's not going to be as number one but we need you to back Tim Howard up and if he gets injured we feel like you can do a job for us." I jumped at the chance. I wasn't getting any younger and it was the chance to play for someone I had supported as a kid. Everton had got me into football and goalkeeping!'

Despite making just the one appearance for his boyhood club, Nash enjoyed his two-year spell on Merseyside. In the same article, he poured scorn on the idea that understudy goalkeepers lack the drive and determination to succeed at the very top, 'I always wanted to play and I always believed I was good enough to play wherever I went. I think that motivation drove me on. It's not an easy position, being a number two, and it is a lot harder than being a number one in certain respects. You train harder, you work harder, you do more than the first-choice keeper does over a week and there's no carrot at the end of it. But I relished the chance and I kept myself fit. When I was at Everton, it was probably the fittest I've been throughout my career even though I was coming towards the end. I felt I was the fittest I've ever been because I had the facilities. I still think I could have gone on a bit longer!'

After leaving Everton in 2010, Nash signed for Stoke and acted as understudy to Thomas Sørensen and Asmir Begović. Three years later, he moved to Norwich and provided cover for ex-Blue John Ruddy. Following retirement, the nomadic custodian, who had received a free curry from his local balti house every time he had kept a clean sheet during his spell with Stockport in the late 90s, returned to the north-west and used his wealth of experience in his goalkeeping coaching roles at Oldham Athletic, Salford City, Port Vale and Accrington Stanley.

In South Africa in 2010, Tim Howard put in a man-of-the-match performance for his country in his first game at a World Cup finals. His saves against England, in the match made famous by Three Lions goalkeeper Robert Green letting Clint Dempsey's tame effort from distance roll through his legs, earned the USA an unexpected point. After a draw with Slovenia and a win over Algeria, Howard and his team-mates qualified for the last 16 of the competition, where defeat to Ghana ended any hopes of them progressing further.

Ján Mucha, signed from Legia Warsaw that summer to provide cover for Howard, also played in the 2010 World Cup, appearing in all four games as Slovakia progressed to the knockout stage of the competition.

On the opening day of the 2010/11 Premier League season, Howard was at fault for the only goal of the game in the away defeat to Blackburn. Having seemingly collected the ball just inside his box, he inexplicably dropped it at the feet of Nikola Kalinić after the softest of contacts from the Croatian forward, who then rolled the ball into the empty net. Nevertheless, in another ever-present league campaign, Howard showed incredible strength of character to bounce back, making several huge saves at big moments in games that season. At home to Manchester United in September, he somehow managed to turn Paul Scholes's deflected strike over the bar with his right foot, having initially dived to his left to keep out the former England ace's venomous effort. It turned out to be a huge turning point in the game as Everton went on to rescue a point with two goals in added time.

Then, in the space of ten days just before Christmas, Howard helped his side earn four points from a possible six, firstly by making a wonderful recovery sprawling save in a 2-1 victory over Manchester City at the Etihad Stadium and then by making himself as big as possible and sticking out a strong right hand to deny Ronnie Stam of Wigan in a goalless draw at Goodison Park. Undoubtedly, a huge feature of Howard's decade at Everton was his strength of character and ability to recover after high-profile errors and poor performances.

Almost exactly a year after his Ewood Park horror show, his redemption was complete when he saved a penalty from Blackburn's Junior Hoilett in Everton's first away game of the 2011/12 season, which they won thanks to an injury-time spot kick of their own, converted by midfielder Mikel Arteta in his final game before joining Arsenal. Just over a month later, Howard, who sported a khaki army-style camouflage strip throughout a fourth successive ever-present league campaign, became the first Everton goalkeeper since George Kitchen in 1902 to save a penalty in a Merseyside derby, when he brilliantly denied Dirk Kuyt at the Park End by diving low to his left to turn the Dutchman's shot behind for a corner.

At the Reebok Stadium in late November, Howard and his defenders were in defiant form, keeping only their second clean sheet of the season in the team's 2-0 victory. After the game, he told the club's official website, 'It's getting harder and harder to get clean sheets now. So many goals get scored in the Premier League and for whatever reason they're hard to come by. It's why you're so happy when you finally get one. There's so much going on in this league – we have some of the world's best players and one moment of hesitation in a game, one slip-up and bang, somebody will capitalise on it.'

Towards the end of the 2011/12 campaign, Howard made one of his greatest saves in an Everton shirt when denying Fulham forward Clint Dempsey, his international team-mate, whose deflected strike looked to have looped over him until he somehow managed to adjust his feet and arc himself backwards to tip the ball on to the bar. Nonetheless, Howard's standout moment that season had most definitely come three months earlier, when he scored from inside his own box with a near-100-yard strike on a ridiculously blustery evening at Goodison Park. Having received a back pass from defender Sylvain Distin, Howard sent the ball towards the Gwladys Street for fellow countryman Landon Donovan and Frenchman Louis Saha to challenge for with the Bolton backline. However, 30 yards from goal, the ball took a nasty bounce and looped over the head of the Bolton keeper, Ádám Bogdán. Mobbed by his team-mates, Howard celebrated in a muted fashion and was clearly embarrassed by the freakish nature of his goal. After the game, he told *The Guardian*, 'It was cruel. You saw the back fours and the keepers not being able to believe balls all night, and at the back one wrong step and it can be a nightmare. For our goal I was disappointed from a Goalkeepers' Union standpoint. You never want to see that happen. It's not nice, it's embarrassing, so I felt for Ádám but you have to move on from it.' Incidentally, Iain Turner scored a similar goal for Preston earlier that season, beating opposing keeper Stuart Nelson with a kick from his own area in the Lilywhites' 2-0 victory over Notts County.

In 2011/12, Everton reached the semi-finals of the FA Cup, losing 2-1 in heartbreaking fashion to Liverpool in the very last minute, having taken an early lead at Wembley through Croatian forward Nikica Jelavić. On the bench for every FA Cup game that campaign was Howard's veteran compatriot Marcus Hahnemann, who signed an eight-month deal in September 2011 after being released by Wolverhampton Wanderers. Five seasons prior to signing for Everton, Hahnemann had made the most saves in the Premier League (139), in Reading's first campaign in English football's top tier. During his lengthy career, the Seattle-born stopper was a regular understudy to Howard on the international front, including at the 2010 World Cup, and won nine international caps of his own between 1994 and 2011.

Following the humbling by Oldham in January 2008, David Moyes took the FA Cup far more seriously in subsequent seasons – playing his first-choice goalkeeper in every game in the competition thereafter. In February 2013, in Moyes's final season in the Goodison Park hot seat before taking over at Manchester United, Everton again faced the Latics. After drawing 2-2 at

Boundary Park, the Blues came out 3-1 winners in the fifth-round replay. However, at Goodison, Howard broke two bones in his back following a nasty landing, which ruled him out of the club's next three matches, including a quarter-final with Roberto Martínez's Wigan. It also brought an end to his incredible run of 210 successive league appearances – just two short of Neville Southall's record.

After seven League Cup appearances over three seasons, including one at Brentford, where he saved a penalty in the third-round loss in 2010, and 103 successive league matches warming the bench as an unused substitute, Ján Mucha finally made his Premier League bow, in the 3-1 victory over Reading at Goodison Park in March 2013. Alas, in his next game, he was beaten three times in four minutes in a disastrous first-half team performance that saw Everton exit the FA Cup to eventual winners Wigan. Seven days later, the mood inside Goodison was far brighter after goals by Jelavić and Leon Osman gave Everton a 2-0 victory over reigning champions Manchester City. On that day, in his tenth and final appearance for the club, Mucha was in fine form, making eight saves and taking the pressure off his defenders by coming out and clearing crosses with effective punches – something many Evertonians often cite as being Howard's biggest weakness throughout his decade at Goodison. Speaking to the club's official website, Mucha stated, 'That game is one of my best memories. I'd waited so long for these chances, so to then take on the best team in England at the time, beat them and secure a clean sheet … that was special.'

Following the expiry of his contract at the end of the season, Mucha signed for Russian side Krylia Sovetov Samara. After spells back in Slovakia and Poland, he had a brief stint in Scotland with Hamilton Academical before retiring in 2019. In total, the Slovakian stopper gained 46 caps for his country.

During Mucha's three-game run in the side, 18-year-old Mason Springthorpe, a £125,000 signing from Shrewsbury Town, sat on the bench, as he did for the 2-1 victory over Southampton midway through the 2013/14 campaign – which took place just three days after Howard had been sent off against bottom side Sunderland for bringing down midfielder Ki Sung-yueng after a mix-up with Leon Osman. The following month, Springthorpe was loaned to Woking. After being released at the end of the 2013/14 season, he joined several non-league clubs, including many back in his home county of Shropshire. Teenager Mateusz Taudul also left the club in 2014, having turned down the offer of a new contract. Speaking to the *Liverpool Echo* in 2020, the Polish-born keeper revealed, 'Everton offered me a six-month deal with an extension and they said that I would go on loan to the lower divisions. Then, in the summer of 2014, I came back to Poland and I met an agent who promised me mountains. I travelled to Everton and said, "I refuse to sign the contract." They looked at me like I was stupid. They kept saying, "Are you sure?" I said I was and came back to Poland.' Unfortunately for Taudul, the move back to his homeland did not work out as expected and over the next decade he would sign for no fewer than ten clubs across the Polish and Cypriot leagues.

Howard's Boxing Day dismissal was one of very few lowlights for him during an excellent first season under Roberto Martínez, whose footballing philosophy very much required both his defenders and keeper to be comfortable playing out from the back. Notwithstanding a couple of incidents – notably against Chelsea at home in September when he had to be rescued by midfielder Gareth Barry after getting his feet in a tangle – the American, working with new goalkeeping coach Iñaki Bergara following Woods's departure to Manchester United, adapted brilliantly to his new manager's demands. There were also some fabulous saves and 'old-school' goalkeeping performances served up by Howard that season. At Villa Park in the autumn, he made an unbelievable stop with his top hand to keep out Christian Benteke's powerful spot kick, and was influential in Everton collecting four points from successive away trips to Manchester United and Arsenal in December, making big saves in both matches as Martínez's stylish team closed in on an impressive ten-game unbeaten run in the lead-up to Christmas. In 37 league games that season, Howard kept 15 clean sheets, his best return since 2008/09, and was a key player in Everton's fifth-placed finish.

At the 2014 World Cup in Brazil, he became an internet sensation after setting a record for the number of saves (15) in a finals game, in the USA's 2-1 quarter-final loss to Belgium. In the days that followed, social media was filled with humorous memes about 'what Tim Howard could save'. Moreover, American fans petitioned for Reagan Airport to be renamed in his honour, and congratulatory calls from US President Barack Obama and secretary of defense Chuck Hagel came his way. For the rest of that summer, Howard appeared to be everywhere.

Sadly, though, in the eyes of many Evertonians, Howard's heroic performance that summer, and all the fame that followed it, sparked the beginning of the end of his time as a top-class Premier League goalkeeper. Despite putting in one of his finest performances at club level, when denying Kevin De Bruyne and his Wolfsburg team-mates with a range of superb stops in the group stage of the Europa League in September, numerous sloppy errors leading to goals were made by a keeper seemingly lacking focus in the early months of 2014/15. As the season progressed, his growing army of critics called for him to be dropped and for Joel Robles to be given a chance to stake his claim for the first-team spot. At Southampton, in a 3-0 defeat in December, Howard's relationship with the fans hit a real low. Having taken a simple catch, he stared angrily back at the section of away supporters who had ironically applauded him for not dropping the ball. After the game, Howard insisted there was no problem with the supporters, 'There will be no change. I love these fans and they are passionate. But I fight with my brother, too.'

In Everton's next fixture, though, a change was indeed required. For the second Boxing Day game in a row, Howard failed to see it out – limping off in the defeat to Stoke City with a calf injury, which would rule him out for the next six weeks. His absence resulted in Spaniard **Joel Robles**, an FA Cup winner with Martínez at Wigan Athletic in 2013, finally being given a run in the side. Although he kept clean sheets in each of his final three appearances during that eight-game spell – including at home to Liverpool in a derby-day stalemate – and stayed at the club for four more years, the Spanish under-21 international is mostly remembered by Evertonians for missing a spot kick (and failing to save any of West Ham's penalties) in the FA Cup third-round replay shoot-out defeat that January. On the bench that evening, and for every fixture during that period, was academy graduate Russell Griffiths, who later moved to Motherwell after spells on loan at five different clubs between 2015 and 2017.

In total, Robles made 65 appearances for Everton before leaving for Real Betis in 2018. Although he would go on to play two Europa League games for the Blues in the 2017/18 season, his final league appearance came against Burnley in April 2017, when he conceded a penalty after needlessly racing off his line and bringing down forward Sam Vokes. After a brief spell back in England with Leeds United, playing in the final four games of their 2022/23 relegation campaign, he joined the Saudi First Division club Al-Qadsiah that summer. The following year, he signed for the Portuguese outfit Estoril. According to BBC Sport's Phil McNulty, 'Joel Robles was an OK shot-stopper but never quite good enough to be the first-choice goalkeeper at a Premier League side' – an opinion shared by many Evertonians.

The final two seasons of Tim Howard's Everton career saw his performances fall well below the standards he had previously set. Though he had been guilty of making mistakes in the past, he had always managed to find a way to bounce back. However, other than the performance against Wolfsburg in the Europa League and a stupendous save against Southampton in April 2015 (mentioned in Chapter 15), there were very few highlights in his final 18 months on Merseyside. In contrast, more and more mistakes crept into his game, resulting in Howard coming in for some scathing criticism in the press and being mocked by many vociferous supporters, not only for his indecision when dealing with crosses but also for his unusual-looking 'star jump' technique when spreading his body in trying to make a block.

In January 2016, after Howard had given away a penalty in the home defeat to Swansea City, many Everton supporters got their wish, when the under-fire Martínez replaced him with Robles for all but two of Everton's remaining 19 games that campaign, including the FA Cup semi-final defeat to Manchester United. For two of those matches, Howard was absent from the squad altogether, with 19-year-old Jindřich Staněk, later to play at Euro 2024 for the Czech Republic, taking his place on the bench. However, after it was made public that Howard would be returning to his homeland and joining Colorado Rapids at the end of the season, the departing goalkeeper was re-instated between the Everton posts for the club's final two home games.

With his relationship repaired with the Goodison Park faithful, Howard was given the greatest of send-offs after his last appearance for the club – in which he kept a clean sheet in the 3-0 victory over Norwich. Afterwards, he was given a guard of honour by both sets of players as the crowd chanted 'USA! USA!' and waved United States flags. It was a fitting end for a goalkeeper who had fully embraced the spirit and ethos of the club throughout his decade on Merseyside.

While being interviewed on the pitch after the game, Howard struggled to hold back the tears, stating, 'Everton has helped to give me an identity in a positive way. In my heart, I hope I have become an Evertonian. It's what I want to be. I know the values of the club, I know the history and if I can be a small part of that fabric, then I've done a good job.'

In a 2016 article for *The Guardian*, journalist Tim Hill wrote an excellent summary of Howard's career in England. It feels fitting to finish the section of this book dedicated to the man who played a total of 414 games for Everton with Hill's words on his time on Merseyside, 'Tim Howard maybe epitomised Everton under Moyes and Martínez: admirable, competent and generally well-liked, but just short of the quality required to be considered truly elite. But we should give him his due. Along with Brad Friedel and Kasey Keller, Howard shaped the perception of US goalkeeping into something positive. USA might be deficient in other areas, but their keeping is solid, and Howard has much to do with that. Ten years in the upper reaches of the Premier League, including a spell of 210 consecutive appearances for his club; 106 caps and counting for the US national team – plus one famous wind-assisted goal against Bolton: that's not half bad.'

After leaving Colorado Rapids in 2019, Howard became Everton's first international ambassador in the United States as the club aimed to raise its profile in his motherland. He combined the role with his work for various sports media outlets, in the UK and overseas, in which he would often be found championing the causes of neurodivergent athletes and shining a light on their many struggles.

In the summer of 2016, Dutchman Ronald Koeman was installed as the new manager at Everton. One of the first players he brought to the club was compatriot **Maarten Stekelenburg**, who was signed from Fulham for a reported £850,000. The veteran stopper had acquired a vast amount of experience, having played in the 2010 World Cup and 2012 European Championship and in Serie A with Roma after moving to the Italian club from Ajax for £5m in 2011. Nonetheless, following his move to Fulham in 2013, the Dutchman's career had stalled somewhat – and after losing his first-team place to David Stockdale, he spent time on loan away from Craven Cottage at Monaco and Southampton.

Stekelenburg started the 2016/17 season ahead of Robles and in October enjoyed the best moment of his Everton career, superbly saving two penalties in the 1-1 draw at Manchester City, denying Sergio Agüero and Kevin De Bruyne, before making two more fine stops from the same players. A nasty leg injury sustained in the December derby resulted in a four-month spell out of the side but after Robles's error at home to Burnley, he returned to the starting XI for the final few games of the season. Koeman told the *Liverpool Echo*, 'We started the season with Maarten. We named him as the first goalkeeper and he did well. He got his injury. It took more time than expected and the team was on a good run. Joel showed really good performances but he dropped his level in the last few weeks and that was the reason to change.'

In the same article, Koeman was asked whether he was happy with his goalkeeping options, which also included Polish youngster Mateusz Hewelt, who sat on the first-team bench seven times during that campaign and won the Premier League 2 Division One title with David Unsworth's talented under-23 side. Koeman replied, 'They are questions for the end of the season. We need to make our mind up, to bring a strong squad in.'

That summer, with Iranian businessman Farhard Moshiri's millions at his disposal, Koeman splashed out massively in the transfer market. Most of the signings turned out to be disastrous purchases for the club, with long-lasting ramifications; however, the acquisition of Jordan Pickford from relegated Sunderland would prove to be one of the most important pieces of business in Everton's modern history. In Goodison Park's final few seasons as the home of the men's first team, Pickford's performances were nothing short of phenomenal and rightly brought about comparisons with those by Neville Southall at the peak of his powers.

13

The End of an Era – But the Grand Old Lady Lives on!

Having reportedly spent in excess of £125m during the summer of 2017, Everton went into the new campaign full of optimism, which appeared founded after Wayne Rooney, brought back to the club after a 13-year spell at Manchester United, netted in the two opening league fixtures – bagging the winner at home to Stoke City on his Goodison Park return and then scoring in a 1-1 draw with future champions Manchester City at the Etihad Stadium nine days later. In both matches, **Jordan Pickford**, signed from Sunderland for an initial payment of £25m, made important interventions – turning a last-minute effort from Stoke's Xherdan Shaqiri around the post with a leap to his left on his Goodison Park debut before saving well from Nicolás Otamendi, Raheem Sterling and Danilo in the away draw with Pep Guardiola's side. Three days later, Everton's new goalkeeper was again in fine form – superbly saving a penalty against Hajduk Split, in a game which saw another of the club's expensive new signings, Iceland international Gylfi Sigurðsson, score from 45 yards to help Ronald Koeman's team advance to the group stages of the Europa League.

In the early weeks of the 2017/18 season, everything seemed to be going to plan for the Dutchman and his backroom staff, which included brother Erwin and goalkeeping coach Patrick Lodewijks. However, not long after the game in Croatia, the wheels began to fall off. After winning just one of their next seven league matches and having made a disastrous start to the Europa League Group E campaign, Everton decided to part ways with their manager and his colleagues – their final game being the 5-2 home defeat to Arsenal in late October, which saw the team drop into the relegation zone and would have been a far heavier loss had it not been for their young goalkeeper's performance that day. Although the Blues were struggling badly, Pickford's fine displays had not gone unnoticed by England manager Gareth Southgate, who handed the 23-year-old his first full international cap on 10 November 2017, in a 0-0 draw with Germany at Wembley.

After saving a penalty in Everton's 4-0 home win over West Ham United in interim manager David Unsworth's final match of eight in charge, Pickford went on a remarkably consistent run of form – keeping clean sheets in four of the next six games that he played in under new manager Sam Allardyce, who, 21 months earlier, had handed him his Sunderland debut. Goalkeeping coach Alan Kelly, who, for a 15-match spell in the last ten weeks of 2017, worked with the first-team goalkeepers under Unsworth and Allardyce, fondly remembers some of Pickford's displays during that period, 'Jordan was on fire. Up at St James' Park, he made a series of brilliant saves in a 1-0 win over Newcastle, as he did at Goodison in the 0-0 draw with Chelsea two days before Christmas. In my last game of that particular spell, at The Hawthorns on Boxing Day, he somehow managed to switch hands mid-air and turn a wickedly dipping shot around the far post in another goalless draw. It was great to be working with him again, 18 months or so after last doing so at Preston. I also really enjoyed working with Joel Robles and Maarten Stekelenburg, the latter of whom went on to star for the Netherlands in Euro 2020. They were both great professionals and fantastic goalkeepers to work with on the training ground. Joel actually saved a penalty in his penultimate game for Everton, against Atalanta in the Europa League, that November. His last game for Everton was also in Europe, away to Limassol, when Ademola Lookman scored twice, and a load of the academy lads made their competitive debuts in a 3-0 win for the Toffees.'

In the new year, Martyn Margetson, Allardyce's regular goalkeeping coach, worked with the first-team goalkeepers for a period of five months before exiting Merseyside along with the manager and the rest of the first-team coaching squad after the final game of the 2017/18 campaign, when the team finished eighth but faced fierce criticism from their own supporters for

Allardyce's widely perceived negative style of play. Although Pickford had found clean sheets harder to come by in the second half of the campaign, his fine performances rightly led to him sweeping the board at the club's end-of-season awards evening. After winning the player of the year, young player of the year and players' player of the year trophies, he told the club's official website, 'I wasn't expecting to walk away with three awards tonight, so I'm delighted and honoured. It means a lot to be voted for awards by the fans and your team-mates. It's been an enjoyable first season for me at a massive club. I'm confident I can keep improving and we will continue to improve as a team.'

In Russia that summer, Pickford became the first England goalkeeper to win a penalty shoot-out at a World Cup, when a superb save to his right with his left hand denied Carlos Bacca in the last-16 tie against Colombia. Earlier in the game, he made possibly the save of the tournament when leaping to his left to fingertip Mateus Uribe's half-volleyed effort from distance away for a corner. Despite his heroics, very little praise came his way in the media, especially as Colombia ended up equalising from the resulting corner. Indeed, several pundits, who had criticised Pickford for not saving Adnan Januzaj's shot in England's group clash with Belgium earlier in the competition, believed that he should not have attempted to save Uribe's strike, as in their eyes it had been heading wide, even before his intervention. It most certainly had not been.

In the next round, against Sweden, Pickford put in an even more impressive display, making three fine saves from Marcus Berg, Viktor Claesson and Berg again late on to help England progress to the semi-finals, where they lost 2-1 to Croatia in extra time after taking an early lead through Kieran Trippier.

On his return to club duties, Pickford found a new man in charge at Goodison Park, with Marco Silva having replaced Allardyce. During Silva's 18-month tenure in charge, Pickford endured an extremely difficult and inconsistent period, which included two of his most uncomfortable moments in the Everton goal, and resulted in scathing criticism frequently coming his way. Firstly, at Anfield in December 2018, he conceded a tragi-comical injury-time winner in front of the Kop, when, seemingly concerned about giving away a corner deep into stoppage time, he tried to catch Virgil van Dijk's sliced effort, only to hit his arms on the crossbar and push the ball back into play for a simple headed finish for Belgian Divock Origi. Then, having played a starring role in the return goalless derby fixture on 3 March 2019, he appeared to lose his head the following week in a 3-2 defeat at Newcastle United, getting caught up in a load of nonsense with the barracking home supporters. Having given away, and then saved a penalty in the first half, Pickford was widely criticised for riling up the crowd and allowing the home team to get back into the game after goals from Richarlison and Dominic Calvert-Lewin had put Everton in a commanding position.

More criticism was soon to follow, when less than a month later he was reportedly involved in a street fracas outside a pub back in Sunderland – an incident which was investigated by Northumbria Police. Despite ending the season strongly (keeping six clean sheets in his last eight matches) and some more penalty heroics for England in the UEFA Nations League finals third-place play-off match against Switzerland that summer, when he saved and then scored from the spot, ramming his penalty high past opposing stopper Yann Sommer after saving splendidly from Josip Drmić, his detractors were once again out in force. In *The Times*, former Celtic and Republic of Ireland forward Tony Cascarino likened Pickford to a UFC fighter, 'When I watch Jordan Pickford, part of me feels like he should be a cage fighter in the Octagon. He is a hothead who makes a brilliant save now and again that gets him out of trouble. The Everton man is too intense.'

Midway through the 2019/20 campaign, Marco Silva was relieved of his managerial duties after a poor run of form culminated in a 5-2 loss at Liverpool, which dropped Everton into the relegation zone. Ahead of the club's next fixture, Duncan Ferguson was placed in temporary charge, and Alan Kelly reprised his role of first-team goalkeeping coach following the departure of Hugo Oliveira. For the previous 18 months, Kelly had worked with the club's younger goalkeepers and is very proud of the work he carried out in his role away from the first-team squad. Kelly explained, 'I had around 18 months with the under-23s from April 2018 onwards. It was a really enjoyable time, and I felt as though I was giving a lot back – passing on my goalkeeping experience of playing professional and international football for 20 years and coaching at the highest level for ten years to goalkeepers at the start of their careers. During that period, we handed the highly rated Joe Hilton his debut in the under-23s and also had the likes of Chris Renshaw, Nicholas Hansen and Mateusz Hewelt, who had sat on the first-team bench a few times in the 2016/17 and 2017/18 seasons, in and around that squad. João Virgínia joined us from Arsenal at the start of the 2018/19 season too – a season in which we won the Premier League 2 title and the Premier League Cup. It was a great group to be involved with. And though Hilton, Renshaw, Hansen and Hewelt had to move away from Everton to further their careers and continue their goalkeeping development – either in league football or slightly further down the pyramid – they can be very proud of their achievements at the club.'

Back with the first-team squad, Kelly was reunited with Pickford, whose understudies during the first half of the season had been Stekelenburg, who would return to the Netherlands and sign for Ajax in July 2020, and Denmark international Jonas Lössl, a free transfer in July 2019 from Huddersfield Town, for whom he had made 69 Premier League appearances over the previous two seasons. However, having been unable to oust Pickford from the first team at Goodison Park, he returned to the Terriers on loan in January 2020, in a bid to keep himself in the thoughts of Denmark manager Age Hareide's plans ahead of the 2020 European Championship. In February 2021, having failed to make a first-team appearance on Merseyside, Lössl left Everton permanently, returning to his homeland to re-sign for FC Midtjylland, for whom he had made his professional debut over a decade earlier.

Five points from matches against Chelsea, Manchester United and Arsenal under Ferguson's temporary stewardship in December 2019 had everyone connected with Everton feeling far better about the club's situation ahead of the festive period. The fanbase's mood was lifted further when Carlo Ancelotti agreed to take over the managerial reins ahead of the home clash with

Burnley on Boxing Day. Under Ancelotti, who kept Ferguson and Kelly on as part of his coaching staff, the team quickly allayed any relegation fears with several positive performances and results in the early months of the legendary Italian's tenure. However, Pickford's form during that period remained patchy, with his performance in the 3-1 home victory over Crystal Palace in the February in many ways a microcosm of his general form during that time – at the Gwladys Street End, he saved both bravely and brilliantly from Belgium forward Christian Benteke just moments after allowing a tame effort from the same player to slip inexplicably under his body.

In February 2020, after decades of speculation and a series of failed proposed moves away from Goodison Park, Everton received planning approval from Liverpool City Council for a magnificent £500m state-of-the-art stadium at Bramley-Moore Dock. Despite looking forward to an exciting new future on the banks of the River Mersey, Evertonians prepared themselves for an emotional long goodbye to the home they affectionately called the 'Grand Old Lady'.

A month later, all domestic football was suspended because of the coronavirus pandemic, and the decision was also made to suspend that summer's European Championship finals for 12 months. When the domestic game did return, in June 2020, all games had to be played inside empty stadia in an attempt to stop the virus from spreading. The first Premier League fixture for Everton behind closed doors was a drab goalless and soulless draw with Liverpool at Goodison Park. Football was back but not really as anyone knew it.

Although supporters were still forbidden from attending matches in 2020/21, Everton's next home derby, on 17 October 2020, proved to be a far more explosive affair. Unfortunately for Pickford, an incident early in the first half gave his detractors yet another stick to beat him with. Six minutes into the game, with eyes only for the ball, he came flying off his line feet first and clattered into the Liverpool captain Virgil van Dijk. The impact of the collision resulted in the Dutchman requiring surgery and spending ten months on the sidelines. Pickford, meanwhile, needed to hire a bodyguard after receiving death threats in the mail, aimed at himself and members of his young family. In the months that followed, in what seemed to be every Everton or Liverpool game televised during that period, reference was made to the undoubtedly reckless but in no way malicious challenge. On Sky Sports, an excess of loaded vocabulary was used in the post-match analysis: Liverpool midfielder Georginio Wijnaldum called the challenge 'extremely stupid' while Graeme Souness described Pickford's actions as 'an assault, not a tackle, an assault'. Moreover, although another former Liverpool player, defender Jamie Carragher, disagreed with Souness that there had been any intent in Pickford's actions, he too went in hard on the Everton man, 'He comes out and makes a crazy decision like he's been doing for the last 12 months and very unfortunately has left one of the top players in the Premier League in a bad way. I really believe Pickford will not be in a good place himself tonight and I hope he isn't in some ways.'

In what most definitely felt like a media witch hunt against Pickford, he would not be allowed to forget the incident in a hurry. Even respected journalist Jonathan Wilson, author of *The Outsider* – a 2013 book about the history of goalkeepers and goalkeeping – let himself down in *The Guardian* by referring to Pickford as 'a human Jägerbomb'. It all felt both extremely unnecessary and deeply personal.

Nonetheless, something needed to change. And it did. Over the remainder of the 2020/21 campaign, Pickford was managed expertly by Carlo Ancelotti and Alan Kelly. A fortnight after the Merseyside derby, he was replaced in the team by experienced Sweden international **Robin Olsen** for the game at Newcastle United – with Ancelotti's decision almost definitely influenced by what had gone on at St James' Park 18 months previously. In October 2020, Olsen joined Everton on a season-long loan from Roma, where two years earlier he had been seen as the ideal replacement for the Liverpool-bound Brazil stopper Alisson Becker. During his time on Merseyside, Olsen performed competently in seven league appearances for the club and played in both domestic cup competitions, including a 5-4 thriller with Tottenham Hotspur in the FA Cup fifth round, while Ancelotti firstly took Pickford out of the firing line and then gave him the opportunity to nurse a persistent rib injury that he had initially picked up after crashing into his goalpost in the home defeat to Newcastle (who else?!) and then aggravated when making a diving save against Burnley six weeks later.

During the 2020/21 season, the manager frequently came out in support of his under-fire goalkeeper, who made two excellent saves in Everton's 2-0 victory at Liverpool in February following his return to the team after a four-game spell out of the side. Ancelotti told *The Guardian*, 'He is a good guy. It is important that he has to show every day and every game the desire to improve. And he will improve. No doubt about this. He is really focused on training. He is a funny guy. In the last period he felt less pressure on him. I have a lot of confidence in Jordan and Olsen. Jordan is younger but he plays a lot of games in the Premier League. Olsen is more experienced, maybe with less individual quality, but I think Everton is in good hands.'

After another three-game spell on the sidelines, Pickford, having come off injured just before half-time in the loss to Burnley in March, returned for the final eight games of the season. Ahead of that summer's European Championship finals, Pickford looked in fine form, having worked extremely hard with Alan Kelly on the training ground and clearly benefitted from several sessions with a sports psychologist. In an interview for *The Telegraph* in the lead-up to the tournament, he explained, 'I just feel in a very good place. I began working with a psychologist earlier in the season. As you know, in football those little one or two per cent gains – just to raise your ability on the pitch and what you can achieve – are crucial. I have to think how lucky I am, all of the work my family have put in – from me being six, seven years old with my parents taking me to football all the time. The amount they have invested in me. It's about how I can keep that level of performance and look back to where I have come from. It's crucial and I feel that I have kicked on this year. I feel calmer, I feel in the moment and I feel great.'

After announcing his squad for the competition, Gareth Southgate told *The Telegraph*, 'I've got to say, Jordan has finished the season really strongly. Since he's come back from his injury, his focus and calmness in goal have really stood out. I'm really pleased with his form.' In England's seven matches that summer, Pickford was in outstanding form – conceding just two goals, keeping five clean sheets (the most in the competition), and saving two penalties in the final against Italy at Wembley as England went agonisingly close to winning the trophy. In the second group match, against Scotland, Pickford made a fine save from Stephen O'Donnell low to his right before making a fabulous block from Timo Werner and then tipping Kai Havertz's rasping shot over the bar in the last-16 victory over Germany. Indeed, even in the build-up to the Italians' equalising goal in the final, he made a terrific reflex save to turn Marco Verratti's close-range header on to the post before being beaten by Leonardo Bonucci's follow-up effort. Incidentally, in the Wales squad that summer was the former Everton youth-team stopper Adam Davies, who enjoyed spells at Barnsley, Stoke City and Sheffield United after leaving Merseyside in 2012.

At the end of the 2020/21 season, Carlo Ancelotti could not resist the lure of returning to Spanish giants Real Madrid, with whom he had won the Champions League, the Copa del Rey, the European Super Cup and the FIFA Club World Cup in 2014. Robin Olsen's time on Merseyside also came to an end that summer when Everton decided not to sign him on a permanent basis. During his brief spell at the club, Olsen and his young family were threatened by a machete-wielding masked gang, who marched the Swede around his home in Altrincham before stealing various items of jewellery and a luxury watch. Despite that terrifying experience, Olsen returned to England the following season, firstly signing for Sheffield United on loan before moving to Aston Villa as backup to Argentina's Emiliano Martínez.

With the highly rated young trio of João Virgínia, Zan-Luk Leban and Harry Tyrer, who had all sat on the first-team bench in the final months of 2020/21, deemed not ready to be regular members of the matchday squad, new manager Rafa Benítez decided to bring in experienced free agents **Asmir Begović** and Andy Lonergan as backup to Pickford for the new season. Bosnia international Begović, with 63 caps to his name and a wealth of experience of playing in the Premier League with Portsmouth,

Stoke City (for whom he scored a goal with a long clearance in 2013), Chelsea and Bournemouth, would go on to make seven appearances that term – playing three times in the league and twice each in the League Cup and FA Cup.

Towards the end of a tense Premier League fixture against Newcastle in March, which Everton won deep into added time thanks to an Alex Iwobi goal, Begović was joined in his goalmouth by Louis McKechnie, a climate change activist, who bizarrely cabled himself to the goalpost in protest against the use of fossil fuels. The 21-year-old, who had to be cut free with an enormous pair of bolt cutters, was later sentenced to six weeks in prison. On the day that McKechnie received his sentence, Begović took to Twitter to say how the activist's actions had 'scared the shit out of me!'. The Just Stop Oil protester's unorthodox antics mirrored those of Ryanair protester John Foley, who, ten years earlier, had handcuffed himself to the Park End goalpost during Everton's 1-0 victory over Manchester City.

Begović would make three further first-team appearances in the first half of 2022/23. In the last of those, on 8 November 2022, he captained the side against his former club Bournemouth, in the 4-1 League Cup third-round defeat at the Vitality Stadium, played just days before a six-week break from domestic football that had been put in place to accommodate the 2022 World Cup, held in Qatar that winter.

After departing Everton in the summer of 2023, Begović signed for Queens Park Rangers and was a huge factor in the Loftus Road club's successful fight against relegation from the Championship. Six months before leaving for London, he told the Blues' official website, 'Coming to Everton, one of the attractions was to work with Jordan and, obviously, to push Jordan. It's honestly been great to work with him and we've formed a great relationship because he's such a good guy. We've got a very healthy respect for each other and I'm a big fan of his and what he's doing right now because he's performing at such a high level. I think Jordan is one of the best goalkeepers in the world. What we have at Everton is a really great goalkeeper group. We push each other every day and that helps everyone. It's an important relationship – these groups are always very small, so being close is important.

I think the environment for him is very good and, naturally, that rubs off on your character.' Unable to stay away from the 'very special football club', a delighted Begović returned to Everton in August 2024, signing a one-year contract and reprising his role as Pickford's understudy.

In his three seasons as an Everton player, veteran keeper Andy Lonergan failed to make a first-team appearance. However, according to Alan Kelly, Lonergan's importance, along with that of the other goalkeepers in the group around that time, should not be undervalued. Kelly explained, 'Although he never played a first-team game for Everton, Andy Lonergan fulfilled a vital role for our goalkeeping group and that was why I recommended him. He maintained the high standards of performance that we expected from the group, in much the same way as Asmir Begović did. Their experience and what they brought to the goalkeeping group was a huge part of what we did on the training ground every single day. I have always trained all my goalkeepers to the same standard, as every single one of them has to be ready and prepared to play. You never know when someone is going to get injured or go down with illness. I think that if you are not the number one goalkeeper, then you want your goalkeeping coach to keep you motivated, fit and as involved in the matchday preparation as you would be if you were playing.

'As a goalkeeper, you have got to feel good about yourself and be thinking, "OK, I'm being prepared properly and being trained hard. I am getting the same amount of technical advice, tactical advice and the same number of repetitions in the drills as the number one goalkeeper here." I'd like to think all the goalkeepers I have worked with have recognised that and also the fact that I have always had an open-door policy. That has hopefully shone through with the goalkeeping groups that I built at Everton. In many ways, that comes down to who you recruit, what you recruit and why you recruit. Andy is a real diamond of a person, who, along with both João Virgínia and young Billy Crellin – a 2022 signing from Fleetwood Town – was part of an unseen engine room we had in the goalkeeping department at Finch Farm. They set excellent standards in training and always showed a willingness to help the team in any way they could.'

Nonetheless, the 2021/22, 2022/23 and 2023/24 campaigns mainly belonged to Jordan Pickford as he reached new levels with his performances and put all his personal troubles of the previous three years behind him to preserve Everton's top-flight status almost single-handedly and ensure that the Grand Old Lady saw out her final days as a Premier League stadium. Unsurprisingly, Everton's glovesman won the club's player of the year award at the end of each of those three seasons – three dramatic and traumatic campaigns for everyone involved with the club.

***

2021/22: The Great Escape

After starting the season in surprisingly fine form and taking 14 points from their first seven matches, Rafa Benítez's side badly began to lose their way in the autumn and, after just one victory and two draws in the club's next 14 league games, the former Liverpool manager, whose appointment had angered a large proportion of the Everton fanbase, was relieved of his duties in January 2022. Although the incoming Frank Lampard managed to unite a fractured fanbase with his positive outlook, there was very little improvement in terms of results in the first two months of his tenure, and, after a shocking defeat to Burnley at Turf Moor in early April, it appeared to everyone looking in from the outside as though Everton had given up and that the club's proud 69-year stint in the top flight of English football was about to come to a sorry end.

Enter Jordan Pickford and the power of the Goodison Park crowd. Against Manchester United, three days after the Burnley debacle, Pickford made a string of smart saves, including a reflex stop with his right arm to keep out Cristiano Ronaldo's stoppage-time effort, which went a long way to earning his side a hard-fought 1-0 win. In the next match, at home to Leicester, Pickford made a crucial save when diving forcefully to his right to repel James Maddison's powerful strike before Richarlison's late equaliser in a 1-1 draw. After defeat at Anfield four days later, Everton sat inside the bottom three with just six games of the league campaign remaining.

In the next two of those matches, which both resulted in Everton victories, Pickford was simply sensational. At home to

Chelsea, in a performance described by David Prentice as 'one of the greatest Everton goalkeeping displays', the England man made two stunning saves in the space of a minute, firstly denying César Azpilicueta before blocking Antonio Rüdiger's goal-bound effort with his face from the resulting corner. Having dived full-length to his right, only to see Mason Mount's arrowed shot strike both posts, Pickford scrambled across his goal line to make a ridiculously difficult save low to his right from Azpilicueta's angled drive. After quickly celebrating with the supporters sitting behind his goal in the Park End, he then showed tremendous speed and courage when spreading himself and blocking with his face Rüdiger's fierce hit from three yards out at the back post.

At the business end of the season, Everton and England's number one, who also saved superbly from international teammate Ruben Loftus-Cheek and then Mateo Kovačić deep into stoppage time, was quite literally putting his body on the line for his club. On referee Kevin Friend's full time whistle, Everton's indefatigable supporters, who had earlier filled the streets surrounding Goodison Park with thick blue smoke on the arrival of the team bus, raucously celebrated the 1-0 victory and began to believe that the Toffees could complete the unlikeliest of escapes from the jaws of relegation.

Speaking about the save from Azpilicueta in an interview with *The Guardian* at Finch Farm the following week, Pickford told the newspaper, 'Hopefully when we look back in five games, that has a bit of legacy. For me it's always nice to have that legacy of a save but I'm a team player, a club player and it's all about staying up. We have got five games, we need to focus on each individual game, but I will look back at the end of the season with a smile on my face and say that was a vital three points and a great save.'

Away to Leicester seven days later, Pickford was in equally exceptional form, saving terrifically from Nampalys Mendy – using his right hand when diving high to his left to claw away the Frenchman's curling effort – before making two even better saves from Harvey Barnes in a precious 2-1 victory.

In their penultimate game of the season, Everton secured their survival in dramatic fashion, coming from two goals down to beat Crystal Palace on a memorable evening at Goodison Park. At 2-1 down, Pickford made an important block from substitute Jean-Philippe Mateta before goals from Richarlison and Dominic Calvert-Lewin late on sent the old stadium into a state of bedlam. Speaking to Everton's official website after his goalkeeper had been awarded the club's player of the year award, Lampard paid credit to Pickford, 'Since we came in, there have been some outstanding performances and efforts from everyone, but the outstanding player has been Everton's number one and England's number one goalkeeper. Jordan has made some ridiculous saves in recent weeks. He is a great lad and this is fully deserved.'

On receiving the award, a delighted Pickford told the website, 'I have a brilliant relationship with our fans and receiving this award from them means a lot to me. They have been right behind me from the day I joined the club and I felt so proud when I walked out on the first day of this season to see the flag they'd created. I know it's been said a lot, but the way they supported us in the closing weeks of the season, when we really needed them, was absolutely incredible. Like most of the lads, I had never seen or experienced anything close to that level of support. I am so pleased I could play my own small part in keeping Everton in the Premier League and repay the fans in some way for everything they did.'

* * *

2022/23: The Great Escape Part II

During the summer of 2022, there had been lots of talk from Everton's players, management and wider staff of them ensuring supporters that the club would never find itself in such a traumatic position again. However, midway through the World Cup-interrupted campaign, Frank Lampard was sacked after failing to win any of his final ten matches in charge. Once more, Evertonians everywhere were about to be put through the wringer.

In regular skipper Séamus Coleman's absence, Pickford started the season as captain and continued his tremendous form from the previous campaign. Against Nottingham Forest in late August, he was credited with his first assist after his accurate long-range pass was latched on to by Demarai Gray at the

Gwladys Street End to salvage a point late on. Then, a fortnight later in the home derby, his seven saves and man-of-the-match performance earned Everton another point following a goalless draw. In doing so, Pickford badly injured his thigh and faced a spell on the sidelines just three months before the start of the World Cup in Qatar. He was forced to miss England's next two warm-up games for the competition – against Italy and Germany. Luckily for Everton, he missed only one club game during that period.

Against West Ham, Asmir Begović made his sole league appearance of the season and looked confident in a 1-0 victory over David Moyes's side. On the bench that day for the only time in his brief Everton career was Eldin Jakupović, the former Leicester and Hull veteran who had been signed on a short-term contract following injuries to Pickford and Andy Lonergan. Initially signed on a season-long deal, the Switzerland international was allowed to leave the club and join MLS side Los Angeles FC in January 2023, when Everton were back to their full complement of goalkeepers. A month earlier, out in Qatar, Pickford had enjoyed another excellent World Cup campaign – keeping three clean sheets in England's five matches before making a series of splendid saves in the 2-1 quarter-final defeat to France. Nonetheless, he would still face unfair criticism from members of the British press, who claimed he should have somehow saved Aurelien Tchouaméni's opening thunderbolt for Didier Deschamps's eventual runners-up.

On 30 January 2023, with Everton sitting second from bottom in the Premier League, former Burnley manager Sean Dyche replaced Lampard in the Goodison Park hot seat. Despite beating title contenders Arsenal in the new boss's opening game, the team found further victories hard to come by over the next few months and went into the final five matches of the season in 19th position in the table. Again, Everton would be indebted to their goalkeeper for saving their skin.

Just before half-time, away at relegation-threatened rivals Leicester, Pickford took the captain's armband after Coleman had been stretchered off following a nasty collision with Boubakary Soumaré. Deep into first-half stoppage time, with Everton 2-1 down, the Foxes were awarded a penalty after Michael Keane was adjudged to have handled a cross from Harvey Barnes. Facing England team-mate James Maddison from 12 yards, Pickford elected to stand tall and did wonderfully well to beat away the effort from Maddison, who had attempted to drive his spot kick down the middle, having banked on Pickford choosing a side to dive to. The save proved to be a massive turning point in the game and an even bigger moment in the season as a whole. After the break, Alex Iwobi grabbed a late equaliser, which kept Everton in touch with the rest of the pack and stopped their opponents from pulling themselves four points clear with only four games remaining.

Seven days later, in a ridiculously open match away at Roberto De Zerbi's free-scoring Brighton & Hove Albion, Pickford, once again captain in Coleman's absence, was in imperious form, making six incredible saves in the second half to deny Julio Enciso, Evan Ferguson and Alexis Mac Allister as Everton faced an onslaught but somehow ran out 5-1 winners. The impressive victory put them the right side of the dotted relegation line with three matches to play. However, after losing at home to Manchester City and then picking up only a point at Wolves – a point gained thanks to a fabulous spreading save by Pickford and an injury-time equaliser from Colombian Yerry Mina – Everton went into the final game of the season at home to Bournemouth knowing that anything other than a victory would more than likely not be enough to survive the drop to the Championship. Ahead of the latest showdown at Goodison Park, every supporter in the country knew that if Leicester were to beat West Ham, then only a win for Everton would keep the Toffees in the Premier League.

After going a goal down early on, the Foxes did all they could at the King Power Stadium – winning their game 2-1. At Goodison, just short of the hour, Abdoulaye Doucouré sent the old stadium into a frenzy when his arrowed strike beat Bournemouth keeper Mark Travers from the edge of the box and fired Everton into the lead. However, a second goal would not come and with everyone inside the ground knowing that Leicester were winning, the atmosphere became even more intolerable. One goal for the opposition inside the last 30 minutes would send Everton down. Unbearably, that final half-hour would be extended by a further ten minutes after a brave save by Pickford at the feet of Dominic Solanke resulted in him needing treatment for a hand injury. Then, with five minutes of the added ten remaining, he pulled off yet another season-saving stop, diving to his left to keep out Matías Viña's hammered volley from just outside the box at the Gwladys Street End. Thanks to their goalkeeper, Everton had yet again just about done enough.

When asked about his protégé's mindset before big games, Alan Kelly told me, 'He is really relaxed, really chilled. Jordan knows that all the preparation has been done, which obviously results in you feeling settled, calm and ready to perform. Forewarned is forearmed, which brings a clarity to what is required at any moment in the game. As we all saw late on in the Bournemouth game, he is ready in the moment to do whatever needs to be done.'

Three months before that final-day drama, Pickford had signed a contract extension at Everton, reportedly with no relegation clause inserted had things not gone to plan. On signing the new deal, he said the following about the club, its supporters and his desire to leave a legacy behind, 'It's massive to sign this new contract at such a special club for me. The support I've had from everyone at the club since I joined as a 23-year-old has been so important to my family and me. I'm happy here and so are my family. We love it at Everton. Everton is a massive club. The past few seasons have not been what we wanted but we now have a manager who I believe will point us in the right direction and get us up the table. It's definitely my aim to be successful at this club. The fans, the staff and my team-mates have been great with me from the moment I joined and I want to be great for them. I just want to keep working hard and performing for Everton. We know we are in a tough place at the moment in the league but I'm eager to help the team improve this season and then aim for success in the future, which will include playing in our new stadium. This contract will take me to more than ten years at Everton and I want to build a legacy here to put myself up there with the likes of Neville Southall to be one of the best keepers to have played for Everton.'

Nonetheless, things were about to become even more challenging.

* * *

2023/24: A ten-point deduction and yet another battle for survival

Three months into the new campaign, Everton were hit with an unprecedented ten-point deduction for breaking Profit and Sustainability Rules (PSR) in the three-year period to 2021/22, a punishment which dropped Dyche's side from 14th to 19th in the Premier League table and once again had the club fighting for its top-flight status. Although the deduction would be wiped out before Christmas – with Everton winning four games in a row in December and Pickford keeping clean sheets in all those victories – and ultimately reduced to eight points after the Blues were handed back four points and then docked a further two, a failure to win another league game until April meant Pickford and his team-mates went into the final month of the 2023/24 season embroiled in a third successive relegation battle. In the early months of the new year, a string of crucial saves earned Everton points in consecutive draws with Aston Villa, Fulham and Tottenham Hotspur. However, after Pickford shipped six goals in his 250th league appearance for the club at Chelsea on 15 April 2024, things once again looked bleak.

In the next three matches, Pickford was unbeatable and Everton collected all nine points as they pulled off yet another relegation escape. Against Nottingham Forest in a proverbial six-pointer, he made a save from forward Chris Wood to rival the one he had made from César Azpilicueta two years earlier in terms of difficulty and importance. Making himself as big as possible, Pickford spread himself magnificently to block Wood's close-range rocket with a strong right hand. In scenes similar to those after the save in the Chelsea game in 2022, he then celebrated with the supporters behind his goal – the only difference being that against Forest the ball was still in play – before seconds later nonchalantly catching a cross that had been whipped into his area. Three days later, in the home Merseyside derby, he pulled off important saves from Darwin Núñez, Luis Díaz and Mo Salah either side of goals from Jarrad Branthwaite and Dominic Calvert-Lewin in Everton's second 2-0 home victory in three days. Then, against Brentford, in the final game of the crucial three-match trilogy, he again spread himself brilliantly to smother the ball and deny Ivan Toney at the Park End before Idrissa Gana Gueye's goal won Everton the points and meant they could go into the final three games of the season knowing that their top-flight status had been secured.

Pickford, whose stoppage-time intervention at Bramall Lane to deny Sheffield United's Oli McBurnie twice in the space of a couple of seconds in early September, had won his side their first point of the season, had once again been the difference between the club staying up and going down. After keeping a clean sheet against the Blades in Everton's final home game of the campaign, he ended the season with an impressive 13 league shutouts (a record bettered only by Arsenal's David Raya) and was crowned as the Blues' player of the year for a third consecutive time.

***

Changes ahead

In the 2024 close season, Andy Lonergan left the club to join Wigan Athletic in a player-coach role, and Alan Kelly's time at Goodison Park also came to an end, after seven hugely influential years on Merseyside. Kelly had been away from the first-team squad throughout the first half of the 2023/24 campaign after undergoing a knee replacement operation. In August 2023, former Rotherham United goalkeeper Billy Mercer, Sean Dyche's goalkeeping coach during his time in charge of Burnley, had been brought in to cover Kelly and handed the responsibility of coaching the club's first-team goalkeepers. Kelly returned to coaching duties at the beginning of January 2024, reprising his 2018 role of working with the club's academy goalkeepers for the remainder of the season. During that period, he oversaw the rapid development of another Pickford – under-18 starlet George Pickford – and the highly rated under-16 stopper Dougie Lukjanciks.

Kelly's role in the development of Pickford as a man and also a goalkeeper cannot be overstated, and his and Lonergan's support shows what can be achieved in the game when players are surrounded by coaches and peers who believe in them and are willing to back them. During the 2024 European Championship finals, Lonergan told the club's official website, 'Jordan's standards every day are phenomenal. He's a great example for me to learn from, and to pass on to the keepers who I'm now working with. England's number one works to a top level every day, so that's what they have to aim for. There's a narrative around him, which is just lazy journalism and people jumping on a bandwagon. Ever since I was young, I've always felt that whoever was England number one was under mad pressure. Mentally, I don't know how it doesn't affect him. But it doesn't. He's so strong mentally. He knows what he can do, and he backs it up. He's quiet – everyone thinks he's something he's not – and he gets on with his work. The performances speak for themselves.'

After his heroics for England in Euro 2024, Pickford returned to Everton less than a fortnight before the start of the 2024/25 campaign – the club's last at Goodison Park ahead of the much-anticipated move to their new 52,888-capacity home at Bramley-Moore Dock. In the opening weeks he looked out of sorts – with a Euros hangover, combined with the fact that he had played just one pre-season friendly behind a weakened backline missing key defender Jarrad Branthwaite, almost certainly responsible for his indifferent form that August. At Spurs, in a 4-0 loss, he was robbed of the ball inside his penalty area by Son Heung-min and a week later he was part of an Everton side that inexcusably blew a two-goal lead at home to Bournemouth with just three minutes of normal time remaining. Moreover, against Aston Villa in their next outing, Pickford and his confidence-bereft team-mates lost by the same 3-2 scoreline, having again been two goals to the good.

In mid-September, Everton sat bottom of the Premier League table, with no points to their name and having conceded 13 goals in just four matches. Despite Pickford performing below the standards he had previously set, there had still been moments of brilliance from him in those catastrophic defeats. Before the error that led to Son's goal, he had expertly saved the South Korean's wickedly deflected effort, and in the Bournemouth collapse he had made several fine stops late on, when Andoni Iraola's side laid siege to the Everton goal in added time. Undoubtedly undercooked at the beginning of the campaign, Pickford would soon be back to his brilliant best. Unfortunately, the same could not be said of those in front of him. Everton were a mess and Goodison Park was going out with a whimper.

With João Virgínia firmly established as the club's number two goalkeeper and the experienced Asmir Begović back on the books, Everton allowed Billy Crellin to join Accrington Stanley on a season-long loan ahead of the summer transfer window closing. Prior to signing for Everton from Fleetwood Town in 2022, Crellin, a former England youth international, had spent time on loan at a trio of north-west clubs – FC United of Manchester, Chorley Town and Bolton Wanderers. His 2020 spell with Bolton proved to be an unhappy one. After scoring an own goal against Cambridge United and making several high-profile errors, the boyhood Evertonian was publicly criticised by manager Ian Evatt, who told the 20-year-old that he needed to 'man up' – a comment that resulted in Evatt receiving a huge online backlash from supporters, ex-players and professionals concerned about the mental health of the young goalkeeper. At Accrington, with the backing of his manager – the ex-Blues academy coach John Doolan – and the Stanley goalkeeping coach, the former Toffee Carlo Nash, Crellin enjoyed a more positive experience. Against Swindon Town in the FA Cup, his penalty-saving heroics, in normal time and the subsequent shoot-out, set up a third-round tie at Liverpool for the struggling League Two side. At Anfield, Crellin was beaten on four occasions by the Premier League leaders but made an impressive ten saves on a busy afternoon.

For a third successive season, 22-year-old Harry Tyrer also went out on loan – signing for Blackpool just days before the close of the summer transfer window. In the two previous campaigns, the Crosby-born stopper had enjoyed successful spells at Chester City and Chesterfield. Indeed, in 2023/24, Tyrer – another boyhood Blue – had played a crucial role in the Spireites reclaiming their status as a Football League side, making 42 appearances in their National League promotion season.

His time at Blackpool would prove to be eventful – with Steve Bruce taking over the managerial reins at Bloomfield Road just days after the young goalkeeper had signed. Bruce would then spend a brief period away from the club following the tragic, unexpected passing of his grandson that autumn. After a couple of unconvincing displays, Tyrer was taken out of the side in late October and replaced by veteran Richard O'Donnell, with assistant manager Steve Agnew telling the *Blackpool Gazette*, 'Harry has done well; he's made saves at crucial times for us in games, and he's a terrific young goalkeeper. It's always a big call because you don't change your goalkeeper very often. Harry has fitted in the dressing room well, but we've got Rich's experience, and we felt we needed that voice behind the back line.'

Despite putting in some excellent performances after returning to the side, and making a crucial penalty save against Harrogate Town in the EFL Trophy, Tyrer endured some more uncomfortable moments that winter. At Shrewsbury Town, he was caught out by a free kick taken from well inside the opponents' half on a blustery evening in December, before finding a greater consistency to his game in the new year. Without doubt, by going out on loan to numerous clubs early in their careers, Tyrer and Crellin, the latter of whom missed the final month of the season through injury, got to experience the exhilarating highs and devastating lows that inevitably come with a career between the posts. Over the coming years, it will be interesting to see how those experiences help to shape the careers of the highly rated pair – either at Everton or away from the club.

Portugal under-21 international **João Virgínia** also experienced a mixed bag of loan moves prior to establishing himself as Everton's second-choice goalkeeper in 2023/24. Having signed from Arsenal in August 2018, the Faro-born teenager was part of Everton under-23s' double-winning squad in 2018/19, keeping a clean sheet in the 1-0 Premier League Cup Final victory over Newcastle. In a bid to gain first-team experience, the youngster joined Reading in July 2019, initially on a season-long loan, but was quickly recalled after losing his place in the Royals' goal following three unconvincing appearances.

Berkshire-based journalist Jonathan Low told the *Liverpool Echo*, 'He looked very nervous, which was perhaps understandable as he had been thrust into the limelight. I don't think he filled the defenders with much confidence though. Three games says it all. It's a shame it never worked out; clearly he has time on his side and could turn into a brilliant keeper. But this move was too soon for him and it wasn't good for any party so it was best for all concerned he went back to Everton early.'

Having made appearances in the League Cup and FA Cup for Everton and replaced the injured Pickford midway through the Premier League home encounter with Burnley towards the end of Carlo Ancelotti's one full season in charge, Virgínia spent the next two seasons away from the club, at Sporting Lisbon in 2021/22 and Dutch outfit Cambuur in 2022/23. With Begović having departed for QPR, he was elevated to the position of first reserve ahead of the 2023/24 campaign. In the FA Cup third round against Crystal Palace that season, the Portuguese was in splendid form in the goalless draw at Selhurst Park and the 1-0 replay victory at home a fortnight later – looking far more confident and commanding than he had done in his previous appearances.

On 17 September 2024, Virgínia lined up in goal for Everton's final League Cup fixture at Goodison Park but was powerless to prevent the Blues from going out on penalties to Southampton following an extremely drab encounter, in which Sean Dyche's side had less than a third of the possession against their fellow Premier League strugglers. In her final season, the Grand Old Lady and her inhabitants deserved far better than the fare they were being served up. As indeed did Jordan Pickford.

Having recovered from his shaky start, or, in the words of Alan Kelly, 'found his zone', Pickford was nothing short of outstanding in the final three months of the calendar year – a period in which Everton kept clean sheets in seven of their 14 matches yet also failed to score in eight of them. In early October, he made a crucial penalty save from former team-mate Anthony Gordon at the Gwladys Street End to earn Everton a point against Newcastle, and five weeks later he pulled off a stunning last-minute save from West Ham's Danny Ings in another goalless stalemate. With Everton offering very little at the other end of the pitch, their goalkeeper's ability to pull off the miraculous was again proving to be vital.

In the week that followed his late heroics at the London Stadium, Pickford replicated his fine club form on the international stage. In Greece, against the same opponents he had looked on edge against at Wembley just a few weeks previously, the former Sunderland man put in his most complete England performance to date, with sound decision-making, confident dealing of crosses and strong distribution all on display, along with two terrific diving saves.

At the end of 2024, at the halfway stage of the Premier League season, Everton, with only one win in their last 12 matches, sat just two points above the relegation zone. Incredibly, considering such a wretched run of results, going into the Boxing Day round of fixtures, Pickford had kept more clean sheets than any other keeper in the top division. Had it not been for his brilliance in the December draws with Arsenal, Chelsea and Manchester City, there is no doubt that the Blues would have sat below the dotted line going into the new year. In all three matches, Pickford made a string of match-saving stops, with his blocks from Arsenal's Bukayo Saka, Chelsea's Nicolas Jackson and penalty save from Manchester City's Erling Haaland being particularly impressive. As one Everton fan rightly pointed out on X over the festive period, 'A lot of the time, it feels as though Jordan Pickford is taking on the opposition all by himself!' Among the frustrated Goodison Park faithful, that supporter was not alone in his thinking.

Nonetheless, during and also after two of those games, several high-profile names working in the media found the opportunity to criticise Pickford – clamouring for him to be sent off for a blocked save/tackle in the goalless draw with Chelsea (in doing so, regurgitating the Van Dijk incident criticism) and describing him as 'jumpy' literally seconds after he had kept out Haaland's penalty.

The tedious 'Pickford pile-on', led by occasional *Match of the Day* presenter Jason Mohammad, after the game with Chelsea was particularly disappointing, especially considering that former Premier League stopper Shay Given was also in the BBC studio that evening. The Irishman did little to defend Pickford against Mohammad's lazy accusations that he was rash, reckless and often guilty of making bad decisions. Furthermore, the day after a 1-0 defeat at Bournemouth on the first Saturday of 2025, in what seemed like another thinly veiled dig at Pickford, who had made half a dozen saves before being beaten by David Brooks's wonderfully executed volley late on, talkSPORT presenter Max Rushden jibed on his Sunday morning show *The Warm Up*, 'The highlights of Bournemouth's game with Everton mainly consisted of Jordan Pickford making lots of saves … and doing lots of shouting.' Rushden's co-host, Barry Glendenning, would further undermine the goalkeeper's performance by stating that none of the saves he had pulled off at the Vitality Stadium had been particularly difficult to make. And though Gary Lineker, the usual *Match of the Day* anchorman, had posed the question 'Does Jordan Pickford get the credit he deserves?' on the programme just four days after Mohammad's rant, Everton's star performer, in the eyes of many, still could not do right for doing wrong; despite his phenomenal form, it still felt, at times, as though Jordan Pickford was taking on the world.

There were, however, some goalkeeping experts willing to put their heads above the parapet and come out in support. When pushed for a comment on Pickford's goal-line antics prior to him facing Haaland's spot kick (he had been caught on camera pulling odd facial expressions before dropping quickly to his right), Joe Hart, a two-time Premier League winner with Manchester City and recipient of 75 England caps, had the following to say, 'We are used to seeing goalkeepers looking calm in the modern game. Jordan is doing things differently, but that's what gets him in the flow, what gets him in the best movement. He's made seven [Premier League] penalty saves for Everton and been their player of the year for the last three years. It's very positive goalkeeping and there's such consistency in his performances.'

On the *Inside the Game* podcast in late 2024, Alan Kelly was keen to address the widely perceived notion of his one-time mentee being guilty of unfairly berating the players in front of him, 'At times Jordan might look as though he is having a go at others but all he is doing is organising. He might be more animated than most, but all he is doing in those moments is making his defenders accountable for their jobs and getting across the game plan. You don't see many of them come back at him and say, "Do one!"

That's because Jordan hasn't got an ego. His actions come from care – caring about his performances, caring about doing things right and caring about the club.'

In an interview for the official matchday programme that winter, Pickford used the word 'passion' when describing his special relationship with the club and its supporters, 'I've been here for a long time now, and I know Evertonians – what they're like and what they're about. I give 100 per cent each game – that's what Evertonians demand of every player – and I'll always give that. The main word I'd use to describe the relationship is "passion". I feel like I'm very passionate and they're very passionate too. I just want to be at my best week in, week out, show my best and keep helping the team in every way possible.'

Another man who could claim to know what Evertonians were all about was returning manager David Moyes – he was given the task of keeping the Blues in the Premier League following the sacking of Sean Dyche by the club's new owners, the Friedkin Group, a privately held consortium of businesses and investments, led by Texan billionaire Dan Friedkin, in the second week of January 2025. Just hours after Dyche's dismissal, club stalwarts Séamus Coleman and Leighton Baines took temporary charge of the team for the home FA Cup third-round home tie with Peterborough United. In what turned out to be his final Everton appearance, João Virgínia kept a clean sheet as Everton ran out 2-0 winners. Five months later, he and Asmir Begović left following the expiry of their contracts. During their time on Merseyside, the two keepers provided excellent service to the club in their roles as understudies to Jordan Pickford.

Moyes's first four matches in charge yielded three victories – the same number that the team had managed in their previous 20. Pickford also returned two more clean sheets in that spell – taking his total to 80 league shut-outs for Everton, a remarkable number for a goalkeeper playing for a club that had been fighting to stay out of the relegation zone almost every season since his debut in August 2017. Incidentally, only Liverpool's Alisson Becker (92) and Manchester City's Ederson (115) kept more clean sheets during the same seven-and-a-half-year period. According to the official Premier League website, Pickford faced over 500 more shots on target than the two title-winning Brazilian keepers in that time – a staggering statistic highlighting just how ridiculously busy he had been.

On the first day of February, ahead of the 4-0 mauling of Leicester, a game in which Pickford was credited with his second Everton assist, after setting up Abdoulaye Doucouré to fire home Goodison Park's fastest-ever goal (recorded at 10.18 seconds), Moyes explained both the importance and power of a united Grand Old Lady in his programme notes, 'Last time we were here against Tottenham, people told me that for 45 minutes Goodison felt like a very different place from how it has been. We are not here for too much longer now and I think it's important that we all play our part in the next few months. Some weeks it will be enough, other weeks it may not be, but we will guarantee we will do everything we can to give this great stadium the send-off it deserves.' In the same notes, Moyes confirmed that former Preston goalkeeper David Lucas had been promoted from his role as head of academy goalkeeping to first-team goalkeeping coach for the remainder of the season.

Under Moyes, both the team and the supporters had regained their mojo, resulting in a far more positive atmosphere inside the old stadium on matchdays. With Everton offering a much greater threat going forward, the Goodison Park faithful, for the first time in a long time, began turning up to games believing that their team could score goals and retained that belief even very late on into matches. Never was that more evident than in Goodison's final Merseyside derby – the old ground's last game under the lights – later that month, when captain James Tarkowski's stunning volley deep into stoppage time at the Gwladys Street End rescued a point and sent the home fans into a state of ecstasy. The jubilant celebrations in the stands were matched on the pitch by many of the Everton players, including Pickford, who sprinted towards the Main Stand in preparation for the longest and most impressive of knee slides. Later that evening, Everton's passionate glovesman took to social media, posting the following message on his Instagram page, 'Insane end to a historic night. Goodison at its very best. Only Everton do it like this.'

He wasn't wrong.

After securing another excellent three points at Crystal Palace just three days later (and another important intervention by Pickford at 0-0, when he dropped quickly to his right and pulled out a strong hand to smother Jean-Philippe Mateta's powerful strike), the Blues could begin to look to the future. On Monday, 17 February 2025, Everton's under-18s took on their Wigan counterparts at the club's state-of-the-art new home at Bramley-Moore Dock, in a test event held ahead of its grand opening in August. Having started the 2-1 defeat, Adam Seve Patrick, aged just 15, holds the title of being the first Everton goalkeeper to play at the stadium, while second-half substitute Goodness Gospel-Eze became the first to keep a clean sheet there. In a second test event, trialist Abdulla Alhammadi – a former captain of the United Arab Emirates' under-18 team – also pulled on the gloves for the Blues at the stunning waterfront venue. Despite making a couple of smart saves and keeping a clean sheet in a 2-0 victory for Everton's under-21s against a Bolton Wanderers B team, Alhammadi failed to earn himself a permanent deal. His opportunity to play in the game had come about after 18-year-old George Pickford (no relation to Jordan) had been ruled out through injury. Youth international keepers Zan-Luk Leban and Fraser Barnsley also missed out on making an appearance, having received call-ups to the under-21 teams of Slovenia and Northern Ireland respectively that week. Along with Billy Crellin, Leban, who had spent the 2023/24 season on loan at National League North outfit Farsley Celtic, was deemed surplus to requirements when his contract expired later that spring.

Three months before the end of 2024/25, Jordan Pickford sat down with Tim Howard at Finch Farm for a remarkably candid interview. In the 30-minute programme, part of Sky Sports' *The Big Interview* series, the two keepers discussed the psychological side of the position, with Howard labelling mental strength 'the strongest trait a goalkeeper has to have' and Pickford emphasising the importance of being able to move on from an error quickly, 'What's happened has happened and there is no bringing that back; it is all about conquering the next moment, the next action. That's where I think I'm strong.'

Pickford also spoke openly about his previous struggles and past work with a sports psychologist, 'When my son Arlo was born [in 2019], it was the greatest moment in my life, but I wasn't in the best of form as suddenly everything changed, and it really affected my football. I needed to change the mentality side of things so started working with a psychologist. We went into things deeply and used vision boards to work out how I wanted to improve and who I wanted to be, but, in simple terms, I knew I needed to be a footballer at football and a family man at home, and not mix the two together. At first, I didn't think I needed a psychologist, but I speak openly about it now. It's made me a better person and a better goalkeeper. It's all about investing in your body and if I'm making myself better, then I'm making the team better.' Towards the end of the programme, in which Howard described Pickford as 'a world-class goalkeeper', the Everton and England number one highlighted his hopes for the future, including his desire to win silverware with the club and bring the 'feel-good factor' back to the blue half of Merseyside.

In March 2025, back-to-back clean sheets in new England manager Thomas Tuchel's first two games in charge took Pickford's international record to 37 shutouts in 75 internationals – sending him two clear of World Cup winner Gordon Banks, in terms of the number of England appearances made as well as international clean sheets kept. Indeed, at the time of writing, only Peter Shilton sits above Pickford in terms of England caps won by a custodian.

Having returned to club duties, Pickford and the rest of the Everton squad prepared themselves for just four more matches at Goodison Park. In the first of them, a 1-1 draw with former Blue Mikel Arteta's talented Arsenal side, Pickford was in terrific form, pulling off two flying saves in the second half to deny Leandro Trossard and Gabriel Martinelli. Frustratingly, though nobody knew it at the time, Trossard's strike would not have actually counted, as the Belgian was adjudged to have fouled defender Jarrad Branthwaite before unleashing a powerful volley, which Pickford did brilliantly to turn over his crossbar at full stretch. Referee Darren England's decision to award a free kick against Trossard most probably cost Pickford the Premier

League's Save of the Season award as it was a truly exceptional piece of goalkeeping.

In Everton's penultimate away game of 2024/25, Pickford, captaining the side in James Tarkowski's absence, was once again on top form as the Blues came from a goal behind at Craven Cottage to beat Marco Silva's Fulham 3-1. Having denied Harry Wilson with a fine diving save low to his left and then shovelled Ryan Sessegnon's powerful effort from inside the penalty area behind for a corner, he displayed phenomenal leg power early in the second half when leaping ridiculously high before using every millimetre of his body to make a fabulous fingertip save from Wilson. At full time, Pickford lapped up the applause coming his way from the travelling Toffees, who showed their appreciation for their goalkeeper by chanting their new 'Jordan Pickford is dynamite!' song at the tops of their voices in the west London sunshine.

On *Match of the Day* that evening, Gary Lineker described Everton's number one as 'a very consistent goalkeeper', with the full-stretch recovery save that denied Wilson also drawing praise from studio guest Shay Given, who had been hugely critical on the same programme less than five months earlier.

The following weekend, after staging close to 3,000 matches across all competitions, Goodison Park readied itself for one final men's first-team fixture. Before the game with Southampton, thousands of teary-eyed Evertonians lined the streets to greet the team bus for the last time in the city's L4 postcode. At full time, following an excellent 2-0 victory, numerous Blues legends, including Peter Reid, Andy Gray, Duncan Ferguson and Neville Southall, entered the Goodison arena one last time and took in the rapturous applause from the Gwladys Street, Main Stand, Bullens Road and Park End stands. It was a fitting way to mark the end of an era at the country's first purpose-built football stadium.

It was also fitting that Pickford kept a clean sheet (after making two outstanding saves in the second half) and finished Goodison's final game wearing the captain's armband, following yet another injury to the unlucky Séamus Coleman. As this chapter has shown, nobody did more than the Toffees' adopted

Mackem to preserve Everton's top-flight status in Goodison's final years as the home of the men's first team. As a result, it is fair to say that nobody has done more to ensure that the club can look forward to a much brighter future on the banks of the River Mersey – a future as a Premier League football club, free from the fears of administration that a lower-division club with an expensive new stadium to pay for but unable to attract investment would have almost certainly faced. As many fans have pointed out on various social media platforms over the last couple of seasons, Everton Football Club's breathtaking new home – officially named the Hill Dickinson Stadium – is very much 'the house that Jordan built'.

Postscript

Between September 1892 and May 2025, 76 'regular' goalkeepers and eight outfielders acting as emergency stoppers guarded the nets for the men's first team in competitive matches played at Goodison Park – bringing up a total of 84 Glovesmen of Goodison. As the opening chapters of this book have highlighted, there were also tens of goalkeepers who appeared in either pre-Football League or wartime fixtures – appearances not counted in official records – and many who turned out for the Blues at their other previous homes. There were also a handful of stoppers whose only appearances came in matches played away from home, and numerous goalkeepers on the club's books who never got to make a competitive first-team appearance.

Be it George Bargery – Everton's first-known custodian; John Angus, David Jardine, Tommy Fern, Ted Taylor, Ted Sagar, Gordon West or Neville Southall – the main guardians of the goal in the club's title-winning seasons; Bobby Mimms, Mike Stowell or Jason Kearton – three of the many keepers who played the role of understudy to Southall in the 1980s and 1990s; Mick Lyons – Everton's courageous centre-half, who once put on the gloves for the final few seconds of a game following injury to Southall; Jordan Pickford – Everton's saviour on countless occasions over the last decade; or any of the other names mentioned in this publication, each and every one of these men has, to a greater or lesser extent, played a part in the club's rich goalkeeping history.

As indeed have all the goalkeepers who have lined up between the uprights for Everton Women (previously known as Everton Ladies) over the last 30 years. Chapter 14 tells their incredible story – from the club taking over an erstwhile pub team in 1995 to them picking up the baton and becoming Goodison Park's new full time occupants from the start of the 2025/26 campaign. A further twist in an already truly absorbing narrative!

At the time of writing, it remains to be seen who will line up in goal for the men's team's first-ever competitive game at Bramley-Moore Dock. In July 2025, 26-year-old Republic of Ireland international Mark Travers joined Everton's new-look goalkeeping engine room from Bournemouth for a fee believed to be around £4m, with David Moyes telling BBC Sport that the club had been looking for 'a goalkeeper with a level of experience to support Jordan' following the departures of Asmir Begović and João Virgínia.

During his time on the south coast, Travers made 82 first-team appearances for the Cherries and picked up the club's player of the year award at the end of their 2021/22 promotion-winning season. Like Begović, Tim Howard and Iain Turner, he once scored with a kick from inside his own half – netting the winner for loan club Weymouth on his senior debut in 2017. The Maynooth-born stopper also went on loan to Swindon Town, Stoke City and Middlesbrough during his nine-year spell as a Bournemouth player.

It also remains to be seen which goalkeeper will start between the Goodison Park goalposts in Everton Women's first game at the Grand Old Lady as permanent residents. Although we don't yet know which men and women will go on to write their names in the next instalment of the Glovesmen of Everton Football Club series, I am pretty certain that, whoever those brave individuals end up being, they will provide the loyal Everton supporters with a new set of fabulous goalkeeping memories – in some ways very similar to, yet also extremely different from, the ones found in the final chapter of this book.

Ability, agility, bravery – both in the physical sense of the word and in terms of the courage required to stand alone, believe in your actions and hold your hands up when things don't go to plan – composure and craziness, the goalkeeping lexicon and skillset is vast and varied.

The number one position on the pitch has given us some of the club's greatest characters.

The Impossible Job – The highly rated Paul Gerrard found Big Nev's gloves too big to fill.

Tommy Boy! Norwegian Thomas Myhre's Everton career fell away after a promising start.

American stopper Tim Howard waves goodbye to Goodison Park after a decade on Merseyside.

Mr Consistent. Nigel Martyn's calmness proved invaluable at both ends of the Premier League table.

The goalie and the guru – A young Jordan Pickford with mentor Alan Kelly at Preston North End in 2015/16. Courtesy of Alan Kelly

Union – Kelly, Pickford and the rest of the Everton goalkeeping department take a break from training in 2022. Courtesy of Alan Kelly

'A modern-day Everton legend' – Jordan Pickford takes in the home applause after a fine showing against Liverpool in April 2024.

In the Grand Old Lady's final season as the home of Everton's men's team, the Gwladys Street displays its love for their mercurial keeper. *Courtesy of Lewis Guy*

Everton and England's Rachel Brown-Finnis with her mentor Mick Payne at the goalkeeper's induction into the National Football Museum's Hall of Fame in 2016. *Courtesy of Mick Payne*

Levelling up. Academy graduate Kirstie Levell – Everton's first full-time female professional goalkeeper.
Courtesy of Kirstie Levell

Court on camera – the outstanding Courtney Brosnan makes history by becoming the first Everton goalkeeper, male or female, to save three penalties in a penalty shoot-out. Courtesy of Everton Football Club

14

She's the One – A History of Everton Women's Goalkeepers

In 1995, chairman Peter Johnson brought the hugely successful Merseyside-based women's team Leasowe Pacific under the Everton banner. Having conquered the north-west throughout the previous decade, winning five consecutive league titles between 1988 and 1992 and proving their capabilities nationally in the FA Cup when losing 3-1 to Doncaster Belles in the 1988 FA Cup Final before going one better and beating Friends of Fulham 3-2 at Old Trafford the following year, the Wirral-based side were admitted to the National League in 1992. After gaining promotion from Division One North in their first season, they found themselves at the top table: the Women's Premier League. Goalkeeper **Gill Parkinson** recalled, 'Our first game in the top flight was against Wembley and I remember getting absolutely pelted in the first half. I had a really good game and managed to keep everything out before getting beaten after the break. I went on to make some more saves and then Louise Thomas equalised. At full time, we were all like "Wow!" The standard of opposition was so different and so much better than what we had come up against before.' After two seasons in the top flight, Leasowe Pacific were renamed Everton Ladies ahead of the 1995/96 campaign.

Although the connection with Everton didn't initially bring any financial rewards, it did provide an identity – a recognisable name, badge and playing kit – which resulted in the club being able to attract better players, even though the kit was only ever really on loan to the squad back then. According to forward Andrea McGrady, 'We still paid our own subs, and the cost of the minibuses was spread out between us. For me personally, as an Everton fan, it was everything I had ever wanted. From being six years old, I had dreamed of playing for the club. It was about wearing the kit, even though it was only on loan. On the Monday morning, we had to hand it back, all dirty and everything. And then we'd pick it up on the Friday evening ready for the weekend.'

In addition to there being access to Everton's training ground at Netherton and the club moving their matches from the Cuemasters Ground in Moreton to better facilities at Rossett Park, the home of Marine FC, another advantage of the merger was that, at Everton, there was a youth structure already in place, meaning there was a continuous flow of talent coming through the system and a pathway for all young players through to the seniors. Nonetheless, the team made an inauspicious start. Despite having been 3-0 up at home to Croydon, manager Billy Jackson's side went down 6-4 on the opening day of 1995/96 and then suffered bitter defeat a fortnight later when Maria Harper, formerly of Leasowe Pacific, scored the only goal in the inaugural women's Merseyside derby at Prenton Park. Bizarrely, because the camera crew had missed the only goal of the game, Harper and Parkinson had to re-enact it after the full time whistle, much to the disgust of the Everton keeper. Parkinson recalled, 'That was worse than losing. I had to go out there, let the ball in on purpose and pretend I was a rubbish goalkeeper!' It was a very slow start by the Blues, who had to wait until 8 October 1995 to record their first victory, a comprehensive 3-0 win over Millwall Lionesses. From then, they began to find a bit of rhythm, finishing the season in fourth position, behind Croydon, Doncaster Belles and Arsenal.

In the club's first two seasons, goalkeeping duties were mainly shared between the old Leasowe duo Gill Parkinson and **Dawn Parkes**, who had been voted the player of the tournament in a 78-team pre-season competition at Moss Farm, Cheshire, days before the start of the 1995/96 season. With Parkinson struggling with a knee injury that would ultimately curtail her Everton career, utility players **Tracie Johnson** and **Terrianne McGrath** also made appearances between the sticks during that period – indeed, Johnson was selected as goalkeeper for the Premier League Cup Final against Millwall Lionesses – before young prospect **Jo**

Fletcher signed for the club in the spring of 1997. By her own admission, Parkinson was 'past her best' by the time Leasowe Pacific's transition to Everton had taken place. Nonetheless, she has extremely fond memories of her time with the club, 'We were a real team – there was never any bitchiness or anger when we were left out of the side. Our manager Billy Jackson could make some odd decisions and you never knew if you were going to play, even the week after having a "worldie", but everybody just bought into it and backed each other up.'

When speaking about those early seasons, Andrea McGrady had nothing but positive comments to say about Everton Ladies' first stopper, 'Gill was a hugely imposing figure and a joy to play with. She was extremely brave and never stopped talking to her defenders. By contrast, Jo Fletcher was a very quiet girl, which was understandable considering her age and the changing-room environment she was entering.'

Fletcher has the distinction of playing for all three senior Merseyside clubs as a teenager. She was also the first Everton Ladies goalkeeper to play at Goodison Park, having played in the 3-1 defeat to Wembley there in April 1997. Born in Cheshire, she joined Everton as a highly rated 16-year-old from Tranmere Rovers in the spring of 1997 and began the 1997/98 campaign as the first choice. After drawing their first game with Arsenal, the team went on a ten-game winning run in the league, defeating the likes of Wembley, Arsenal and Liverpool (twice in a fortnight – including a 2-0 victory at Anfield) before the festive break. However, early in the new year, after the FA Cup exit to Liverpool and defeat to Croydon in the Women's Premier League Cup, Billy Jackson decided a change was needed in goal and **Annie Wright** replaced Fletcher in the side away at Millwall. Wright stayed in the team for the rest of the season and was outstanding on numerous occasions, including in their only league defeat that campaign, against Doncaster Belles, when she played on despite sustaining a deep cut above the eye. In the 'Girl Talk' section of Everton's official matchday programme that March, goalkeeping coach John Pickering stated, 'It's always a pleasure working with Annie as she always wants to listen and learn. It's no surprise that she has improved so much.'

In a cruel twist of fate, Wright broke her leg in the final game of the season away at Millwall, with Everton having already wrapped up the title seven days earlier. McGrady stated, 'There was a collision in our box and Annie ended up breaking her leg. Annie was another top keeper – very similar to Gill in terms of her bravery and communication with the team.'

On the final day of the men's 1997/98 campaign, Everton Ladies paraded their title at half-time at Goodison Park. It should have been one of the greatest days in lifelong Evertonian McGrady's life but with Howard Kendall's side in great danger of being relegated from the Premier League, it was an occasion that she could not really enjoy at the time. McGrady told me, 'I am coming out in a cold sweat just thinking about it now! Walking around Goodison and receiving my medal, it should have been a very, very special day. Even though it turned out all right in the end, thanks to Gareth Farrelly's brilliant goal, I was extremely tense all day. Nearly all the pubs in the area had closed on police advice [in case Everton had gone down] but one opened in Liverpool city centre for us and I was desperately in need of a drink when I got in there.'

At the end of the ladies' victorious season, Jo Fletcher, in search of first-team football, joined rivals Liverpool for a season before moving to the United States to study biology and play in the much-lauded US college soccer system. While out there, she played at the University of Kentucky in the Southeastern Conference for two years before moving to Oregon State University in the Pacific Coast Conference. Having returned to the north-west of England in 2002, Fletcher, by that point studying for a master's degree in sport and nutrition at the University of Chester, re-signed for Tranmere Rovers before moving to Doncaster Belles and then Birmingham City. In 2005 she made nine appearances for England, including two at the European Championship finals held on home soil that summer, but joined the British Army later that year, effectively bringing an end to her international career. At club level, Fletcher continued to provide sterling service well into her 40s, with Charlton Athletic, Lincoln and Watford all benefitting from her wealth of experience and expertise between the sticks. In 2017, she played against Everton Ladies at Goodison Park.

After Fletcher's departure and Wright's injury, **Andie Worrall** made the switch from Stockport County ahead of the 1998/99 campaign. Worrall, who had come through the Tameside Centre of Excellence – alongside future Manchester United right-back Michael Clegg – was already known to Billy Jackson after impressing for Stockport in a cup tie against Leasowe Pacific a few years earlier. According to Andrea McGrady, Worrall was the most talented goalkeeper she played with at Everton, 'Andie was another vocal keeper and had this incredible ability to spring for balls heading for the top corner. She was a very agile girl.'

By the time she arrived at Everton, the Ashton-under-Lyne-born goalkeeper was a regular in the Wales international camps, having opted to represent the birthplace of one of her grandparents over England earlier that year. Worrall stated, 'After having a good game for Stockport against Barry Town, one of their players came over and asked me, quite on the off chance, whether I was Welsh. When I told her that my nanna had been born in Merthyr Tydfil, her head nearly fell off and it set the ball rolling for the Welsh FA to get in touch.'

Although Worrall spent time at an England training camp in April 1998, after Stockport had told the English FA that their Welsh contemporaries were sniffing around their highly rated keeper and recommended that they came and had a look at her, the promise of being outright number one was too big an invitation for the 21-year-old to turn down, 'I did one session with England and thought I was good until I saw [first-choice goalkeeper] Pauline Cope train! She was just another level. Then Wales basically told me that I would play every game, so my mind was made up. Looking back, though, I should have been patient and backed myself to play for England.'

Worrall's Wales experiences were far from ideal. On one occasion, the players were left stranded in Edinburgh and told to find their own way home, even though, according to Worrall, FA councillors travelling with the squad 'were flown home and treated like kings on the FA dime!' Furthermore, training kit was always at a premium. Worrall explained, 'They gave me one pair of socks for a five-day training camp and [men's international forward] John Hartson's massive old T-shirt with the sleeves cut off!' It was a similar story when it came to matchday kit: 'You were given your first shirt but then told you had to give everything else back. One day, the kit man had forgotten to bring the goalkeeper shirts so he headed off to JJB Sports and came back with the most horrendous tops you could find. No badge on them or anything. When he told me I could keep them, I told him he could stuff it!'

Although Everton failed to retain their title in 1998/99 and finished fourth in each of the three seasons she spent at the club, Worrall has fond memories of her time on Merseyside, 'I loved it at Everton. I was now playing at the highest level possible, with players I used to watch on Channel 4's women's football programme. As a kid, I loved watching Karen Burke play for Knowsley [who later became Liverpool Ladies] on television. All of a sudden, I was a team-mate of hers at Everton. I made my debut at Wembley in the inaugural AXA Challenge trophy against Arsenal and saved a penalty from Faye White in front of a massive crowd as we played directly before the men's Charity Shield game between Manchester United and Arsenal. We lost the game and weren't treated brilliantly – we couldn't get on the pitch before the match and were then told to get straight off it afterwards – but to play at Wembley was some experience, even if loads of people only really viewed it as some kind of exhibition game. It was easily the most beautiful playing surface I got to play on.'

In January 1999, backup keeper **Sarah Fabian** returned to the US, with the official club programme citing work commitments and visa requirements as the reasons behind her departure. The season ended with another cup final defeat to Arsenal as the Gunners ran out 3-1 winners at Prenton Park in the League Cup. Although Worrall accepts that Arsenal were a terrific side, she does believe that Everton should have won more during her three-year spell, 'We had a very talented team at Everton. Mo Marley was the best defender I ever played with and players like Louise Jackson and Becky Easton were superb. It was just difficult as Arsenal were a machine, but, having won the league the year before, we really should have kicked on with the players that we had in our squad. Keith Marley, Mo's husband, took over from Billy Jackson as coach not long after I joined, and the two of them really looked after us all.'

At Everton, Worrall received goalkeeper training for the first time in her career and enjoyed having access to Bellefield on Friday evenings during the season. However, conversations with her highlight the many difficulties female footballers experienced during that period, 'I remember travelling down to play Southampton and then going straight to work a 12-hour night shift at a petrol station on my return. Also, we only trained twice a week, on Tuesdays and Fridays, and the players would often go to training straight from working long hours – car-sharing and picking up team-mates from various service stations along the way. I hope people remember all of this and the sacrifices the forerunners to the 2022 England Lionesses made. Players around at that time – the likes of Marieanne Spacey and Jayne Ludlow – were incredible footballers but they didn't train all day every day like the players of today do. I remember bumping into Izzy Christiansen, who played for both Manchester City and Everton, on the train 18 months after she had gone full time and you could see how her physique had changed, through professional training and eating and drinking properly. She ended up being crowned PFA Player of the Year in 2016 and then won the treble, including the Champions League, after moving abroad to play with Lyon.'

Although Worrall continued to enjoy an excellent career for a further 17 years after leaving Everton in 2001, she believes that she 'was born 20 years too early' and that her style of play would have suited the modern game, 'I was always good with my feet and a sweeper keeper before Ederson made it fashionable. I look back on my career fondly. I loved it at Everton and I got to play for my team, Manchester City, for a considerable number of years. However, the more serious it got, the less I started to enjoy it, and, in all truthfulness, some of my favourite football memories are the ones where I played three-a-side with my mates at a barbecue. I was comfortable with both feet and could stun the ball around people with ease, but by the time I was in my 30s I had stopped doing things like that as we were all too scared to try stuff that might have resulted in us making mistakes. It just wasn't as enjoyable anymore. Also, City didn't treat the players who didn't go full time brilliantly. We were left out of WhatsApp groups and not told when meeting times got changed. It all felt a little childish, and it left a bitter taste, to be honest, but they clearly made their point that we were no longer required.'

After Worrall departed, **Carly Timmins**, who had been sent off against Tranmere in the Premier League Cup quarter-final defeat in February 2001, took over in goal for the 2001/02 season. In a goalless draw with Leeds United in Everton's fourth game of the new campaign, Timmins made a superb late save to deny Lucy Ward from the edge of the box to earn her side a much-deserved point. At the other end of the pitch was **Clare Farrow**, whose outstanding stops from Amanda Barr and Chantel Woodhead that day left such a lasting impression on the Everton management staff that they signed her the following year. However, despite an excellent performance by Farrow in a 3-1 victory over her old club in October 2002, the Blues decided another change in the goalkeeping department was required midway through the 2002/03 campaign. After several changes between the sticks over a short period of time, including outfielders Sara Whewell, Sara Bayman and Mo Marley donning the gloves in 2002, the club's next signing – already a seasoned international – would become a mainstay in the team.

In January 2003, 22-year-old England international **Rachel Brown** (now **Rachel Brown-Finnis**) signed for the club following her return to England after five years in the United States. A decade earlier, the Burnley-born stopper had attended ex-Arsenal keeper Bob Wilson's goalkeeping school in Hertfordshire and blown away the coaches with her passion for the position, desire to improve and willingness to mix it with the boys. Particularly impressed by both her attitude and ability was coach Mick Payne, a former Chelsea youth-team goalkeeper who went on to become head coach at the University of Alabama at Birmingham and then the England C goalkeeping coach for over two decades. Payne explained, 'Call it fate, luck or destiny, but Rachel ended up in my group. She might have been the first female goalkeeper I'd ever worked with, but right from the start I treated her the same as everybody else. I saw her first and foremost as a goalkeeper, not "a girl goalkeeper", and even at 12 years old, it was clear to see she was a naturally gifted technician with a drive and enthusiasm that was going to take her far in the game.'

After Brown attended the three-day residential course for a second time, she was put in touch with Liverpool secretary Sylvia Gore and subsequently invited for a trial at the club. Brown recalled, 'I remember there being only seven players there on my first day and me thinking, "We're going to need more than this!" Then a few weeks later, lots of Liverpool players returned from the 1995 World Cup wearing England tracksuits. I was amazed as I didn't even know there was an England team or World Cup at that point! It spurred me on even more knowing there was a national team.' Before joining Liverpool, Brown had only trained and played locally to Burnley, 'It was good practice playing for Accrington Stanley Ladies as I was only just a teenager and we weren't very good so I always had lots to do! Before that I hadn't played for any team as girls were banned from playing at secondary school. The only football I got was down at the "Big Recca" in Burnley when I joined in with goalkeeper sessions there.'

The step up in quality from Accrington to Liverpool was a real eye-opener for Brown, who, having just turned 15, was expecting to start the season as backup to experienced England international Tracey Davidson. However, that summer, Davidson unexpectedly retired from the game, leaving Brown as the only keeper left at the club. 'I had gone there really looking forward to learning lots from Tracey, but then she left and I was thrust into the first team. I made my debut at Anfield against the champions Arsenal, so it was a real baptism of fire. We got turned over 6-0 and I learned just how high the standard was. Kelly Smith was sensational up front for the Gunners that day.'

The season ended with an FA Cup Final appearance against Croydon, losing on penalties after a 1-1 draw, and GCSE exams in the same month, before Brown flew out to the States to meet up with old mentor Payne, 'May was a busy month! I played in the FA Cup Final, which went completely under the radar at school. My school never really discouraged my football but you couldn't say they were ever behind it. I remember my teachers saying that it wouldn't ever come to anything and that I would probably just keep getting injured. I sat my GCSEs days later and then the day after my final exam flew out to Alabama for the summer.' There, she assisted Payne on his goalkeeping camps and stayed with a host family, whose own daughter played football for Alabama Angels. After playing a couple of games for the Angels that summer, on her return to England, Brown received several letters offering her scholarships at US universities following the completion of her A levels. 'This was everything I wanted. I knew I wanted to go to university and knew I wanted to play football. In the UK that wasn't really an option, so two years later, in 1998, I went back out there.'

The only potential sticking point for Brown was the possibility of her international career being put in jeopardy. However, her fears were allayed when the FA agreed to fly back the stopper, who had made her international debut at the age of 16 the previous year at Preston North End's Deepdale, for any future international games. Brown stated, 'The game at Preston was ideal for me as it was so close to home. I remember having lots of family at the match and coming off my line, smashing into forward Birgit Prinz, who was a massive name at the time, and beating her to a through ball. It felt fantastic! More call-ups followed over the next 18 months. By the time I went out to the US, I was an established squad member but it was still great to get that assurance from the FA about me coming home for England games.'

Having stayed in Alabama for two years, playing for Alabama Crimson Tide during her time in the Deep South, Brown transferred to Pittsburgh to study sports science in 2000, turning out for Pittsburgh Panthers and being named Goalkeeper of the Year in the Big East Conference League every season she played there, before returning to England in January 2003. Notwithstanding certain cultural issues (Brown experienced intolerable racism and religious hypocrisy during her time in Alabama), she has extremely fond memories of her time in the US, especially from a playing perspective, '*Forrest Gump* had not been out that long and I found myself living where it had all been filmed, spotting landmarks on a daily basis. It was brilliant. The daily goalkeeper work was absolutely fantastic too. At Liverpool, specialised keeper training was intermittent at best, so to be working on my position day in, day out felt very special, even though the heat at times was unbearable.'

However, despite the positive experiences, Brown knew she didn't want to settle in the States permanently. She explained, 'Whilst out there, I was diagnosed with epilepsy, which obviously brought a load of uncertainties, and was something I both wanted and needed to get on top of. Thinking further ahead, I knew I didn't want to build a life out in America. I couldn't see myself marrying, settling and bringing up a family out there. Also, I had seen how huge female soccer was in the States and wanted to make a difference back home. I wanted to be a female footballer who not only made it in England but also made a huge difference to how the female game was portrayed here. I went to the 1999 World Cup Final between USA and China as a fan and remember thinking, "Wow, these guys are supposed to be my peers, yet their experiences are completely different from the ones we as England internationals are having." They were playing in front of 90,000 supporters that day and were household names in their countries. On my return to England, Kelly Smith and I went to the FA telling them how unjust everything was, how things needed to change and how women's football needed to become far more visible in the UK.'

Playing a huge part in Brown's move to Everton was new manager Mo Marley, who had played with her for England for over half a decade and taken over managerial duties from husband Keith earlier in the season. Brown recalled, 'Mo knew I was thinking of coming home and so got in touch. She was a gifted coach and trying to build something special at Everton. It wasn't easy for her, though, as there was no capacity to offer full time training or financial incentives, so she really had to think outside the box to attract players. She put me in touch with Liverpool John Moores University, who granted me a scholarship for a teacher training course, which was a massive selling point for me.'

Having played the second half of the 2002/03 season for Everton and then gone out to Iceland to play for ÍBV during the summer season, Brown started 2003/04 in fine form before suffering a sickening cruciate injury, which curtailed her campaign and resulted in her having to defer from her PE teacher training course after just three months: 'It was a frustrating time as I had really enjoyed the summer on loan at ÍBV – learning new training methods and picking up bits of a new language – and started the new season well. Obviously, being out of action meant I couldn't continue with my course, so I ended up moving out of my digs in Liverpool and headed back home to Burnley.'

On reflection, Brown feels that she rushed her return from injury in 2004, 'Physios were thin on the ground. The club were great in the sense of getting the operation sorted on the NHS but there was a huge difference between how the male players were treated and how we were. I tore my cartilage just nine months later and scar tissue started to build up. By the time I was 27 [in 2007], my knees were wrecked. I remember a physio telling me that if I had been a professional male goalkeeper, who had enjoyed a similar career and had the financial security that such a career would have brought me, he would have told me to retire at that point. I didn't, though, and I am proud to say that I played in goal for Everton for ten years.'

Throughout that decade, there were numerous highlights as Everton began to close the gap on Arsenal and Brown established herself as the country's leading goalkeeper. After finishing 2004/05 in third spot, the Blues would end up as runners-up to Arsenal in the next five seasons. During that time, the number of goals conceded decreased massively, coming down from 36 and 24 in 2003/04 and 2004/05 respectively, to just 20, 15, 14, ten and 19 between 2005/06 and 2009/10. Considering the huge difference in terms of resources available to the two clubs, Brown is very proud of how she and her team-mates managed to run the Gunners close over a sustained period, 'They had a winning mentality and knew how to get the job done. Many of their players had been there a long time and were used to winning – loads of league titles and FA Cups. We ran them close and it really was neck and neck at times. But they could fly players in from all over the world and were training together five times a week. I was teaching all day at school, then going to my friend's for a bite to eat before training with Everton on a night, often until around 10.30pm, and then making use of the library to plan my teaching lessons for the next day. It was far from ideal and I was knackered a lot of the time. But we had a group of top girls in a similar position to me, and our desire and determination to succeed got us very close to winning the league on more than one occasion.'

In 2010, Everton finally did manage to get the better of the north London club and bring silverware back to Merseyside. Unsurprisingly, when asked for her favourite moment as an Everton player, Brown was very quick with her response, 'The FA Cup Final 3-2 win over Arsenal in 2010, without a doubt. We'd run them close so many times in the league without managing to beat them to the title, so this felt very, very special. We had actually beaten them two years earlier to lift the Premier League Cup, but this one meant so much more. Straight after the game, we went out celebrating in our Everton tracksuits. Nobody knew who we were or what we had just done but the camaraderie in the squad and the collective sense of achievement we all felt was tremendous. Mo had worked tirelessly to get us to that point and the team spirit she had fostered was our real strength during that period.'

European adventures were also a high point for Brown during that period. She revealed, 'Some of my best stories come from the European games. We never went to Paris or Munich. We played in countries like Serbia and Lithuania and were really close to the cultural bones of the places, staying in high-rises with bullet holes on the outside of the building. Nonetheless, we were super proud to be representing the club away from England. I remember coming across my old mate Birgit Prinz, from my England debut well over a decade earlier, and she smashed two goals past me for Frankfurt. But these were often professional players we were coming up against and we maximised everything we had. We did really well in our European campaigns.'

On the international stage, Brown played a huge part in helping England to qualify for the 2007 World Cup in China, beating France to the top spot by just three points, after both games between the teams finished as draws. According to Brown, her greatest performance came in the goalless draw with the French at Ewood Park, where she crashed her head on the post after tipping Marinette Pichon's powerful header on to the woodwork and then kept out the follow-up effort. In China, England won one and drew two of their three group games, advancing to the knockout stages after finishing as runners-up to Germany, with whom they had drawn 0-0 in Shanghai. In the quarter-finals, England were well beaten by the United States, but the experience of playing in front of a crowd of 30,000 supporters is one that will live long in Brown's memory, 'I loved it out in China and it took me back to 1999, when I had been a spectator out in the USA World Cup. The crowds were incredible and a far cry from what was happening at club level. Although the game was growing back home, we were still playing in front of very small crowds at Marine, which was a bit of a comedown and a bit depressing at times.'

A year before the World Cup in China, Brown started to combine training and playing with working for Everton in the Community on their education programmes. Her work with the charity is something that she is immensely proud of. She stated, 'Between 2006 and 2010, along with many of the other girls in the squad, I was able to use my teaching background to work on the different education programmes run by Everton in the Community. It was a really positive move for the women's team as I was a regular female face around the club, which meant that I could push for certain changes to be made. We started training at Finch Farm around that time, which was massive really. It was more coincidental than by design how I came to be in a position to push for change but once in place I certainly wanted to be a voice for the women's team.'

After four successful years on the programme, Brown relinquished the role in order to concentrate all her efforts on making the Team GB squad for the 2012 Olympics. Interestingly, despite being in the twilight of her career by that stage and not actually making an appearance at the Olympics, she regards the London 2012 experience as the highlight of her career, 'I grew up loving everything about the Olympics and was fortunate enough to be a ball girl in 1996 in Atlanta, where I told Everton forward Daniel Amokachi, who was out there playing for Nigeria, that I played for Everton, even though I was a Liverpool player at the time, so that he would give me his shirt! London was truly incredible – the whole of the UK seemed so up for sport that summer. I am so pleased it was quite literally 'a once-in-a-lifetime experience for me' as I have talked to some of the girls who played in the Tokyo Olympics in 2021, and they said it was all very disappointing.'

After suffering further niggling injuries, marrying golf caddie Ian Finnis in 2013 and enjoying a brief loan spell at old rivals Arsenal the following year, Brown-Finnis – as she became after her wedding – retired from football in 2014. She and the Gunners seem inextricably linked as when pushed to provide details of her greatest save, she recalled the time she pulled off a fabulous diving stop low to her left, just minutes after dislocating her finger and needing 'to get it popped back in'. Since hanging up the gloves, she has enjoyed a very successful career as a football pundit, often found giving refreshing goalkeeping insight into incidents involving last lines of defence. She told me that her goalkeeping background has helped her massively in her media work, 'Sometimes I have to remember to take the blinkers off and watch the game as a whole, not just from the viewpoint of a goalkeeper, but I like the pressure of being put on the spot and not letting my emotions get the better of me. Just like when I was a goalkeeper, it helps me to visualise being both an army major and a snake! It might sound odd, but the army major visualisation reminds me that I need to be assertive, clear and concise with what I am saying, just like I did when communicating instructions to my back four, whereas the slithering snake image reminds me that I have to remain calm and relaxed. It has always worked for me, as have other psychological techniques, for example wiping my forehead as a way of "wiping the slate clean", whenever I made an error as a keeper.'

Brown-Finnis has used her roles as a television pundit and newspaper columnist to champion several female keepers, including former Lioness Mary Earps, whose style of play is not too dissimilar to that of her own, 'Mary has done a lot better for herself out of it. She has won the Euros, saved a penalty in a World Cup Final and been voted World Goalkeeper of the Year, but I suppose you could say that we are quite similar goalkeepers! We are roughly the same height as each other and therefore would have maximised and focused on similar areas of our games.

Certainly, from my point of view, I tried to make myself as springy as a cat. Plank, power and agility work were what I focused on. I was never out of the gym in that respect as, unlike most of the male keepers, I couldn't rely on a huge reach. I needed to cover the ground more quickly, get across my box as fast as possible and find different ways to make saves. During my time at Everton, I would often train with Kevin O'Brien, who ran goalkeeping sessions for the younger male keepers at the club. The conversations I had with him and my goalkeeping coach Keith Rees about starting positions were very different from the ones Kev would have had with his male, 17-year-old, six-foot-four-inch keepers!'

When asked what Everton means to her, Brown-Finnis told me that she is half Claret and half Toffee, 'Burnley is where I am from so I will always have affection for them, but I am immensely proud of Everton Football Club. I think the work that we do in the community cannot be matched by any other organisation, and my time at the club is a period of my life that I look back on with great pride, for what we achieved both on and off the pitch.'

Brown-Finnis was inducted into the England Hall of Fame in 2016. Fittingly, she asked mentor Mick Payne to present her with her award. Payne looks back on his protégé's career with a great sense of pride. He explained, 'Rachel was a pioneer for female goalkeepers – a role model, ambassador and connoisseur of the position, who maximised her ability and made the most of every opportunity that came her way. She took nothing for granted and had the mental strength to fight back from numerous knock-backs, mainly horrific injuries that would have ended the careers of players with less mental strength than she had. Things didn't ever play on her mind. I have always said that goalkeepers have to be born, not manufactured, and Rachel was definitely born to be a goalkeeper. She knew when she signed on that dotted line exactly what she was signing up for – the ups and downs, the injuries and pitfalls that the career of a goalkeeper brings. Her character on and off the field is that of a winner, understanding what to say and how to say it, and always putting things out there in the right way.'

For the first five years of Rachel Brown's Blues career, **Danielle Hill** served as her able understudy. A product of the

Everton academy, the Liverpool-born keeper made her debut for the senior side at the age of 15. Although first-team opportunities were at a premium over the next five seasons, whenever Hill was called upon the youngster impressed team-mates and opponents alike with her sound handling, positional play and ability with her feet. Having deputised for Brown in the 2005 FA Cup Final defeat to Charlton Athletic, Hill played a massive role in the Blues defeating Arsenal in the Premier League Cup Final three years later, tipping over Kelly Smith's long-range effort not long after Amy Kane had given Everton the lead, before thwarting England forward Lianne Sanderson and her strike partner Julie Fleeting in quick succession with smart saves in the second half. Indeed, Hill's performances were so assured during the second half of the 2007/08 season that they resulted in her being called up to the England squad.

However, with Brown back to full fitness, Hill decided to leave Everton in the summer of 2008 and sign for Blackburn Rovers. Sadly, in only her second game for her new club, she suffered a cruel cruciate injury against Chelsea, which ruled her out for the rest of the season.

After two years away, Hill returned to Everton in September 2010, ahead of their Champions League campaign. Over the next two and a half years she would reprise her role as Brown's understudy, taking over from full time firefighter **Nicola Hobbs**, who, following another injury to Brown, had joined Everton on loan from Doncaster Rovers Belles two months into the 2009/10 campaign. Hobbs made her debut and kept a clean sheet in the 3-0 victory over Bristol Academy in November 2009, a week after outfielder Emily Westwood had played in goal in the 5-3 defeat to Chelsea. Having performed well in Brown's absence, Hobbs was disappointed only to make the bench for the 2010 FA Cup Final victory over Arsenal. She told me, 'When Rachel got injured, Mo Marley got in touch and asked whether I fancied joining Everton for the rest of the season. I was at the start of my England journey, having been called up for a few training camps, and jumped at the chance of playing week in, week out with established international players. Things went well for me there. Although I understood why Rachel came back into the side a month or so ahead of the final, it was very frustrating for me as I had performed well and, being the understudy goalkeeper, I knew I was never going to come on for the last 15 minutes or so of an FA Cup Final unless, of course, she got injured again.'

Sitting on the bench was something Hobbs was not prepared to do throughout her lengthy career, which took in spells at Lincoln, Norwich City, Blackburn Rovers, Doncaster Rovers Belles, London Bees and Sheffield United, as well as Everton. She added, 'I often travelled for over two hours to and from training and matches and would have to take annual leave or pay my work colleagues to cover my shifts on matchdays so, obviously, I always wanted to play. I loved it at Everton – the cup final victory, even though I didn't play, was a tremendous experience – but I needed to be playing regularly, so when Rachel returned to full fitness, I went back to Doncaster Rovers Belles and hit the ground running following my Everton experience. Being at the start of my England journey, I also needed the minutes to stay in their thoughts.'

Although she enjoyed her brief spell with the club, Hobbs admitted that she often experienced the feeling of 'imposter syndrome' while at Everton, 'Sometimes I felt a little insignificant as a goalkeeper there. Many of the players were seasoned internationals and, in my mind, I was "just little Nic Hobbs from Lincoln". I often found myself questioning whether I really had the right to be instructing my more esteemed team-mates where to position themselves on the pitch. Not being able to train every week because of my shifts also resulted in me not building a real rapport with everyone there, though Tash Dowie remains a close friend all these years later. I suppose I just felt far more comfortable at Belles. Yes, we had England international Sue Smith playing for us at the Keepmoat, but she was the exception rather than the norm, so I felt more of an equal to the girls in the Donny Belles squad.'

Despite not making a full international appearance, Hobbs represented England up to under-23 level and enjoyed an excellent club career, before retiring at Sheffield United just before the Covid pandemic hit the UK. She stated, 'I was winding down my career by the time I joined Sheffield United and couldn't commit to the demands the club wanted to place on us to bring us more in line with the professional game. I didn't want to take the place of a younger goalkeeper who could possibly develop and push the first-choice keeper more, so I decided to hang up my gloves at that point.' When asked whether she would have gone professional had the opportunity arisen earlier in her career, Hobbs had the following to say, 'I think so, but I would not have enjoyed the social media side of things or the pressure that today's female players have to cope with. I was never asked about or had to read about errors I had made in matches as there obviously wasn't the coverage that there is today. You never know how you will cope with a situation until you actually have to, but that is one side of the game I do not think I would have enjoyed.'

In her second spell at the club, Danielle Hill played eight games, before an alleged altercation at Everton's 2012 Christmas party resulted in her and youth-team coach Mick O'Brien leaving the club. After spending the 2013/14 season playing in Norway for Avaldsnes IL, Hill returned to England, re-signing for Blackburn Rovers after short spells at Durham, Liverpool Feds, Doncaster Rovers Belles and Notts County. Her second spell at Blackburn proved to be far more successful. Between 2015 and 2018, she was firmly established as the club's first-choice goalkeeper, making 80 appearances before hanging up her gloves and shifting her focus to coaching Rovers' goalkeepers.

When Hill left Everton in December 2012, **Lizzie Durack** edged out **Anna Moorhouse** to take on the role as the main understudy to Rachel Brown, as Everton, now competing in the Women's Super League (the WSL) and under new management following the resignation of Mo Marley, who wanted to concentrate on her England duties, seriously fell away from the leading pack. Many of Everton's rivals decided to go full time during that period and were able to lure many of the club's top talent away from Finch Farm with offers of professional and semi-professional contracts. Under new manager Andy Spence, the emphasis was placed on developing talented young players. Although born in Sydney, Durack was a member of the England under-19 squad and secured a move to Everton while training with the international set-up. After making ten appearances for the Blues, Durack moved to the US to study human development regenerative biology at Harvard University before briefly heading back to Merseyside at the conclusion of her studies. Her return to Everton in 2017 coincided with the club turning professional and their return to the top flight after relegation in 2014. At first, Durack seemed extremely happy to be back. Speaking to the club's official website, she said, 'It feels like I'm coming home. It's familiar but, at the same time, the club has come such a long way that it feels like a new environment. It's a nice balance of both. I'm very excited to be joining the WSL 1 League. I've had my sights on it for the last couple of years and I've been lucky in terms of the timing of the season and Everton's promotion. It was perfect timing.' However, less than a year after re-signing, Durack, a full England international by that point, moved to Chelsea, only to retire from the game at the age of 25, to pursue a career in finance. Incidentally, after leaving Everton in 2013, Anna Moorhouse took in brief spells with Durham, Doncaster Rovers Belles, Arsenal and West Ham United before moving abroad to play at Bordeaux and then Orlando Pride. In 2024, at the age of 29, she received her first call-up to the England squad and set a new record for the number of clean sheets in a US National Women's Soccer League (NWSL) season.

Vying with Lizzie Durack for the number one spot at the start of Everton Ladies' inaugural professional campaign was academy graduate **Kirstie Levell**, who had excelled between the sticks and been an ever-present during the team's successful 2017 Spring Series, gaining promotion back to the top division after winning the WSL 2.

Levell joined Everton at 12 years old, opting for the Blues over Liverpool, the team she has always supported, because of how welcoming Andy Spence had been towards her at an earlier trial. She told me, 'I had gone for trials at both Everton and Liverpool when I was ten and been offered a place at both clubs but turned them down as it didn't feel right at the time. I was really enjoying playing football for my grassroots teams at the weekends and didn't want it to get too serious too soon. Andy had made a big impression on me, though, so when I decided that I did want to take the next step two years later, I only trialled at Everton.'

Over the next few years, Levell would train twice a week, receiving goalkeeper training every Tuesday evening from Danielle Hill and then joining in with the outfielders every Thursday night. She believes the two very different sessions were the perfect mix for her early football development, 'Dan Hill worked us really hard from a fitness point of view and it was great to get goalkeeper-specific training, but I enjoyed working with the rest of the team as well. It really helped with the distribution side of my game and helped me to socialise with the rest of the girls too.'

At the age of 16, Levell started to train with the first team. She recalled feeling extremely anxious about making the step up to the seniors at such a young age, 'When I got home from college, my mum and dad told me that they had received a message from the club saying they wanted me to train with the first team. I tried to come up with a hundred reasons why I couldn't go before switching my thinking to "Just go and give it your best shot!" We knew Rachel Brown was retiring and there was only one other keeper at the club, **Meg Walsh**, so there was a good chance for both me and Walshy to stake a claim for the first-team spot.'

Over the next couple of years, the two pushed each other hard before Walsh moved on to Notts County at the end of the 2014/15 campaign – the club she had played against at Goodison Park in Everton's 3-0 FA Cup semi-final defeat that season. After two years with the Magpies, Walsh signed for Yeovil Town, where she established herself as one of the country's top goalkeepers. She would later play for Brighton & Hove Albion and West Ham United. In 2022, the Bromsgrove-born keeper made her international debut, for the Republic of Ireland, having previously played for England at under-17, under-19 and under-23 levels.

Following Walsh's departure, **Delyth Morgan** and **Alex Brooks** came in to provide short-term competition for Levell. However, Levell quickly cemented her place as the club's undisputed first-choice stopper with some impressive displays, including one at Goodison Park in May 2017 when she kept a clean sheet in the Blues' penultimate match of the Spring Series, a 4-0 win over Watford Ladies. She explained, 'The Goodison Park experience was hugely significant for me as it showed how much the club was backing the women's team. It was quite unusual back then for women's games to be played at the grounds of men's teams, so it showed everyone that Everton were serious about pushing the team forward, and gave us a great starting point.'

Incidentally, earlier that season, outfielder Danielle Turner had replaced the injured Levell in an FA Cup tie at Durham – and was voted SSE Women's FA Cup player of round four for her heroics during extra time and in the penalty shoot-out victory. On receiving her award, Turner told the FA's official website, 'It was crazy. We'd discussed it in the warm-up, what we would do if Kirstie got injured. At half-time, she was struggling, so we made the decision then, but I was happy to go in. In training, I'm always the first one to get stuck in, and I'm fairly agile. I'm not afraid in the tackle, and I'm not afraid to throw myself around in goal either. We were not blessed with a lot of height on the day, I was one of the tallest, and so it probably didn't leave many options. I loved it – I had 75 minutes in net and kept a clean sheet. If it was to ever happen again, I'd certainly volunteer!'

In July 2017, Levell became the first female goalkeeper to sign a professional contract with Everton. She recalled how things changed pretty much overnight for her and her team-mates that summer, 'It was a crazy transition from training maybe two or three nights a week after long days at college to being in at Finch Farm every day from 9am until 3pm. There was gym work, loads of analysis meetings and at least 45 minutes of goalkeeper work every single day. It was bloody brilliant, to be honest, and it showed how far I had come from being that nervous girl four years earlier, who hadn't really wanted to go and train with the first-team squad!'

During the 2017/18 season, Levell had to be patient as the experienced Durack was preferred for most of the league fixtures. Levell revealed, 'Lizzie was knocking on the door of the England first-team squad at the time so I just had to wait for my chance and took it as an opportunity to learn what I could from her. She was extremely athletic and agile, so I took what I could from her, developing my spring and footwork to make up for my lack of inches. When her form dipped a little, like all keepers' form does at times, I was ready to step in and fight for the jersey.'

Having caught the eye in the impressive FA Cup run to the semi-finals in 2018, Levell, backed up by ex-Liverpool stopper **Becky Flaherty**, was installed as Everton's first choice at the start of the 2018/19 campaign and quickly showed the rest of the league what she was about, with some outstanding displays against the division's big hitters. Although Spence's young side struggled against their more experienced opponents, Levell's form reached new heights in games against the likes of Arsenal, Manchester City and Chelsea in particular. She explained, 'I always felt the pressure was off in those big games, as we were undoubtedly the underdogs, which resulted in me being able to relax that bit more.' As the women's game started to gain more coverage across various media platforms, with games being broadcast live on terrestrial television, and magazine shows starting to appear on numerous television channels, Levell began to receive a great deal of coverage and was regularly nominated for save of the month awards on the WSL's Twitter platform, with her fast feet often enabling her to scramble across her goal before pushing off into brave full-length dives.

Even when old mentor Spence lost his job in the autumn of 2018, there seemed little to suggest that things were about to take an unexpected downward turn. However, after positive experiences with interim managers David Unsworth and Jen Herst – Levell's old goalkeeping coach – and a superb session with Alan Kelly, in which she made a series of stupendous saves from Unsworth's highly rated under-23 male players, Levell found her time at Everton was coming to an end when new manager Willie Kirk decided he wanted to make a major change in the goalkeeping department at the end of the 2018/19 season.

That summer, Kirk decided to bring experienced Finland international **Tinja-Riikka Korpela** to the club and quickly established her as his first-choice goalkeeper. At first, Levell remained unfazed, 'He told me that he liked me, that I had done well for him and that I would learn a lot from Tinja, who is more than ten years older than I am, and I certainly did learn a great deal as she is without doubt the most professional goalkeeper I have ever worked with. He kept telling me that my time would come but I soon worked out that he wanted me gone.'

Over the next two Covid-hit campaigns, Korpela, who had previously played for German giants Bayern Munich, made 16 league appearances for the Toffees. In November 2019, she played a starring role at Anfield in front of a near-25,000 crowd, as Everton, who had dropped the word 'Ladies' from their name at the start of the 2019/20 season, beat their bitter rivals 1-0 thanks to Lucy Graham's long-range strike and a fine diving save to her left from Korpela. However, in the summer of 2021, she moved on to WSL rivals Tottenham Hotspur, making her 100th international appearance not long after leaving the Blues, before moving to AS Roma in 2023.

Partly the reason Kirk felt he could let the experienced Finn leave was due to the return to England of Everton youth product **Sandy MacIver**, who, after a spell in the States on a soccer scholarship between 2016 and 2019, re-signed for the club at the beginning of 2020. Levell told me, 'When Sandy came back, I knew I had no chance. How were all three of us going to play? Then Covid came and I got the call over the telephone that I wasn't being kept on, which was a really sad way to end my Everton career. I couldn't say a proper goodbye to the girls or anything. Spurs had wanted to take me on loan, but I turned them down as I wanted to stay in the north; the Wirral was my home and I didn't want anything to change, really.'

In the summer of 2020, Levell signed for Championship side Leicester City and won the Golden Glove award as her new club gained promotion to the WSL in her first season. However, after Kirk left Everton and took over the Leicester managerial reins from Lydia Bedford in 2022, she knew her place in the team was again in jeopardy and in 2023 signed for semi-professional outfit Burnley. She explained, 'It is clear that Willie never really fancied me as a goalkeeper. Whether it was a clash of characters or down to a perceived vulnerability under a high ball because of my lack of height, I do not know. After all, a lot of managers have a type of goalkeeper that they want. They're often looking for a tall keeper with a big presence, but my leg power has always been very good, and my spring has always been one of the strongest parts of my game and made up for any lack of inches. It's frustrating but you cannot really sit around and get annoyed about genetics.'

Sandy MacIver was in goal when Everton Women played their first game at new ground Walton Hall Park in February 2020, and played a starring role in the 2-1 FA Cup quarter-final victory over Chelsea at Goodison Park in the September that year. Just a month later, she put in the performance of her career as Everton, playing their first competitive game at Wembley, lost out to Manchester City after extra time in the 2020 FA Cup Final. Despite finishing on the losing side, MacIver was named the player of the match by BBC pundit Sue Smith after producing a string of fine saves. Her recovery save from ex-Blue Chloe Kelly's fizzing strike was particularly impressive and left Smith and commentator Jonathan Pearce momentarily gobsmacked as the goalkeeper's lightning-quick footwork got her back into position to tip Kelly's shot over the crossbar, having already done brilliantly to tip Caroline Weir's initial strike on to the post.

On the back of those strong displays, MacIver, who had already been capped at youth level and awarded the Golden Glove for her outstanding performances in the 2018 FIFA under-20 Women's World Cup, gained a full England cap in February 2021. Against Northern Ireland, she came on for the last 30 minutes of the 6-0 victory, only to switch allegiances to Scotland in 2023. Her terrific performances, not only in the 2020 FA Cup Final but also at Goodison Park on the opening day of the 2021/22 season, had made such an impression on opponents Manchester City that they submitted an offer for her in July 2022. However, after moving down the East Lancs Road, MacIver's career stalled massively and she found herself behind England international Ellie Roebuck and young starlet Khiara Keating in the pecking order.

With MacIver, Korpela and reserve goalkeepers **Faye Kirby**, **Anna Pedersen** and **Cecilía Rán Rúnarsdóttir** all having left the club within a 12-month period, Everton were in need of an overhaul of their goalkeeping department ahead of the 2022/23 season. Incoming manager Brian Sørensen decided to put his faith in US-born Eire international **Courtney Brosnan** and **Emily Ramsey**, the latter of whom Sørensen initially brought in on a season-long loan from Manchester United. Prior to Ramsey sustaining an injury while training with the England squad in early 2023, Sørensen had alternated his two keepers in the first half of the season, with both showing the quality that had brought them international recognition. Ramsey, having already been capped by England at under-17, under-19 and under-21 levels, received her first competitive senior call-up for the Arnold Clark Cup fixtures in February 2023 but had to withdraw after sustaining an ankle injury in training. It was a cruel blow for Ramsey, who had certainly caught the eye in the opening months of the season, with two penalty saves against Aston Villa in the Continental League Cup and a majestic performance away at Arsenal in the league, a game in which she made a series of fine saves to keep the scoreline down to 1-0. According to the BBC Sport website, Ramsey had the highest save percentage (82.5 per cent) of all the goalkeepers in the WSL in 2022/23.

Ramsey's spell on the sidelines gave Courtney Brosnan, gearing up for a summer at the World Cup finals in Australia after saving a penalty in the qualifier against Scotland in October 2022, the opportunity to have a sustained run in the team. Like Ramsey, Brosnan had performed brilliantly before the winter break and continued to show her international class in the second half of the campaign, performing heroically in the 0-0 draw at Manchester United as well as in the Friday night derby draw under the floodlights at Goodison Park, where she made several brave saves at the feet of Liverpool's onrushing forwards.

With Ramsey unavailable throughout February and March, Sørensen brought in Scotland international **Eartha Cumings** on an emergency loan from Liverpool to bolster his substitute goalkeeper options. The ex-Charlton and Bristol City stopper, who had developed compartment syndrome and almost had to have both her legs amputated during her teenage years, would share understudy duties with youngster **Peyton Henderson** in Ramsey's absence before signing for Swedish side FC Rosengård in the close season. In April, Ramsey returned to the fold, again sharing goalkeeping duties with Brosnan for the last six games of the 2022/23 campaign.

2023 was a special year for Courtney Brosnan, at club and international level. Her penalty-save heroics that helped to clinch World Cup qualification for the Republic of Ireland came within a run of seven consecutive international clean sheets, a phenomenal sequence which went a long way to her being crowned FAI International Player of the Year ahead of the summer tournament in Australia. At the World Cup she added to her impressive haul of clean sheets, keeping out Nigeria in Ireland's final group game. Although Eire failed to qualify for the knockout stages of the competition, having narrowly lost to both Australia and Canada before drawing with Nigeria, Brosnan and her team-mates returned home as heroes, having matched their more illustrious opponents in all three matches.

Appearing at the World Cup and being named her country's player of the year had probably felt a long way off for Brosnan when she was released by West Ham only two years earlier. Speaking to the *Irish Times* ahead of appearing at the finals, she said, 'It's unbelievable – a really proud moment for me. I've seen the penalty save back a few times, for sure. It's nice to have saves and things to look back on. It's just about speaking to yourself positively and looking at things you are able to do, knowing you can do them.' Her off-the-field work with Everton in the Community also saw her named the PFA Community Champion of the 2022/23 season. On receiving her award, Brosnan told the official website, 'The fans at Everton are absolutely amazing. I've had a lot of opportunities to work with Everton in the Community. What they do is so special.'

On returning to club duties ahead of the 2023/24 campaign, Brosnan found a familiar face waiting for her on the training ground. That summer, Brian Sørensen decided to make Emily Ramsey's move to Everton permanent. Yet again, the pair, under the supervision of head goalkeeping coach Ian McCaldon, would battle it out for the starting spot at Walton Hall Park. The Brosnan–Ramsey partnership is one of the strongest examples of a Goalkeepers' Union, with both keepers enjoying each other's company and pushing the other goalkeeper to improve. In interviews with the media, both women have been extremely complimentary about their 'rivals'. Brosnan told the *Irish Times*, 'Working with Emily has been amazing; she's an unbelievable goalkeeper so having that competition to push me every day, whether I was playing or not, helped me improve my game. And it was great to get plenty of minutes under my belt and get top competition in the WSL – it's been a great year all round for both of us.' On her return to Everton, Ramsey told the official website, 'We get on really well together and actually help each other in terms of pushing each other on. We were both in and out of the team last year, but it wasn't so tough in those moments as it may have been working with other people, because we have that level of understanding. I know that Courtney is a great goalkeeper, and I respect that if she's playing well then the manager may want to play her as that is what's best for the team. I really enjoy the relationship we have and the way we are able to work with each other and I'm looking forward to keeping that going.'

Ramsey started the first two matches of 2023/24 before Brosnan returned to the side for the next five games as the Blues made a slow start to the new campaign. Speaking to the BBC Sport website for an article about the rotation of goalkeepers by many clubs in the WSL, Sørensen had the following to say, 'This year we decided to start with Emily because she did really well in pre-season so she had the first two games. Courtney is still an excellent keeper so she got the next two. It's not that there is a pattern to it or anything. Both goalkeepers are good. It's more about their skillsets in terms of what type of game we think it will be. Are we going to be on the ball a lot or is it more transitional? They are the things we take into consideration.'

Ramsey returned for the humiliating 7-0 defeat to former employers Manchester United in the Continental League Cup and further heartbreak was to follow just four games later when she hobbled off in the defeat to Liverpool in the same competition after injuring her ankle trying to keep out Yana Daniels's scrambled effort, having already made a trio of fabulous saves. Forced into a long spell on the sidelines, Ramsey was replaced in the matchday squads by young keeper **Libby Hart**, who had signed for the club three months earlier. Speaking to the official website soon after completing her move, Hart, previously of Birmingham City and Manchester City, said she was 'really looking forward to getting started', while Sørensen said that he was confident his new signing would 'develop into a top-class goalkeeper and hugely benefit from working closely with the elite experienced goalkeepers we already have at Everton in Courtney and Emily'.

In April 2024, after over four months out of action, Ramsey suffered a devastating blow while stepping up her rehabilitation, injuring her other ankle just 24 hours before she was expected to play in a friendly. Such a cruel setback highlights the fragility and vulnerability of the goalkeeper position, and Ramsey's Everton career to date perfectly encapsulates the ups and downs that those who play between the posts frequently experience. In sharp contrast to Ramsey's misfortune, at the end of the 2023/24 season, after yet another incredibly impressive campaign, Courtney Brosnan made it a goalkeeping double when she took home the club's women's player of the year award, just as Jordan Pickford did in the men's category. After signing a new contract with the club in the close season, Brosnan, who made the most saves – 95 – of any WSL goalkeeper in 2023/24, told the official website how much Everton means to her, 'I'm really excited to be continuing as an Everton player. I think everyone knows how much this club, the players and the fans mean to me. It's safe to say this club is a second home. I've made a great group of friends here. The coaching staff have been great mentors for me and I'm grateful to have a special bond with the fans, too. For me, Ian [McCaldon] is a goalkeeping coach at Everton who has helped me to develop massively. I'm really looking forward to continuing that relationship with him to become a better version of myself this season.'

In July 2024, Brian Sørensen signed 25-year-old Portugal international **Inês Pereira** following the expiry of her contract with Swiss side Servette but immediately loaned his new goalkeeper to Spanish outfit Deportivo de La Coruña for the 2024/25 Liga F season. He told the club's official website, 'Inês is a player I've been tracking for a while, from around the age of 18. We have two excellent goalkeepers with us now in Emily and Courtney, and Inês is one we see making an impact to our squad in the future. She has a lot of experience – playing at the Euros and the World Cup – but she is still young and has a lot more to give. Inês is a talented goalkeeper, excellent with her feet, and plays with a lot of courage. One of the first things I noticed with her was her mentality, the way she conducts herself. She is a good character on the pitch and demands a lot from her team-mates. Speaking to her, I can tell she's a quality human being and I'm excited to see how she gets on in her loan spell in Spain before playing for us in the future.'

Ten months later, after a series of eye-catching displays for Deportivo, Pereira was named in the Liga F team of the season. Early in the new year, she had replicated her fine club form on the international front, making a couple of superb saves in Portugal's surprising 1-1 draw with England in the UEFA Nations League. However, in the return match at Wembley in May, she was left helplessly exposed by her backline as Portugal fell to a comprehensive 6-0 defeat.

Another goalkeeper who spent time away from Merseyside during the 2024/25 campaign was youngster **Lily Groves**, who signed for Bury on dual registration forms in August 2024. Groves, who had sat on the Everton bench as a schoolgirl for the WSL fixture against West Ham United six months previously, was voted the Shakers' player of the match in their season opener against Salford City.

With Ramsey still recovering from injury, and Hart having departed, Everton brought in former Liverpool goalkeeper **Rylee Foster** on a short-term deal as cover for Brosnan for the first half of 2024/25. The Canadian's story is a truly inspiring one. Having sustained life-threatening injuries in a horrific road traffic accident in Finland in October 2021, when she was thrown through the windscreen after her seatbelt had malfunctioned, Foster needed emergency spinal surgery to mend seven neck fractures. She told BBC Sport, 'It was catastrophic. The doctor said he had never seen it this bad. He said, given the injuries I had, I should not have been breathing or talking on my own. Football just wasn't a thing. I was just trying to fight for a quality of life at this point.'

Miraculously, Foster went on to make a full recovery. After spending several months wearing a halo device to immobilise her neck, she returned to action in 2023/24, making 19 appearances for the appropriately named New Zealand outfit Wellington Phoenix. Following her departure from Everton in January 2025, she extended her stay in England by signing for Championship side Durham WFC.

In early October, against Newcastle United in the first round of the Continental Cup, Courtney Brosnan made history by becoming the first Everton goalkeeper, male or female, to save three spot kicks in a penalty shoot-out (four if both saves from Georgia Gibson's twice-taken effort are counted). The following month, for the first time in the club's history, Everton Women played back-to-back home games at Goodison Park – losing heavily to reigning champions Chelsea before coming out on top in the Merseyside derby a fortnight later. Against Liverpool, in front of the Sky Sports cameras, Brosnan was simply terrific and made a series of fine saves in Everton's 1-0 victory, the pick of which being a fine double sprawling stop to deny midfielder Fūka Nagano at the Park End early in the second half. The derby win, clean sheet and player of the match award capped off a magnificent week for the Republic of Ireland star, who had been named the FAI Senior Women's International Player of the Year for the second year running just four days earlier.

After her splendid showing in a 2-0 victory at Aston Villa at the beginning of March, Brosnan led the table for the number of saves made in the 2024/25 WSL season – with 70 – though did show she was human in the 2-0 away loss to Manchester United four weeks later, when an uncharacteristic handling error gifted the Red Devils their opening goal. Showing exceptional mental strength and an ability to move on from mistakes quickly, Brosnan then went on to make a series of first-class saves. Speaking on *Upfront: A Women's Football Podcast* about her ability to recover from errors not long after making the mistake at Leigh Sports Village, Brosnan explained, 'Football is a game of mistakes. My goalkeeping coach at Everton tells me, "It is a drop in the bucket of who you are as a goalkeeper and who you are as a person." So it is something you can switch on quite quickly.'

In the same interview, Brosnan provided the following sage piece of advice for any aspiring goalkeepers, 'As you mature, it's important to realise that mistakes happen. The journey isn't always constantly moving up and up. There are valleys and there are peaks. And it's really important to take those failings and setbacks as they make you who you are.'

After the Manchester United defeat, Brian Sørensen came out in defence of his goalkeeper, telling the BBC Sport website, 'She [Brosnan] has been excellent for us all season. These things, unfortunately, happen sometimes. We can't be 100 per cent perfect in everything, but I think she bounced back really well.' Nevertheless, for Everton's next fixture, away to Manchester City, Emily Ramsey was handed her first league start in 18 months and performed brilliantly in a battling 1-1 draw. The returning Ramsey's performance reminded everyone of her outstanding ability and again highlighted the strength of the club's goalkeeping department.

At Anfield a fortnight later, it was Brosnan's turn to once again show her class. In the Blues' 2-0 victory, she was a colossus – thwarting the old enemy on three separate occasions with a trio of saves that went a long way to winning her side all three points and securing Everton's fifth win from five matches played at Anfield. On a more personal level, Brosnan's tip on to the bar of former Toffee Taylor Hinds's dipping long-range effort, reaction stop low to her left from Austrian Marie-Therese Höbinger's fizzing strike and brave block to deny Olivia Smith, after staying big when the Canadian forward broke into the box in front of the Kop, helped to secure her fifth clean sheet in six derby appearances.

Before the season was over, both keepers once again paid tribute to the Everton goalkeeping group, headed by their coach Ian McCaldon. Ramsey told the Voice on Soccer YouTube channel, 'We have got a great little union going on here and train to a high standard out on the pitch. Courtney's consistency in training throughout the week is fantastic. She is definitely one of the best keepers I have worked with. Working together while competing for the shirt with her here is fantastic. Ian knows how to get the best out of us.' On *Upfront: A Women's Football Podcast*, Brosnan, who made more saves than any other WSL keeper for a second successive campaign in 2024/25, had the following to say about the connection between the club's last lines of defence, 'The goalkeeper is such a unique position. The people you're competing with day in, day out are also the only ones who really understand what it is like to be in your position, which helps to form a special bond in that union.'

At the end of the women's team's 30th season in existence, and less than a week before the men's team's final fixture at Goodison Park, the club announced that the 133-year-old stadium would be saved from demolition and become the new home of Everton Women – with alterations to the old ground set to be made over the coming years. On the official website, the following statement appeared, 'This long-term vision reflects the club's commitment to investing in the women's game and ensuring that Goodison Park continues to play a vital role in both football and the community. The club's regeneration plans will retain Goodison Park's proud identity while giving Everton Women a world-class platform in the heart of Liverpool 4. For supporters, it offers the chance to be part of a new era in one of football's most iconic venues. The ambition is to create a team capable of challenging for honours – backed by high-quality facilities and a world-renowned home.'

Angus Kinnear, the club's CEO, added, 'We know how treasured Goodison is, not only to every Evertonian, but to the game itself, and being able to keep such an iconic stadium at the heart of the legacy project is something that has been incredibly important to us.'

In the week that the extraordinary news broke, perhaps the most fitting lines came from one of the club's former goalkeepers. Rachel Brown-Finnis told BBC Radio 5 Live, 'It is fantastic news. The women's team including myself have played at Marine Football Club; we've played at Widnes rugby league; we've played at lots of different homes but they have never felt like homes. It feels like this is Everton Women coming home. The statement the Friedkin Group have made since coming in by refurbishing Goodison Park to make it fit for purpose for the women's team absolutely shows they want to invest in women's football and keep moving it along that upward trajectory that we have seen in these past five or six years.'

From Gill Parkinson to Courtney Brosnan, via the likes of Annie Wright, Andie Worrall, Rachel Brown-Finnis and Kirstie Levell, Everton's female goalkeepers have always worn the club's shirt with real pride and distinction. As the women's game continues to grow, it will be interesting to see who follows in their footsteps and pulls on the gloves to guard the Goodison Park goalposts in the future.

Exciting times ahead.

15

Fans' Goodison Goalkeeping Memories

Between 1892 and 2025, countless memorable moments involving Everton and opposing goalkeepers were witnessed by supporters inside Goodison Park. From match-winning saves and brilliant individual performances to moments of madness and occasions when things did not go as planned, inhabitants of the Grand Old Lady saw it all.

Over the next few pages, you will find an incredible anthology of goalkeeping memories, superbly written by the Everton supporters who witnessed them. Thank you to everyone who contributed to this chapter.

I've looked everywhere for this and I can't find a single bit of footage, so you'll have to trust me. It was October 1987 and Everton went into the home game against Watford in eighth place. Importantly, they also went into it with **Neville Southall** back in goal after a spell out of the side through injury. The game itself was 'routine' and Everton brushed their opponents aside with a 2-0 win in a game they didn't need to leave second gear in. But the standout moment for me was a save Neville made in the second half. It wasn't his most famous save. It wasn't even close to his best. But diving low to his right, he plucked a well-struck shot from Kenny Jackett, I think, out of the air, one-handed and stood up as though nothing had happened. Imagine that now. A keeper. Catching a shot. Arrowing towards the bottom corner. With one hand! People around me laughed and I will never forget that. It was the essence of the man, making the routine look easy, to the point where it was almost contemptuous. Imagine being an opponent and facing someone who could make your best efforts look so utterly futile. Those who saw him at his best were lucky. I'll always be grateful for that.

Miles Shackley

The final match of the 2022/23 season against Bournemouth was another nerve-wracking battle for survival. The must-win game is often remembered for a wonder goal by Abdoulaye Doucouré in the 57th minute – and the resulting raucous celebrations which have become part of Everton folklore. However, Doucouré's goal would have counted for nothing if it had not been for the remarkable wonder save by **Jordan Pickford** deep into added time. Everton and England's number one displayed immense concentration and agility to thwart a thunderbolt drilled from the edge of the box by substitute Matias Viña. The impact of his heroics is immeasurable as it preserved the club's participation in the top flight – albeit by the skin of their teeth – for another season.

Dr David France

In the FA Cup tie at Wolverhampton Wanderers in 1967, our revered keeper **Gordon West** played the game of his life to keep Everton in the game in a 1-1 draw. There were no pundits then – just Jimmy Hill commenting that it was the best performance by a keeper he had witnessed. The replay on the following Tuesday sees the teams having to change ends due to Wolves winning the toss. So Westy picks up his gloves and runs to the Park End, accompanied by 60,000 fans on their feet applauding his efforts the previous weekend. Everton won the replay and in the next round beat Liverpool.

Tom Evans

One of my favourite memories was walking around Goodison in August 1995 with the 1950s goalkeeper **Bert Harris** and his son Vin. All of a sudden, there was a shout, 'Bert, are you playing today?' After turning around, I realised it was George Scanlan. George had played with Bert for Bootle and had just acted as Andrei Kanchelskis's interpreter the day before, when the Russian winger had signed for Everton from Manchester United. George's words to Bert that day were wonderful, 'He's good is Andrei, but he wouldn't score past you!'

Ian Maher

I witnessed history being made when Aston Villa's **Peter Schmeichel** volleyed in from a corner in 2001 to become the first goalkeeper to score in the Premier League, causing myself and many other Blues to have a nervous final few seconds before the whistle eventually went and we won the game 3-2.

Christopher Scott

For me, if it wasn't for Big Nev, then **Nigel Martyn** would be my number one. A similar build to Nev and everything you would want in a keeper. Moyes's best signing and how things could have been different if he had signed in 1996 instead of being given a tour of Park Foods and then directions to Leeds! In terms of a standout save at Goodison, Martyn's tip-over from James Milner at the Gwladys Street End in the game when we clinched Champions League qualification in 2005 lives long in the memory. It looked even better in slow motion!

Steve Smith

When I was a very young lad, a performance by Borussia Mönchengladbach's **Wolfgang Kleff** in the 1-1 European Cup draw was just incredible, despite him being partly at fault for the goal Johnny Morrissey scored after just 25 seconds. That night, Kleff made a save from Joe Royle that was unbelievable. In domestic cup competitions, I remember a performance by the most unlikely-looking goalkeeper ever, a small, squat guy called **Nigel Batch**, who had the game of his life for Grimsby Town at Goodison in the League Cup in 1984. Everton peppered him all night in one of the most one-sided matches I have ever seen, but Batch kept everything out – before Paul Wilkinson scored a winner for Grimsby in the final minute.

Phil McNulty

Neville Southall was always my hero growing up. He was world-class then and when everyone in my class at school said 'I want to

be Ian Rush' or 'I want to be Gary Lineker', I always wanted to be
Nev. He became an even bigger hero to me when my goalkeeping
son, aged seven or eight at the time, broke his wrist. I didn't know
how to rehabilitate him so tweeted Big Nev on the off chance that
he would respond, which he did, with some really sound advice.
My son, Harvey, became a goalkeeper at the age of five, after an
incident at Goodison before his first game. As the players entered
the ground at the Park End, Harvey held up his ball and **Tim
Howard** asked him if he wanted it signed. From that moment on,
he was his number one fan!

Nev made so many memorable saves that won us trophies, but
I think Howard's stop against Southampton, when he somehow
clawed the ball out from behind him before it crossed the line, is
the best save we have seen at the Grand Old Lady.

Michael and Harvey Todd

On 9 September 2006, Everton were leading the 175th league
Merseyside derby 2-0 at Goodison Park when in added time a
speculative shot from future England manager Lee Carsley, who
had famously scored the only goal in the last Everton derby win,
seemed to trouble the Liverpool goalkeeper **Pepe Reina** far more
than it should have.

Having parried Carsley's shot, Reina lost his bearings between
the sticks of the Park End goal, and in an effort to keep the ball
out of the net he rather panicked. As I watched his efforts from
my seat, I saw him comically push the ball upwards and outwards.
But, before he could catch it again, the ever-alert Andy Johnson
headed the ball home to score his second goal of the game, and
the Blues' third, to the ecstatic delight of Evertonians everywhere,
and delivered Everton's biggest win against them for over 40 years.

John Blain

Jordan Pickford brings the high energy of the north-east music
scene to Merseyside, and this attitude seems to make him a
divisive character; some find him too much but others find him
inspiring. In my opinion, if you tried to tame him, you'd lose him,
as the intensity is what makes him great. Without the constant
noise and movement, you couldn't have the moments of laser

precision under extreme pressure. England's number one thrives on chaos and sometimes he has to make his own, like in 2024, when he celebrated his incredible save from Nottingham Forest's Chris Wood with the Gwladys Street End while the ball was still in play and then caught the cross straight after. The mad cat. But calm or crazy, the aim remains the same. Keep the ball out of the net, by any means possible, and that is something Pickford excels at.

Rose-Heather Mikhail

As a fan, three names stick out for me which provoke instant memories: **Georgie Wood**, **Neville Southall** and **Jordan Pickford**. Wood was a character when I was growing up as a Blue, Neville needs no explanation except to say he influenced my life both personally and professionally (and still does to this day) and Pickford, for me, has been a saviour for our club in modern times. I will never underestimate the penalty save at Leicester, which I believe kept us in the Premier League in 2023. However, my standout save at Goodison will always be an odd one. During Mick Lyons's testimonial, a substitution was made and on came a blanket-covered stretcher. They ran it over to the goalmouth and off jumped Gordon West to rapturous applause. He then made one of the best saves I have ever seen – and the crowd was just in awe. Despite being retired, Big Westy still had it!

Alan Myers

It's rare that an exceptional goalkeeping performance begins with an error leading to a goal but, unfortunately for us, that was exactly the case as Everton welcomed Fiorentina for the UEFA Cup last-16 second leg in March 2008. The Blues were 2-0 down from the first leg a week earlier, but halved the aggregate deficit just 16 minutes into the Goodison Park fixture, as Andy Johnson profited from a howler by Fiorentina keeper **Sébastien Frey**. However, it would be Frey's first and last error of the tie, as the Frenchman's defiant resolve denied the Blues a deserved equaliser. Producing a string of saves throughout the opening period, Frey alone prevented Everton from having the fixture wrapped up by half-time, firstly saving a Mikel Arteta free kick, before making a remarkable point-blank save from a Yakubu effort. Andy Johnson then came close to doubling his tally for the game, but Frey was once again equal to it and it would eventually take a special strike from Arteta midway through the second half to finally beat a keeper having the game of his life, as Goodison's deafening noise levels went up a decibel. With an aggregate score of 2-2, Frey made a dramatic double save deep in the second half to once again deny Yakubu. All square after extra time, Frey's heroics ultimately decided the tie, as the Fiorentina keeper made one final save of the evening, stopping Phil Jagielka's penalty and sending the Blues out of Europe. Another 'what if' fixture in the frustrating history of the club and the most memorable performance from an opposition goalkeeper in my match-going experience.

Lou Reed Foster

Everton and Borussia Mönchengladbach are level on aggregate after extra time in the second round of the 1970/71 European Cup. Penalty shoot-outs have been introduced by UEFA this season. This is the first time they will be utilised in this tournament. Everton's Sandy Brown has just scored to give Everton a 4-3 lead. One penalty remains.

Ludwig Müller approaches the penalty spot as the Gwladys Street launches a cacophonous tirade of vitriolic abuse. The Everton custodian **Andy Rankin** composes himself. When Müller steps up to take his kick, Rankin moves slightly off his line. The ball is dispatched hard and low but somehow Rankin launches himself to his right and palms the ball away to safety. Cue bedlam as players and fans mob the hero of the hour. Andy Rankin has just become the first English keeper to make a save in a European Cup penalty shoot-out and Everton are in the quarter-finals!

Eight years later, in the third round of the League Cup, Everton faced Fourth Division Darlington with the home fans expecting a comfortable victory. In goal for the visitors was **Martin Burleigh**, who had been an outstanding prospect for Newcastle United but had struggled with fitness issues before being released in 1974. Now aged 27, this was a chance to put himself back in the spotlight. Under the floodlights, he produced one of his best performances, defying everything the Blues could throw at him with a string of breathtaking saves. He was finally beaten on 53 minutes when Martin Dobson managed to chip the ball over him to earn Everton a 1-0 win.

On the final whistle, Burleigh received a rousing round of applause from the home crowd after his impressive display. Joe Harvey, the Newcastle boss, had once said, 'The point is Martin is a great keeper.' That night showed why he said that!

Paul McParlan

Tim Howard's save versus Southampton comes to mind first, with Jordan Pickford's incredible stop against Chelsea in 2021/22 being a close second. In terms of overall performances, Pickford versus Chelsea was spectacular. As for away keepers, many of them save their best games for when they play us! Bernd Leno for Fulham on the opening day of the 2023/24 season was amazing and José Sá for Wolves a few weeks later was also very solid.

Alfie Fitzsimmons

Pretty much all the great goalkeeping performances I can remember from over 50 years of going to Goodison are by our own boys: George Wood, Martin Hodge, Neville Southall, of course, Nigel Martyn, Tim Howard and Jordan Pickford. My memory is selective: I seem to have airbrushed out the heroics of opposing keepers. That said, I do recall **Gary Bailey** of Manchester United playing a blinder against us once or twice, and it was always fun seeing nutty **John Burridge** at Goodison. But my EFC bias is such that the two moments I most vividly remember involving opposition goalies are **Ray Clemence** diving in vain to stop Andy King's famous derby winner in October 1978, and six months earlier, **Peter Bonetti** failing – thank goodness – to stop Bob Latchford's penalty against Chelsea, his 30th goal of the season, winning a £10,000 prize from the *Daily Express* at a time when ten grand meant more to top footballers than the cost of a low-key night out!

Brian Viner

George Burnett and **Jimmy O'Neill** were very good keepers, whom I regularly got to see play at Goodison Park. However, my main goalkeeping memory is of **Ted Sagar** getting annoyed with T.G. Jones over his casual headers back to him. Around that time, I played with **Albert Dunlop** for Liverpool Schoolboys. He was often overlooked as the selectors preferred Farnworth (Roscoe School), who went on to play for Lancashire Schoolboys, but never reached international level. Strangely, Albert and I came together again later in life, when we were both posted to Deysbrook Lane in Liverpool during our national service days. He was a physical training instructor and I was a common lance corporal. I remember the runs he used to take us on all round West Derby! He wasn't well liked, probably because of his runs! He also played cricket for Liverpool Cricket Club and some other clubs.

Raymond Terry

We played Southampton on 20 November 1971. It was snowing and freezing. We won 8-0 but during the game a fan jumped out of the Park End and offered **Gordon West** a cup of tea.

Ian Richards

In a routine 2-0 victory against Sunderland, I vividly remember the performance of a 22-year-old **Jordan Pickford**. As Idrissa Gana Gueye and Romelu Lukaku secured the three points for Everton, the margin of victory would have been far greater if not for the rising star between the sticks for Sunderland. Considering this was a season that saw the Mackems relegated from the Premier League, Pickford's performances went slightly under the radar. Everton's goalkeeper choices were average during the 2016/17 season, and it was obvious we were going to enter the market for a new number one in the summer. After the match, I remember discussing with my dad if Pickford was a viable option; it was clear he was raw but you could see potential oozing from him. Little did we know he would go on to be one of our most pivotal signings and become a national hero.

James Kellett

Because of Tim Howard's remarkable consistency, it took Slovakia's first-choice goalkeeper **Ján Mucha** 984 days to make his Premier League debut – finally playing in a 3-1 victory over Reading in 2013 having sat on the bench for over 100 league games. His only other league performance – against reigning champions Manchester City just seven days after THAT embarrassing FA Cup quarter-final defeat to Wigan Athletic – is my standout Goodison goalkeeping performance. Everton won courtesy of a goal from Leon Osman that requires knowledge of algebraic curves to explain and a scrappy finish – immortalised by crowd footage – from the out-of-form Nikica Jelavić, though it could be said, that, in a cult performance from our Slovakian stopper, the game was really won at the other end. Mucha made eight saves that day including two smart one-on-one smothers. Thank you for your patience, Ján, and for a performance that lives long in the memory.

Tom Slater

It was the last home game of my debut season, 1970/71, the first of what I'd envisaged in my young mind of being many years of unrelenting success for my wonderful Toffees. The champions were expected to dominate the league for years. But it was a season of disappointment and a precursor of what was to come, as we had heartbreaking exits in the FA Cup and European Cup, allied to a poor league placing of 14th. We at least expected to sign off with a win against relegated Blackpool, especially as they were fielding an unknown on-loan 19-year-old goalkeeper. **John 'Budgie' Burridge** would become a legendary character but at that time it was definitely a case of 'John Who?' But what a game he had! He stopped everything the Blues threw at him to secure a 0-0 draw and was the talk of the ground after the game. He would go on to be a very popular figure, always appreciated by the Gwladys Street and renowned for his unique behaviour. He made a great start to his career that day.

Trevor Edwards

Jordan Pickford continually demonstrates that keepers are as important as any superstar striker. However, he is edged out in the 'greatest' Everton goalkeeper debate by two league championship and FA Cup winners: **Gordon West** and **Neville Southall**. It's almost impossible to separate them, but Westy solved it in his own inimitable way at a now famous football dinner attended by both of them. With a wry smile, he brilliantly declared, 'OK, Nev. Let's just say I was the best in black and white and you were the best in colour!'

In September 1980, Mick Lyons staged his testimonial game at Goodison – Everton Present taking on Everton Past. Dai Davies was between the posts for the former stars when an unexpected second-half change was made. The mysterious sub entered the field of play on a stretcher, covered by a blanket. When the covering was whipped off at the Street End, it was none other than the now portly and substantial figure of Westy.

The fans roared their delight while instinctively fearing for him. Almost immediately, John Bailey lashed a volley towards the top corner. Gordon, having perfectly narrowed the angle as he had done so many times before, defied gravity to tip over at full stretch. For one glorious moment, we had travelled back in time to 1969/70. If you know your history, as you clearly do, those were days we will never forget.

Ken Rogers

I remember **Tim Howard** scoring a goal at Goodison Park from his own area against Bolton Wanderers, with a fair bit of help from the wind that swirled around the old ground that night. We still got beat 2-1.

Gary Swain

Although he once kept a stunning clean sheet at the Camp Nou as a youngster for Celtic, it is a March afternoon in 2014 Evertonians will most likely remember **David Marshall** for. The Champions League-chasing Toffees faced his relegation-threatened Cardiff City that day, although the Scot looked Champions League quality for a day. He denied Kevin Mirallas with a fine stop early in the first half, before making an even better save from Gerard Deulofeu. The Spanish winger cut in from the right with a low left-footed drive that Marshall superbly repelled. He then tipped over a curling effort from Lukaku just outside the box to keep the game goalless at half-time.

He was eventually beaten by a deflected Deulofeu effort just after the hour mark, when it felt like Everton needed such luck to beat the Scot. Cala then looked to have earned the Bluebirds an unlikely point shortly after. Marshall again excelled when he somehow tipped Lukaku's deflected, low right-foot effort round the post. Indeed, it would take a slice of luck to beat Marshall again. Séamus Coleman sliced an effort that deceived the Scot from a Gareth Barry knock-down at the very death. It was cruel on him, as most who attended Goodison that day would have agreed that Marshall did not deserve to be on the losing side.

Curiously, the Scot was linked with Everton in 2015 and 2016 as Tim Howard declined and Joel Robles failed to impress, but his heroics for Cardiff will be the biggest impression he left on the Blues.

Liam Knight

One of my earliest memories of being an Everton fan isn't a particular save, though there have been plenty that stick in the memory, but a talent of the first goalkeeper I recall, **Gordon West**. I remember his ability to throw a ball with amazing accuracy and distance. Maybe it's a case of blue-tinted spectacles, which are now some 55 years old, but I have an enduring belief that he threw with a greater distance and accuracy than most others kicked.

Paul Wright

Some of the performances of the women's team goalkeepers at Goodison Park over the years have been very special. **Kirstie Levell** and **Sandy MacIver** were in fine form in games at the Grand Old Lady, but the save that instantly comes to mind is the brilliant **Courtney Brosnan**'s courageous block at the feet of Liverpool's Fūka Nagano at the Park End. Brosnan put everything on the line to preserve the clean sheet and make sure we came out on top against our closest rivals. What a goalkeeper! I am looking forward to seeing her make more saves like that one at Goodison next season!

Grace Allen

Every Everton fan can immediately recall **Neville Southall**'s performances at Sheffield Wednesday in 1985 and Coventry in 1988. My immediate go-to game is the 1984 FA Cup Final, when he was superb, plucking crosses with one hand and making saves one-on-one. His performance that day inspired me to become a goalkeeper. Ultimately, the game that sticks in my mind at Goodison is the December 1987 match against Derby County, who themselves had England's number one, Peter Shilton, in goal. In that game, Nev showed why he was the best in the world with some breathtaking saves, and, if I remember rightly, he was wearing tracksuit bottoms as well!

Joseph Pierce

It sounds easy if you say it quickly: 'Give us your favourite Goodison goalkeeping performance.'

Except you can't have Jordan Pickford's peerless performance against Chelsea. That's already gone.

So has Gordon West's portly cameo in Mick Lyons's testimonial. Oh, and your old *Liverpool Echo* colleague Phil McNulty has claimed Nigel Batch, the Grimsby keeper who produced the unlikeliest of shut-outs in a 1984 League Cup tie. If games away from Goodison had been allowed, it would have been easy. Big Nev produced comfortably the greatest goalkeeping performance I've ever witnessed – at Coventry. Martin Hodge produced one of the best reaction saves – at Villa Park, while Georgie Wood astonishingly and repeatedly repelled one of the greatest Liverpool teams of all time in March 1979 – except it was at our original home, Anfield.

So I'm going to opt for a performance which was as important as it was significant: **Hans Segers**.

No further description is necessary. Everyone knows the match we're talking about. Not many footballers have a single match identified purely by their name. But of the 363 league appearances Segers made in his career he is synonymous with one – the last match of the 1993/94 Premier League season, the original Great Escape. It was an afternoon when nerves were shredded, when straight-thinking minds went walkabout:

tension wrapped Goodison like a suffocating straitjacket and when nerve ends sparked like firecrackers. And that atmosphere is why talk of 'match-rigging' and 'a fix' was, and still is, erroneous. Segers was subsequently accused of being involved in a match-rigging plot in 1995. Except Everton versus Wimbledon wasn't one of the matches he was quizzed about. And he was cleared of all charges at a Winchester Crown Court trial in August 1997.

So what was the fuss about? Quite simply Everton needed to beat Wimbledon on the last day of the season to stay in the Premier League. And they trailed 2-0 after 20 minutes. The circumstances surrounding that early deficit underlined the strange forces at work that day. The whole day was surreal. The Park End of Goodison Park resembled a building site with a backdrop of fans hanging precariously from Stanley Park trees. But it wasn't just fans behaving unusually. Anders Limpar insanely flapped an innocuous cross away with his hand to concede a penalty after four minutes. David Unsworth and Dave Watson over-zealously challenged for the same aerial ball resulting in Gary Ablett slicing the resulting shot from Andy Clarke into his own net – the Wimbledon striker's shot was going wide. The only sound which could be heard when the ball plopped sickeningly into the net was a lone Street End supporter's primeval scream. The atmosphere was unique.

The night before, Wimbledon's team coach had been torched outside their hotel, presumably by Blues fans keen on sending a grim message of the ramifications of sending their team down.

Of course, the Crazy Gang weren't easily intimidated, but John Fashanu's demeanour at the final whistle as he urgently ushered his club-mates off the pitch showed that the message had landed.

And up until the 81st minute, Hans Segers had done his job professionally and precisely. Until he had his brain freeze. He'd already plucked a Gary Ablett Exocet out the air as if it was catching practice. He'd parried a fierce near-post Graham Stuart drive, and he'd collected a punt from Ian Snodin 'serenely', according to BBC commentator Barry Davies, in a collision which knocked out Paul Rideout.

If Segers really had been intent on 'throwing' the match, leaving it until nine minutes from time was cutting it mighty fine. The moment which subsequently attracted so much attention came when Stuart exchanged passes with Tony Cottee on the edge of the Gwladys Street penalty area. Except the ball came back to 'Diamond' sharply. He didn't have time to set himself as two Wimbledon players converged on him, so it was almost a block tackle he produced rather than a shot, which sent the ball spinning towards Segers. The goalkeeper's vision was obscured by a thicket of players, so he fell to his right, arms outstretched, in a technically sound goalkeeping position. Except he didn't stretch his arms out far enough and the ball spun past his fingertips.

'Hans Segers, to tell the truth, made a bit of a mess of that,' said Barry Davies on that night's *Match of the Day*. But that was all. A mess, nothing sinister.

And it was a goalkeeping moment with enormous ramifications for Everton Football Club. It wasn't Jordan Pickford racing from one goalpost to the other before flinging himself at Antonio Rüdiger's shot. It wasn't Neville Southall making a ridiculous double save in a 1989 derby. And it wasn't Tim Howard clawing back a Graziano Pellè shot almost from behind his own goal line. But it was perhaps the most important goalkeeping intervention in Everton's history. Or should that be non-intervention?

David Prentice

In the 1964/65 derby at Anfield, Everton were missing Alex Parker, Ray Wilson, Roy Vernon and Alex Young. Liverpool were champions and favourites to win. We were clinical and three up before half-time, but a young **Andy Rankin** was the hero, making save after save, with the Kop singing, 'We're gonna hang Andy Rankin from the Kop.' Andy's fine form continued and in the home game against Wolves in the snow and rain, he was caught out of position when Melia hit a shot that was arrowing into the top corner. However, in typical acrobatic style, he flung himself high to his left, turning the ball over with his right hand.

Frank Keegan

I was a ten-year-old mad Everton fan living in Anglesey. I'm now in my 50s. My teacher told us to write a letter to somebody, so I wrote a letter to **Neville Southall**. Four weeks later, I received a white envelope through the post. I was quite excited as I never ever got mail. In the envelope was an autograph from Neville and a handwritten letter from him, thanking me for my letter and telling me to do my best at football but also at school. I have still got the letter. I did better at school than at football, but he's still the GOAT!

In my opinion, although Big Nev made countless incredible stops in front of the home supporters, all his very best saves were actually made away from Goodison Park. There were the ones at Spurs and Sheffield Wednesday in 1985 and a save from Gary Pallister's header in the FA Cup Final a decade later, when he nearly cracked a smile afterwards. He came up with the goods when he was needed away from home. I think this probably says a lot more about him as a player and person.

Dion Thomas

I have so many fond memories of Goodison Park and will really miss the place. My first game was in 1959 and I saw some brilliant goalkeeping performances over the next 65 years or so. **Westy** was an incredible goalkeeper in a side packed with star players. I actually played with **Neville** at Llandudno Swifts for a short period in the 1970s. Even though he was only 15 and playing in men's football, you knew he was going to be something special. I got to see that for myself at the Grand Old Lady, where he saved us on numerous occasions. However, I have got to say that **Tim Howard**'s save versus Southampton, when he clawed the ball out at the Gwladys Street End, is the best save I saw at our old ground.

Johnny 'Scouse' Jones

Her first match. An hour on the clock. Standing, cradling my little girl in my arms in the front row of the Family Enclosure, rocking her close to my chest. She lives on a remote Scottish isle of 500 people and had never seen anything like 35,000 Evertonians going berserk. Turning my back to the pitch we looked up at the Main Stand visibly shaking above us. Men, women and children off their seats, warm embraces between strangers, unbridled delight. Goodison Park at its swelling, sea-of-limbs best. A fabulous sight. And it wasn't even in celebration of a goal. **Jordan Pickford** had just saved Crystal Palace captain Luka Milivojević's penalty with the game poised at 0-0. Two late goals snatched the win for Everton, but it was our brilliant goalkeeper who provided her first exposure to the Goodison Roar. She was enthralled.

Jamie Yates

Goalkeepers. It's funny that of all the positions in the team, goalkeeper is the one I've thought about the least during my 40 years as an Evertonian. Perhaps this is because the first few years of my fanaticism saw the position held by **Big Nev**, a constant in the ever-decreasing circle of the club. My only observations were my uncle getting his autograph on a programme pull-out at a wedding and – me never getting – his shirts (most prominently in my memory, the 1990 NEC zigzag example) and then him nearly trapping my arm in his car door after the Coventry debacle in the autumn of 1994. I don't think I, nor many of my generation, truly appreciated his greatness until the mixed fortunes of the following years since.

Other keepers throughout the time, though, stick in my mind, such as **Stephen Reeves** (whom my mum X-rayed after an arm injury he sustained in a Central League victory over Morecambe) and **Sander Westerveld** (who walked past my balcony on the day he controversially signed), and before them **Gordon West**, who we found out used to live around the corner. Also **Rachel Brown-Finnis**, who now does, and we regularly see on the school run or buying stickers in the local Co-op and then the next day doing excellent punditry on the television.

Everyone rightly lauds the centre-forwards of our club's great history, but the keepers of yesteryear and now deserve equal status. Their position, especially in front of the Gwladys Street at its baying best (or worst), means that it takes a special person to handle the pressure and it's been a pleasure to introduce my son to football with Jordan Pickford between the sticks. He's even toyed with the idea of playing in goal because of our current custodian, although I don't think his personality matches the specialist position.

I remember reading an article about the mindset of goalkeepers, their alternate psychology, and there are so many examples of unusual characters across the world. I think their kits are part of their unique attraction, but their concentration levels and courage add to the intrigue.

I'm delighted to have the opportunity to share my thoughts on those brave individuals who have worn the green, black, yellow, even red shirts (and, most importantly, gloves) for our beloved blue boys and girls at Goodison Park. I'll certainly think about them more in the future, at Goodison and in the new stadium.

Jonathan Greenbank

Appendix – A Statistical History of Everton Men's First-Team Goalkeepers

Chapter 2

Goalkeeper (not including outfielders playing as goalkeepers or goalkeepers who played before the inception of the Football League in 1888)	First-team career (not including the seasons played before 1887/88 – Everton's first in the FA Cup)	Games (not including appearances made before the inception of the Football League other than those made in the FA Cup in 1887/88)	Major honours won as an Everton player and full international honours record
Charles Jolliffe	1887/88–1889/90	7	
Robert Smalley	1887/88–1890/91	40	1891 First Division winner
Walter Cox	1889/90	4	
John 'Jack' Angus	1890/91	12	1891 First Division winner
David Jardine	1890/91–1893/94	37	1891 First Division winner
Richard 'Dick' Williams	1891/92–1894/95	70	
Archibald Pinnell	1892/93	3	
William Thomas	1892/93	1	
Murray	1892/93	2	
Alex Rennie	1892/93	4	
John Whitehead	1893/94	2	
Tom Cain	1894/95	12	
William Sutton	1894/95	1	
William John 'Jack' Hillman	1894/95–1895/96	38	1 cap for England (earned after leaving Everton)

Henry Briggs	1895/96–1896/97	11	
Bob Menham	1896/97	23	
John Patrick	1896/97	1	2 caps for Scotland (both earned after leaving Everton)
John Palmer	1896/97	1	
Robert 'Rab' Macfarlane	1897/98	9	1 cap for Scotland (earned before joining Everton)
Willie Muir	1897/98–1901/02	137	1 cap for Scotland (earned after leaving Everton)

Chapter 3

Goalkeeper (not including outfielders playing as goalkeepers)	First-team career	Games (not including appearances made during the wartime period)	Major honours won as an Everton player and full international honours record
George Kitchen	1898/99–1903/04	90	
Jack Whitley	1902/03–1903/04	14	
William 'Billy' Scott	1904/05–1911/12	289	1906 FA Cup winner 25 caps for Ireland (16 earned while at Everton)
Leigh Richmond Roose	1904/05	24	24 caps for Wales (2 earned while at Everton)
Harry Collins	1905/06	3	
Robert Depledge	1906/07	1	
Donald Sloan	1906/07–1907/08	6	
Clarence Berry	1908/09–1911/12	3	
Walter Scott	1909/10–1910/11	18	
James Caldwell	1912/13	36	
William Hodge	1912/13–1913/14	10	
William Bromilow	1912/13	1	
Frank Mitchell	1913/14–1919/20	24	1915 First Division winner
Tommy Fern	1913/14–1923/24	231	1915 First Division winner

Benjamin Howard Baker	1920/21; 1926/27	13	2 caps for England (1 earned while at Everton)
Ernie Salt	1921/22	4	
Alfie Harland	1922/23– 1925/26	70	2 caps for Ireland (earned before joining Everton)
Jack Kendall	1923/24– 1925/26	23	
Robert 'Bob' Jones	1924/25	3	
Charles 'George' Menham	1925/26	3	
Harry Hardy	1925/26– 1927/28	45	1928 First Division winner 1 cap for England (earned before joining Everton)
Arthur Davies	1926/27– 1929/30	94	1928 First Division winner
Ted Taylor	1926/27– 1927/28	42	1928 First Division winner 8 caps for England (all earned before joining Everton)

Chapter 4

Goalkeeper (not including outfielders playing as emergency goalkeepers)	First-team career	Games (not including appearances made during the wartime period)	Major honours won as an Everton player and full international honours record
Ted Sagar	1929/30– 1952/53	497	1932 First Division winner 1933 FA Cup winner 1939 First Division winner 4 caps for England (all earned while at Everton)
Billy Coggins	1929/30– 1933/34	56	1931 Second Division winner
George Bradshaw	1934/35	3	
Frank King	1934/35– 1936/37	14	
Harry Morton	1936/37– 1938/39	29	
George Burnett	1945/46– 1950/51	54	

Chapter 5

Goalkeeper (not including outfielders playing as emergency goalkeepers)	First-team career	Games	Major honours won as an Everton player and full international honours record
Jimmy O'Neill	1950/51–1959/60	213	17 caps for Republic of Ireland (all earned while at Everton)
Harry Leyland	1951/52–1955/56	40	
Bert Harris	1955/56	5	
Albert Dunlop	1956/57–1962/63	231	1963 First Division winner

Chapter 6

Goalkeeper (not including outfielders playing as emergency goalkeepers)	First-team career	Games	Major honours won as an Everton player and full international honours record
Gordon West	1961/62–1972/73	402	1963 First Division winner 1966 FA Cup winner 1970 First Division winner 3 caps for England (all earned while at Everton)
Andy Rankin	1963/64–1970/71	104 (+1 as sub)	
Geoff Barnett	1965/66–1967/68	10	

Chapter 7

Goalkeeper (not including outfielders playing as emergency goalkeepers)	First-team career	Games	Major honours won as an Everton player and full international honours record
David 'Dai' Davies	1970/71–1976/77	94	52 caps for Wales (16 earned while at Everton)
David Lawson	1972/73–1976/77	152	
Drew Brand	1975/76–1976/77	2	
George Wood	1977/78–1979/80	126	4 caps for Scotland (3 earned while at Everton)
Martin Hodge	1979/80–1980/81	31	
Jim McDonagh	1980/81	48	25 caps for Republic of Ireland (4 earned while at Everton)

Chapter 8

Goalkeeper (not including outfielders playing as emergency goalkeepers)	First-team career	Games	Major honours won as an Everton player and full international honours record
Neville Southall	1981/82–1997/98	751	1984 FA Cup winner 1985 First Division winner 1985 ECWC winner 1985 FWA Footballer of the Year 1987 First Division winner 1995 FA Cup winner 92 caps for Wales (all earned while at Everton, though one of those Wales appearances was made during Southall's loan spell at Port Vale in 1983)
Jim Arnold	1981/82–1983/84	59	

Chapter 9

Goalkeeper	First-team career	Games	Major honours won as an Everton player and full international honours record
Bobby Mimms	1985/86–1987/88	37	1987 First Division winner
Mike Stowell	1988/89	1	
Jason Kearton	1992/93–1994/95	5 (+3 as sub)	1995 FA Cup winner (unused substitute)

Chapter 10

Goalkeeper	First-team career	Games	Major honours won as an Everton player and full international honours record
Paul Gerrard	1996/97–2002/03	98 (+1 as sub)	
Thomas Myhre	1997/98–2000/01	82	56 caps for Norway (20 earned while at Everton)
Steve Simonsen	1999/00–2003/04	35 (+2 as sub)	
Richard Wright	2002/03–2006/07	69 (+2 as sub)	2 caps for England (both earned before joining Everton)
Espen Baardsen	2002/03	1	4 caps for Norway (all earned before joining Everton)

Chapter 11

Goalkeeper	First-team career	Games	Major honours won as an Everton player and full international honours record
Nigel Martyn	2003/04–2005/06	99 (+1 as sub)	23 caps for England (all earned before joining Everton)
Iain Turner	2005/06–2006/07	5 (+1 as sub)	
John Ruddy	2005/06	0 (+1 as sub)	1 cap for England (earned after leaving Everton)
Sander Westerveld	2005/06	2	6 caps for the Netherlands (all earned before joining Everton)

Chapter 12

Goalkeeper	First-team career	Games	Major honours won as an Everton player and full international honours record
Tim Howard	2006/07–2015/16	414 (1 goal)	121 caps for United States of America (93 earned while at Everton)
Stefan Wessels	2007/08	7	
Carlo Nash	2009/10	1	
Ján Mucha	2010/11–2012/13	10	46 caps for Slovakia (16 earned while at Everton)
Joel Robles	2013/14–2017/18	62 (+3 as sub)	
Maarten Stekelenburg	2016/17–2018/19	26	63 caps for the Netherlands (4 earned while at Everton)

Chapter 13

Goalkeeper	First-team career	Games (correct as of 31st May 2025)	Major honours won as an Everton player and full international honours record (correct as of 31st May 2025)
Jordan Pickford	2017/18–time of writing	319	75 caps for England (all earned while at Everton)
João Virgínia	2020/21–2024/25	7 (+1 as sub)	
Robin Olsen	2020/21	11	76 caps for Sweden (10 earned while at Everton)

| Asmir Begović | 2021/22–2022/23 | 10 | 63 caps for Bosnia and Herzegovina (all earned before joining Everton) |

Unfortunately, there is no authoritative statistical data available for the complete history of Everton Women's goalkeepers. As a result, the names of all the keepers in Chapter 14 have been emboldened – not just those of the women who are known to have made first-team appearances.

Bibliography

Interviews:
Jim Barron
Rachel Brown-Finnis
Bert Harris
Nicola Hobbs
Alan Kelly
Kirstie Levell
Andrea McGrady
Phil McNulty
Bobby Mimms
Alan Myers
Gill Parkinson
Mick Payne
David Prentice
Kevin Ratcliffe
Lou Reed Foster
Brian Viner
Dave Watson
Andie Worrall

Books:
Buckland, G., *Boys from the Bluestuff: Everton's Rise to 1980s Glory* (deCourbetin, 2021)
Buckland, G., *Money Can't Buy Us Love: Everton in the 1960s* (deCourbetin, 2019)
Buckland, G., *The End: From Glory to a Whole New Ball Game* (Toffeeopolis, 2024)
Corbett, J., *Faith of our Families: Everton FC, an Oral History* (deCourbetin, 2017)
Corbett, J., *The Everton Encyclopedia* (deCourbetin, 2012)
Coton, T., *There to be Shot at: An Autobiography* (deCourbetin, 2017)

Davies, D., *Never Say Dai* (Siop y Siswrn, 1987)

Foster, L., *Fear and Loathing at Goodison Park: Everton FC under David Moyes* (Pitch Publishing, 2023)

France, D., *Alex Young – The Golden Vision* (Skript Publishing, 2008)

France, D., *Everton Crazy* (deCourbetin, 2016)

France, D., *Everton Proud* (deCourbetin, 2017)

France, D., *Gwladys Street's Hall of Fame* (Skript Publishing, 1999)

France, D., Griffiths, D. and Sawyer, R., *Toffee Soccer: Everton and North America* (deCourbetin, 2021)

France, D. and Prentice, D., *Dr Everton's Magnificent Obsession* (Trinity Sport Media, 2008)

France, D. and Prentice, D., *Everton Treasures* (Skript Publishing, 2007)

France, D. and Tallentire, B., *Gwladys Street's Holy Trinity: Kendall, Harvey and Ball* (Skript Publishing, 2001)

Gibson, A. and Pickford, W., *Association Football and the Men who Made it* (Caxton Publishing, 1906)

Hart, S., *Here We Go – Everton in the 1980s: The Players' Stories* (deCourbetin, 2016)

Harvey, C., *Colin Harvey's Everton Secrets: 40 Years at Goodison from Catterick to Moyes* (Trinity Mirror Sport Media, 2006)

Howard, T., *The Keeper: A Life of Saving Goals and Achieving Them* (Harper, 2014)

Johnson, S., *Everton: The Official Complete Record 1878–2016* (deCourbetin, 2016)

Keates, T., *History of the Everton Football Club 1878–1928* (Desert Island Books, 1998)

Keith, J., *Dixie Dean: The Inside Story of a Football Icon* (Robson Books, 2001)

Kendall, H., *Notes on a Season: 1984/85* (Reach Sport, 2020)

Kendall, H. and Corbett, J., *Love Affairs & Marriage: My Life in Football* (deCourbetin, 2013)

Keoghan, J., *Highs, Lows and Bakayokos* (Pitch Publishing, 2016)

Keoghan, J., *Everton Greatest Games: The Toffees' Fifty Finest Matches* (Pitch Publishing, 2017)

Latchford, B., *A Different Road* (deCourbetin, 2015)

McCall, S., *The Real McCall: Stuart McCall's Own Story* (Mainstream Publishing, 1998)

McParlan, P., *The Forgotten Champions: Everton's Last Title* (Pitch Publishing, 2021)

O'Brien, M., *The Everton Miscellany* (Vision Sports Publishing, 2012)

Orr, G., *Everton in the Sixties: The Diary of an Evertonian* (Tobin, 1997)

Osborne, S., *Making the Grade* (Legends Publishing, 2014)

Ponting, I., *Everton Player by Player* (Hamlyn, 1992)

Prentice, D., *A Grand Old Team to Report: 45 Years of Following Everton* (Reach Sport, 2021)

Reid, P., *Cheer up Peter Reid – My Autobiography* (Reacher, 2018)

Rogers, K., *Everton Greats* (Sportsprint Publishing, 1989)

Royle, J., *The Autobiography* (BBC Books, 2005)

Sawyer, R., *Broken Dreams: Everton, the War and Goodison's Lost Generation* (Toffeeopolis, 2024)

Sawyer, R., *Harry Catterick: The Untold Story of a Football Great* (deCourbetin, 2014)

Sawyer, R., *The Hope Robertson Chronicles* (Amazon, 2022)

Sheedy, K., *So Good I Did it Twice: My Life from Left Field* (Trinity Mirror Sport Media, 2014)

Southall, N., *In Search of Perfection* (Black and White Publishing, 1995)

Southall, N., *Mind Games: The Ups and Downs of Life and Football* (HarperCollins, 2020)

Southall, N. & George, R., *Everton Blues: A Premier League Diary* (B&W Publishing, 1998)

Southall, N. & Corbett, J., *The Binman Chronicles* (deCourbetin, 2012)

Tallentire, B., *Talking Blue: A Collection of Candid Interviews with Everton Heroes* (Breedon Books, 2000)

Tallentire, B., *Still Talking Blue: A Collection of Candid Interviews with Everton Heroes* (Transworld Publishers, 2001)

Tallentire, B., *Real Footballers' Wives: The First Ladies of Everton* (Mainstream Publishing, 2017)

Thompson, P. and Hale, S., *Everton in the 1980s* (Tempus Publishing, 2003)

Vignes, S., *Lost in France: The Remarkable Life and Death of Leigh Roose, Football's First Superstar* (Stadia, 2007)

Viner, B., *Looking for the Toffees: In Search of the Heroes of Everton* (Simon & Schuster UK, 2014)

Weir, D., *Extra Time – My Autobiography* (Hodder & Stoughton, 2011)

West, G., *The Championship in My Keeping* (Souvenir Press Ltd, 1970)

Wilson, B., *You've Got to be Crazy: On Goalkeepers and Goalkeeping* (Weidenfeld & Nicolson; First Edition, 1989)

Wilson, B., *Behind the Network: My Autobiography* (Hodder Paperbacks, 2004)

Wilson, J., *The Outsider: A History of the Goalkeeper* (Orion Publishing, 2013)

Young, A., *Goals at Goodison* (Pelham Books, London, 1968)

Zocek, S., *For the Boys in the Royal Blue Jersey 2* (Lulu.com, 2019)

Newspapers and periodicals:

Aberdeen Press and Journal
Athletic News
Belfast Evening Telegraph
Birmingham Mail
Blackpool Gazette
Bristol Evening Post
The Clarion
Cricket and Football Field
Daily Citizen
Daily Mirror
Daily Telegraph
Derry Journal
Edinburgh Evening News
Evening Express
Everton: A Celebration of Winning the 1986/87 League Championship – Official 25th Anniversary Souvenir Special
Everton: The Official Monthly Magazine
The Evertonian
These Football Times
FourFourTwo
Glasgow Herald
Goal
The Guardian
The Independent
Ipswich Star
The Irish Times
Lancashire Evening Post

Lancashire Evening Telegraph
Lancashire Telegraph
Liverpool Courier
Liverpool Daily Post
Liverpool Echo
Liverpool Evening Express
Liverpool Mercury
Liverpool Post
London Echo
Morning Leader
Newcastle Daily Journal and North Star
The People
Rugby Paper
Scottish Referee
Sheffield Star Green 'Un
Shields Daily News
Sunday Dispatch
Sunday Mirror
Sunday People
Sunderland Echo
The Telegraph
The Times
The Weekly News
Western Daily Express
Yorkshire Evening Post

Websites:
bbc.co.uk
chelseasupporterstrust.com
cheshire-live.co.uk
efcheritagesociety.com
efcstatto.com
evertoncollection.org.uk
evertonfc.com
evertonia.com
evertonresults.com
mightyleeds.co.uk
premierleague.com
royalbluemersey.sbnation.com

spartacus-educational.com
theexecutionersbong.wordpress.com
toffeeweb.com

Other:

BBC Radio 5 Live
City of Leeds YouTube channel
Everton FC Official Matchday Programmes – author's own
  collection
Everton: Great Games, Great Goals (VHS)
Great Save: The Essential Guide to Brilliant Goalkeeping (VHS)
Howard's Way – Rob Sloman's 2019 documentary on the 1984/85
  season
Inside the Game football podcast
Instagram
Match of the Day
*Saves Galore: The Best 110 Saves of the 1988/89 Barclays League
  Division One Season* (VHS)
*Saves Galore: The Best 110 Saves of the 1989/90 Barclays League
  Division One Season* (VHS)
Sky Sports – *The Big Interview: Tim Howard and Jordan Pickford*
Sky Sports News
talkSPORT
Upfront: A Women's Football Podcast
Voice on Soccer YouTube channel
X (formerly known as Twitter)